LET THE
NATIONS
BE GLAD!

Other Books by John Piper

God's Passion for His Glory
The Pleasures of God
Desiring God
The Dangerous Duty of Delight
Future Grace
A Hunger for God
A Godward Life
Pierced by the Word
Seeing and Savoring Jesus Christ
What's the Difference?
Brothers, We Are Not Professionals
The Supremacy of God in Preaching
Don't Waste Your Life
The Passion of Jesus Christ
Life as a Vapor
When I Don't Desire God
Taste and See
Fifty Reasons Why Jesus Came to Die
God Is the Gospel
What Jesus Demands from the World
Battling Unbelief
When the Darkness Will Not Lift
Spectacular Sins
Finally Alive
John Calvin and His Passion for the Majesty of God
Rethinking Retirement
This Momentary Marriage
Velvet Steel
A Sweet and Bitter Providence

LET THE
NATIONS
BE GLAD!

THE SUPREMACY
OF GOD
IN MISSIONS

THIRD EDITION

JOHN PIPER

Baker Academic
a division of Baker Publishing Group
Grand Rapids, Michigan

© 1993, 2003, 2010 by Desiring God Foundation

Published by Baker Academic
a division of Baker Publishing Group
P.O. Box 6287, Grand Rapids, MI 49516-6287
www.bakeracademic.com

Printed in the United States of America

Library of Congress Cataloging-in-Publication Data

Piper, John, 1946–
    Let the nations be glad! : the supremacy of God in missions / John Piper.—3rd ed. rev. and expanded.
       p. cm.
    Includes bibliographical references and indexes.
    ISBN 978-0-8010-3641-5 (pbk.)
    1. Missions—Theory. 2. God (Christianity)—Worship and love. I. Title.
BV2063.P55 2010
266'.001—dc22
                                                    2009043303

In keeping with biblical principles of creation stewardship, Baker Publishing Group advocates the responsible use of our natural resources. As a member of the Green Press Initiative, our company uses recycled paper when possible. The text paper of this book is comprised of 30% post-consumer waste.

green press INITIATIVE

10   11   12   13   14   15   16   7   6   5   4   3   2

To
Tom Steller

in the precious partnership
of worship, prayer, and suffering
for the supremacy of God in all things,
for the joy of all peoples
through Jesus Christ
crucified and risen

Contents

7. The Inner Simplicity and Outer Freedom of Worldwide Worship 239

Conclusion 255
Afterword: The Supremacy of God in Going and Sending *Tom Steller* 261
Subject Index 265
Person Index 269
Scripture Index 273
A Note on Resources: Desiring God 281

Preface to the Third Edition

My passion is to see people, churches, mission agencies, and social ministries become God-centered, Christ-exalting, Spirit-powered, soul-satisfied, Bible-saturated, missions-mobilizing, soul-winning, and justice-pursuing. The supremacy of God in all things for the joy of all peoples through Jesus Christ is the central, driving, all-unifying commitment of my life.

This vision is as clear and firm in my heart in 2010 as when this book was first published in 1993 and revised in 2003. In fact, this vision has been deeply solidified in the intervening years by the completion of another book relating to world missions, *What Jesus Demands from the World*.[1] What drove that book was Jesus' command in the Great Commission: "Teach them to observe all that I have commanded you" (Matt. 28:20). That book is my effort to sum up from the four Gospels what Jesus meant by "all I have commanded you." It is a handbook for discipling the nations in obedience to that part of the Great Commission.

So the vision has not faded. And I am thankful that God has been merciful to use *Let the Nations Be Glad!* to make himself more central in missions and more satisfying in the hearts of those who give their lives for the sake of his name.

I am thankful to Baker Publishing Group again for the privilege of partnering with them in an expanded and refined third edition. If I were to guess why this book continues to be useful it would be because it is mainly biblical reflection rather than methodological application. Meth-

---

1. John Piper, *What Jesus Demands from the World* (Wheaton, Ill.: Crossway Books, 2006).

ods change. But worship, prayer, suffering, unreached peoples, the gospel, faith, heaven, and hell remain.

John Stott has sounded the note I love to hear and echo:

> The highest of missionary motives is neither obedience to the Great Commission (important as that is), nor love for sinners who are alienated and perishing (strong as that incentive is, especially when we contemplate the wrath of God . . .), but rather zeal—burning and passionate zeal—for the glory of Jesus Christ. . . . Only one imperialism is Christian . . . and that is concern for His Imperial Majesty Jesus Christ, and for the glory of his empire.[2]

He said this in relation to Romans 1:5. There the apostle Paul sums up his calling as a missionary: "[I am called] to bring about the obedience of faith *for the sake of his name* among all the nations." Notice: "For the sake of his name!" Stott exults again in this great Pauline passion:

> We should be "jealous" . . . for the honour of his name—troubled when it remains unknown, hurt when it is ignored, indignant when it is blasphemed. And all the time anxious and determined that it shall be given the honor and glory which are due to it.[3]

O for the day when more pastors and scholars and missionaries would not just say that but feel it as the driving force of their lives!

The apostle John applies this Christ-exalting passion to all missionaries when he says, "They have gone out for the sake of the name" (3 John 7). My friend and comrade in the Greatest Cause for over thirty years, Tom Steller, wrote an afterword for this book based on that text in 3 John. I have dedicated this book to Tom with deep affection.

As we get closer and closer to the finish line together, we want to give our lives to creating, sending, and sustaining world Christians who live and die "for the sake of the name." Increasingly, what burns inside us is the question, *Where do such God-centered, Christ-exalting, missions-driven people come from?* We believe they come from God-besotted, Christ-addicted, Bible-breathing homes and churches and schools and ministries. That is what this book aims to nurture.

There is a God-enthralled, Christ-treasuring, all-enduring love that pursues the fullness of God in the soul and in the service of Jesus. It is

2. John Stott, *Romans: God's Good News for the World* (Downers Grove, Ill.: InterVarsity, 1994), 53.
3. Ibid.

not absorbed in anthropology or methodology or even theology—it is absorbed in God. It cries out with the psalmist, "Let the peoples praise you, O God; let all the peoples praise you! Let the nations be glad and sing for joy. . . . Sing praises to our King, sing praises! For God is the King of all the earth" (Pss. 67:3–4; 47:6–7).

There is a distinct God-magnifying, Christ-exalting mindset. It is relentless in bringing God forward again and again. It is spring-loaded to make much of the Triune God in anthropology and methodology and theology. It cannot make peace with God-ignoring, God-neglecting planning or preaching or puttering around.

Such God-entranced people are what we need. For example, even after all these years, I am still happy to say that *Let the Nations Be Glad!* is like a little skiff riding on the wake of the massive undertaking of Patrick Johnstone and Jason Mandryk and their team in publishing *Operation World*. Would that every Christian used this book to know the nations and pray.

I look at this great, church-wakening, mission-advancing book, and I ask, "What kind of mindset unleashes such a book?" Listen.

> All the earth-shaking awesome forces unleashed on the world are released by the Lord Jesus Christ. He reigns today. He is in the control room of the universe. He is the only Ultimate Cause; all the sins of man and machinations of Satan ultimately have to enhance the glory and kingdom of our Saviour. This is true of our world today—in wars, famines, earthquakes, or the evil that apparently has the ascendancy. All God's actions are just and loving. We have become too enemy-conscious, and can over-do the spiritual warfare aspect of intercession. We need to be more God-conscious, so that we can laugh the laugh of faith knowing that we have power over all the power of the enemy (Luke 10:19). He has already lost control because of Calvary where the Lamb was slain. What confidence and rest of heart this gives us as we face a world in turmoil and such spiritual need.[4]

There it is. Where are the teachers and preachers and mission executives and seminary presidents who talk like that? Their number is increasing. I want to be one. I want to breathe any little spark of Godward zeal I can into the reader's soul. Feel free to ransack this book for wherever you feel that breath. It doesn't have to be read straight through.

Let it be clear: This book is not just for missionaries. It is for pastors who (like me) want to connect their fragile, momentary, local labors to

---

4. Patrick Johnstone, *Operation World* (Kent, England: STL, 1987), 21. The regularly updated online version is at http://www.operationworld.org/.

God's invincible, eternal, global purposes. It's for laypeople who want a bigger motivation for being world Christians than they get from statistics. It's for college and seminary classes on the theology of missions that really want to be *theo*logical as well as anthropological, methodological, and technological. And it's for leaders who need the flickering wick of their vocation fanned into flame again with a focus on the supremacy of God in all things.

Tom Steller and I love Jesus Christ, we love the church, and we love missionaries. Our united prayer and commitment, from the home base of a missions-mobilizing local church, and the newly founded Bethlehem College and Seminary, is that God will be merciful to us and make our labors fruitful for Christ's "Imperial Majesty." May he raise up generations of world Christians who are willing to lay down their lives to make the nations glad in the glory of God through Jesus Christ.

Acknowledgments

I am surrounded by people who energize me because they share the vision to spread a passion for the supremacy of God in all things for the joy of all peoples through Jesus Christ.

This third edition would not have been possible without the steady help and encouragement of my executive pastoral assistant, David Mathis. Thank you, David, for keeping my feet to the fire and holding back the ever-pressing demands.

Thank you to Bethlehem Baptist Church, who, under the leadership of visionary, globally minded, God-centered elders, give me the freedom to write.

Thank you, Carol Steinbach, friend and fellow-fighter for joy, for making the book more accessible and useful with the text and person indexes.

Thank you, Noël and Talitha, who strengthen my hand for the Great Work, and accept my imperfect efforts to love you as husband and father.

Thank you most of all, dear Jesus, that you have buttressed the command, "Teach them to observe all that I have commanded you," with the double promise, "All authority in heaven and on earth has been given to me," and, "I am with you always, to the end of the age" (Matt. 28:18–20).

Introduction to the Third Edition

New Realities in World Christianity and Twelve Appeals to Prosperity Preachers

Missions is not the ultimate goal of the church. Worship is. Missions exists because worship doesn't. Worship is ultimate, not missions, because God is ultimate, not man. When this age is over, and the countless millions of the redeemed fall on their faces before the throne of God, missions will be no more. It is a temporary necessity. But worship abides forever.

So worship is the fuel and goal of missions. That has been the signature thesis of this book since its first edition in 1993. With all the change in the world, *that* has not changed. Worship has always been and will always be the ultimate purpose of God in the universe. It has always been the fire that fuels our passion to reach peoples who do not worship the true God through Jesus Christ. That's where we're headed in chapter 1.

But before we go there a new situation in world Christianity commands our attention. Lamin Sanneh, professor of history and world Christianity at Yale University, uses the word "breathtaking" to describe the new situation.

> Among the many breathtaking developments in the post-World War II and the subsequent colonial eras, few are more striking than the worldwide Christian resurgence. With unflagging momentum, Christianity has become, or is fast becoming, the principal religion of the peoples of the world. Primal societies that once stood well outside the main orbit of the faith have become major centers of Christian impact, while Europe and North America, once

considered the religion's heartland, are in noticeable recession. We seem to be in the middle of massive cultural shifts and realignments whose implications are only now beginning to become clear.[1]

Europe and America are not the center of gravity in world Christianity any longer. The center is shifting south and east. The churches of Latin America, Africa, and Asia are experiencing phenomenal growth and are becoming the great sending churches.

Introducing the Global South

Philip Jenkins, professor of history and religious studies at Pennsylvania State University, has clarified this development perhaps more than anyone. The new terminology that has been introduced into our vocabulary is the term "Global South," a reference to the astonishing growth of the Christian church in Africa, Latin America, and Asia while the formerly dominant centers of Christian influence in Europe are weakening. For example:

- At the beginning of the twentieth century, Europeans dominated the world church, with approximately 70.6 percent of the world's Christian population. By 1938, on the eve of World War II, the apparent European domination of Protestantism and Catholicism remained strong. Yet by the end of the twentieth century, the European percentage of world Christianity had shrunk to 28 percent of the total; Latin America and Africa combined provided 43 percent of the world's Christians.[2]
- In 1900, Africa had 10 million Christians representing about 10 percent of the population; by 2000, this figure had grown to 360 million, representing about half the population. Quantitatively, this may well be the largest shift in religious affiliation that has ever occurred, anywhere.[3]
- The number of African Christians is growing at around 2.36 percent annually, which would lead us to project a doubling of the continent's Christian population in less than thirty years.[4]

1. Lamin Sanneh, *Disciples of All Nations: Pillars of World Christianity* (Oxford: Oxford University Press, 2008), xix.
2. Dana L. Robert, "Shifting Southward; Global Christianity Since 1945," *International Bulletin of Missionary Research* 24, no. 2 (April 2000): 50.
3. Philip Jenkins, "Believing in the Global South," *First Things* 168 (December 2006): 13.
4. Ibid., 12.

- By 2050, Christianity will be chiefly the religion of Africa and the African diaspora. By then, there will be about three billion Christians in the world, and the population of those who will be white and non-Latino will be between one-fifth and one-sixth the total.[5]
- At the 1998 Lambeth Conference, the highest consultative body of the Anglican Communion, 224 of the 735 bishops were from Africa, compared with only 139 from the United Kingdom and Europe. Anglicans in Nigeria report 17 million baptized members, compared with 2.8 million in the United States.[6]

The New Shape of World Christianity

Mark Noll has an even more striking way of drawing our attention to the new realities of the Global South.

- "Active Christian adherence has become stronger in Africa than in Europe."
- "The number of practicing Christians in China may be approaching the number in the United States."
- "Live bodies in church are far more numerous in Kenya than in Canada."
- "More believers worship together in church Sunday by Sunday in Nagaland than in Norway."
- "More Christian workers from Brazil are active in cross cultural ministry outside their homelands than from Britain or from Canada."
- "Last Sunday . . . more Christian believers attended church in China than in all of so-called 'Christian Europe.'"[7]
- "This past Sunday more Anglicans attended church in each of Kenya, South Africa, Tanzania, and Uganda than did Anglicans in Britain and Canada and Episcopalians in the United States combined."
- Last Sunday "more Presbyterians were in church in Ghana than in Scotland."[8]

5. Ibid.
6. Robert, "Shifting Southward," 53.
7. Mark Noll, *The New Shape of World Christianity: How American Experience Reflects Global Faith* (Downers Grove, Ill.: InterVarsity Academic, 2009), 10.
8. Ibid., 20.

- "This past week in Great Britain, at least fifteen thousand Christian foreign missionaries were hard at work evangelizing the locals. Most of these missionaries are from Africa and Asia."[9]

"In a word," Noll says, "the Christian church has experienced a larger geographical redistribution in the last fifty years than in any comparable period in its history, with the exception of the very earliest years of church history."[10]

The Day of Western Missionaries Is Not Over

This is a cause for Christians to rejoice in the sovereign grace of God. But the news is not all good. For example, one of the effects of this kind of news is to make many Christians in the West think that the day of sending missionaries from our churches is past. This is tragic. Presumably, what we should do now is support missions from the Global South. My way of putting that would be: Let them shed *their* blood. We will just send *money*.

Many have embraced the uninformed notion that it is always more efficient and culturally effective to support local churches and ministries of the Global South to do the work of missions rather than to pay tens of thousands of dollars each year to send Western missionaries.

I am not opposed to partnering with indigenous missions of the Global South. There are many reputable churches and agencies that make that possible. But it is uninformed to assume that local churches or nearby missionaries can always reach a people better than Western missionaries.

It is uninformed, first of all, because in pioneer missionary situations there *are* no local churches to do the work. That's the *meaning* of an unreached people.[11] Moreover, there is no assurance that a nearby missionary will be more effective than you in learning the new language and crossing the culture teaching the truth. This is especially true if there are old tribal hostilities to be overcome locally. Such a strategy may sometimes be best, and other times not.

The day of Western missions is not over. There are many ways to partner with believers around the world besides simply sending money. There are, as I write in 2009, according to the Joshua Project, 6,645 unreached people groups in the world out of a total of 16,309 ethno-linguistic peoples. And of

9. Ibid., 21.
10. Ibid.
11. See chapter 5 for an extended discussion of the biblical understanding of "unreached peoples."

these 6,645, Joshua Project lists 1,540 of these as unengaged. You can find out the ever-changing, current statistics by checking www.JoshuaProject.net.

The Global South and the Prosperity Gospel

Another ambiguity in the present magnificent expansion of Christianity is that not all the forms of this faith are based on what the apostle Paul calls "sound doctrine" (Titus 1:9; 2:1). Michael Horton makes this sobering observation:

> Celebration of the much-advertised expansion of Christianity in the two-thirds world (most notably in recent years in Philip Jenkins's *The Next Christendom*) should at least be tempered by the fact that the prosperity gospel is the most explosive version of this phenomenon.[12]

> The prosperity gospel is the most sweeping movement within the continent of Africa.[13]

What I mean by "the prosperity gospel" is a teaching that emphasizes God's aim to make believers healthy and wealthy in this life, while it overlooks or minimizes the dangers of wealth, the biblical call to a wartime mindset, and the necessity and purposes of suffering.

The prosperity gospel would be represented by one leading African prosperity preacher who says, "Many are ignorant of the fact that God has already made provision for his children to be wealthy here on earth. When I say wealthy, I mean very, very rich. . . . Break loose! It is not a sin to desire to be wealthy."[14]

I am deeply concerned when a preacher encourages a crowd to give $200 to "open themselves to the blessing" in a culture where a schoolteacher earns $150 a month. Yet more than 300 people come forward to receive the speaker's oil and "within minutes, the church nets tax-free $60,000."[15]

The extent of the teaching in Africa is remarkable. In a 2006 survey, Pew asked participants if God would "grant material prosperity to all believers

12. Michael Horton, *Christless Christianity: The Alternative Gospel of the American Church* (Grand Rapids: Baker Academic, 2008), 45.
13. Quotation from Bonnie Dolan, founder and director of Zambia's Center for Christian missions. Ibid., 25.
14. Isaac Phiri and Joe Maxwell, "Gospel Riches," *Christianity Today* 51, no. 7 (July 2007): 23.
15. Ibid.

who have enough faith." Eighty-five percent of Kenyan Pentecostals, 90 percent of South African Pentecostals, and 95 percent of Nigerian Pentecostals said yes.[16]

"The worst brand of African prosperity teaching is, perhaps unsurprisingly, an American export."[17] Television has become Africa's religious classroom. "People turn it on and assume that TBN is American Christianity, and Americans know everything, so why not listen to it?"[18] And of course prosperity teaching is not unique to America and Africa. It has its Latino and Asian forms and can be found throughout the Global South from Seoul to São Paulo.[19]

What Shall We Say about the Prosperity Gospel?

The first thing we should say about the prosperity gospel is that wealthy Westerners are probably as guilty of its excesses as are the poor in the Global South. The difference is that the poor *don't* have wealth and want it, while the rich have it, expect to keep it, and get angry if God takes it. Both have their hearts set on prosperity. It's just more subtle in the West because we can take prosperity for granted. This is why I spend more time calling our church to live differently than I do calling the Global South to think differently.[20] I am more responsible for the sins at home.

Prosperity Is Relative and the Paths to It Diverse

But this is a book about global missions. And what we think about money and possessions is profoundly important in the way we do missions and the way we disciple converts. So I would like to provide a biblical response to the prosperity gospel. As I point out some of its weaknesses, I aim to keep in mind my own sins, and I hope to remember that it is not a monolithic movement and that "prosperity" is a relative term.

16. Ibid., 24.
17. Ibid.
18. Ibid., 25.
19. Arlene Sanchez Walsh, "First Church of Prosperidad," *Christianity Today* 51, no. 7 (July 2007): 26–27; Ondina E. González and Justo L. González, *Christianity in Latin America: A History* (New York: Cambridge University Press, 2008).
20. For example, see the chapter on "Money: The Currency of Christian Hedonism" in John Piper, *Desiring God: Meditations of a Christian Hedonist* (Sisters, Ore.: Multnomah, 2003); and the chapter on "Living to Prove He Is More Precious than Life" in John Piper, *Don't Waste Your Life* (Wheaton, Ill.: Crossway Books, 2003).

Prosperity in one part of the world would mean a roof over your head, nourishing food on the table a couple times a day, and clean drinking water. "Currently, about 315 million sub-Saharan Africans live on less than a dollar a day."[21] And what we would call a modest lifestyle in America (with a home, a car, electricity, refrigeration, indoor plumbing, clean drinking water, central heating, a computer, a phone, several changes of clothes, and unheard of choices in groceries) would be wildly opulent in most of the world. This is one reason why criticisms of the prosperity preachers must be nuanced and cautious.

Another caution for critics is that there are different ways to think about how Christianity brings prosperity. Few would disagree that a gospel-driven movement of honesty, hard work, patience, generosity, perseverance, and love for excellence would over time lift a culture from the dysfunction of corruption and bring more stable and prosperous times. If that is what the prosperity preachers were saying, there would be little controversy.[22]

But given the lavish way that prosperity preachers often live, even by Western standards—flying in personal jets, living in palatial homes with eight bathrooms, and staying overnight in $5,000 suites—and given the way they clothe the eternal gospel of Christ in the garments of worldliness, it seems wise to provide a measured biblical response. I will put this response in the form of twelve appeals. I am not eager to vilify but to redeem and transform.

Twelve Appeals to Prosperity Preachers

1. Don't preach a gospel that puts unnecessary obstacles in the way of people getting into heaven.

Jesus said, "How difficult it will be for those who have wealth to enter the kingdom of God!" His disciples were astonished, as many in the "prosperity" movement should be. So Jesus went on to raise their astonishment even higher by saying, "It is easier for a camel to go through the eye of a needle than for a rich person to enter the kingdom of God." They responded in disbelief: "Then who can be saved?" Jesus says, "With

21. Phiri and Maxwell, "Gospel Riches," 27.
22. For example, Wayne Grudem has developed a series of lectures titled "50 Factors Within Nations that Determine Their Wealth or Poverty." The point of these lectures is that biblical faithfulness leads a culture in general away from poverty and toward prosperity. http://www.christianessentialssbc.com/messages/.

man it is impossible, but not with God. For all things are possible with God" (Mark 10:23–27).

This means that their astonishment was warranted. A camel can't go through the eye of a needle. This is not a metaphor for something requiring great effort or humble sacrifice. It can't be done. We know this because Jesus said, *Impossible!* That was his word, not ours. "With man it is impossible." The point is that the heart-change required is something man can't do for himself. God must do it—". . . but [it is] not [impossible] with God."

We can't make ourselves stop treasuring money above Christ. But God can. That is good news. And that should be part of the message that prosperity preachers herald before they entice people to become more camel-like. Why would a preacher want to preach a gospel that encourages the desire to be rich and thus confirms people in their natural unfitness for the kingdom of God?

2. Don't preach a gospel that kindles suicidal desires in people.

The apostle Paul warned against the *desire* to be rich. And by implication, he warned against preachers who stir up the desire to be rich instead of helping people get rid of it. He warned, "Those who desire to be rich fall into temptation, into a snare, into many senseless and harmful desires that plunge people into ruin and destruction. For the love of money is a root of all kinds of evils. It is through this craving that some have wandered away from the faith and pierced themselves with many pangs" (1 Tim. 6:9–10).

These are very serious words, but they don't seem to find an echo in the preaching of the prosperity gospel. It is not wrong for the poor to want measures of prosperity so that they have what they need and can be generous and can devote time and energy to Christ-exalting tasks other than scraping to get by. It is not wrong to seek Christ for help in this quest. He cares about our needs (Matt. 6:33).

But we all—poor and rich—are constantly in danger of setting our affections (1 John 2:15–16) and our hope (1 Tim. 6:17) on riches rather than Christ. This "desire to be rich" is so strong and so suicidal that Paul uses the strongest language to warn us. My appeal is that prosperity preachers would do the same.

3. Don't preach a gospel that encourages vulnerability to moth and rust.

Jesus warns against the effort to lay up treasures on earth; that is, he tells us to be *givers*, not *keepers*. "Do not lay up for yourselves treasures on earth, where moth and rust destroy and where thieves break in and steal, but lay up for yourselves treasures in heaven, where neither moth nor rust destroys and where thieves do not break in and steal" (Matt. 6:19–20).

Yes, we all keep something. Jesus assumes that. He does not expect, except in extreme cases, that our giving will mean we will no longer be able to give. There may be a time when we will give our life for someone and thus no longer be able to give any more. But ordinarily Jesus expects us to live in a way that there is an ongoing pattern of work and earning and simple living and continual giving.

But given the built-in tendency toward greed in all of us, Jesus feels the need to warn against "laying up treasures on earth." It looks like gain, but it leads only to loss ("moth and rust destroy and thieves break in and steal"). My appeal is that Jesus' warning find a strong echo in the mouths of prosperity preachers.

4. Don't preach a gospel that makes good work a means of getting rich.

Getting rich is not what work is for. Paul said we should not steal. The alternative was hard work with our own hands. But the main purpose was not merely to hoard or even to *have*. The purpose was "to have *in order to give*."

"Let the thief no longer steal, but rather let him labor, doing honest work with his own hands, *so that he may have something to share* with anyone in need" (Eph. 4:28). This is not a justification for *being* rich in order to give more. It is a call to make more and keep less so you can give more. There is no reason why a person who prospers more and more in his business should increase the lavishness of his lifestyle indefinitely. Paul would say, Cap your expenditures and give the rest away.

I can't determine your "cap." But in all the texts we are looking at in this chapter, there is an impulse toward simplicity and lavish generosity, not lavish possessions. When Jesus said, "Sell your possessions, and give to the needy" (Luke 12:33), he seemed to imply not that the disciples were wealthy and could give from their overflow. It seems they had so few liquid assets that they had to sell something in order to have something to give.

Why would preachers want to encourage people to think that they should possess wealth in order to be a lavish giver? Why not encourage them to keep their lives more simple and be an even more lavish giver? Would that not add to their generosity a strong testimony that Christ, and not possessions, is their treasure?

5. Don't preach a gospel that promotes less faith in God's promise and diminishes the glory of God's help.

The reason the writer to the Hebrews tells us to be content with what we have is that the opposite implies less faith in the promises of God. He says, "Keep your life free from love of money, and be content with what you have, for he has said, 'I will never leave you nor forsake you.' So we can confidently say, 'The Lord is my helper; I will not fear; what can man do to me?'" (Heb. 13:5–6).

On the one hand, we may trust in the Lord to be our helper. He will provide and protect. And in that sense there is a measure of prosperity he will give us. "Your heavenly Father knows that you need them all" (Matt. 6:32). But, on the other hand, when it says, "Keep your life free from love of money, and be content with what you have" *because* God promises never to leave us, it must mean that we can easily move from trusting God for our *needs* to using God for our wants.

The line between "God help me," and "God make me rich," is real, and the writer to the Hebrews doesn't want us to cross it. Preachers should help their people to remember and recognize this line rather than speaking as though it weren't there.

6. Don't preach a gospel that contributes to people being choked to death.

Jesus warns that the word of God, the gospel, which is meant to give us life, can be choked to death by riches. He says it is like a seed that grows up among thorns: "They are those who hear, but as they go on their way they are choked by the . . . riches . . . of life, and their fruit does not mature" (Luke 8:14).

Prosperity preachers should warn their hearers that there is a kind of financial prosperity that can choke them to death. Why would we want to encourage people to pursue the very thing that Jesus warns can make them fruitless?

7. Don't preach a gospel that takes the seasoning out of the salt and puts the light under a basket.

What is it about Christians that makes them the salt of the earth and the light of the world? It is not wealth. The desire for wealth and the pursuit of wealth tastes and looks just like the world. Desiring to be rich makes us *like* the world, not different. At the very point where we should taste different, we have the same bland covetousness that the world has. In that case, we don't offer the world anything different from what it already believes in.

The great tragedy of prosperity preaching is that a person does not have to be spiritually awakened in order to embrace it; one needs only to be greedy. Getting rich in the name of Jesus is not the salt of the earth or the light of the world. In this, the world simply sees a reflection of itself. And if they are "converted" to this, they have not been truly converted but only put a new name on an old life.

The context of Jesus' saying shows us what the salt and light are. They are the joyful willingness to suffer for Christ. Here is what Jesus said,

> Blessed are you when others revile you and persecute you and utter all kinds of evil against you falsely on my account. *Rejoice* and be glad, for your reward is great in heaven, for so they persecuted the prophets who were before you. You are the salt of the earth. . . . You are the light of the world.
>
> Matthew 5:11–14

What will make the world *taste* the salt and *see* the light of Christ in us is not that we love wealth the same way they do. Rather, it will be the willingness and the ability of Christians to love others through suffering, all the while rejoicing because their reward is in heaven with Jesus. "*Rejoice* and be glad [in hardship] . . . You are the salt of the earth." The saltiness is the taste of joy in hardship. This is *unusual* life that the world can taste as different.

Such life is inexplicable on human terms. It is supernatural. But to attract people with promises of prosperity is simply natural. It is not the message of Jesus. It is not what he died to achieve.

8. Don't preach a gospel that conceals the necessity of suffering in the Christian life.

Missing from most prosperity preaching is the fact that the New Testament emphasizes the necessity of suffering far more than it does the notion of material prosperity.

Jesus said, "Remember the word that I said to you: 'A servant is not greater than his master.' If they persecuted me, they will also persecute you. If they kept my word, they will also keep yours" (John 15:20). Or again he said, "If they have called the master of the house Beelzebul, how much more *will they malign* those of his household" (Matt. 10:25).

Paul reminded the new believers on his missionary journeys, "through many tribulations we must enter the kingdom of God" (Acts 14:22). And he told the believers in Rome that their sufferings were a necessary part of the path to eternal inheritance.

> The Spirit himself bears witness with our spirit that we are children of God, and if children, then heirs—heirs of God and fellow heirs with Christ, *provided we suffer with him* in order that we may also be glorified with him. For I consider that *the sufferings of this present time* are not worth comparing with the glory that is to be revealed to us.
>
> Romans 8:16–18

Peter too said that suffering is the normal pathway to God's eternal blessing.

> Beloved, do not be surprised at the *fiery trial* when it comes upon you to test you, *as though something strange were happening to you*. But rejoice insofar as you *share Christ's sufferings*, that you may also rejoice and be glad when his glory is revealed. If you are *insulted for the name of Christ*, you are blessed, because the Spirit of glory and of God rests upon you.
>
> 1 Peter 4:12–14

Suffering is the normal cost of godliness. "Indeed, all who desire to live a godly life in Christ Jesus will be persecuted" (2 Tim. 3:12). I am aware that these words on suffering move back and forth between a more general suffering as part of the fall (Rom. 8:18–25) and specific suffering owing to human hostilities. But I will argue later in chapter 3 that when it comes to God's purposes in our suffering there is no substantial difference.[23]

Prosperity preachers should include in their messages significant teaching about what Jesus and the apostles said about the necessity of suffering. It must come, Paul said (Acts 14:22), and we do young disciples a disservice not to tell them that early. Jesus even said it before conversion so that prospective believers would count the cost: "So therefore, any one of you who does not renounce all that he has cannot be my disciple" (Luke 14:33).

9. *Don't preach a gospel that obscures the God-ordained purposes of suffering in the Christian life.*

The New Testament not only makes clear that suffering is necessary for followers of Christ, it is also at pains to explain why this is the case and

23. See pp. 108–25.

what God's purposes in it are. These purposes are crucial for believers to know. God has revealed them to help us understand why we suffer and to bring us through like gold through fire.

Later, in the chapter on suffering, I will unfold these purposes.[24] So here I will only name them and say to the prosperity preachers: *Include the great biblical teachings in your messages.* New believers need to know why God ordains for them to suffer.

1. Suffering deepens faith and holiness.
2. Suffering makes your cup increase.
3. Suffering is the price of making others bold.
4. Suffering fills up what is lacking in Christ's afflictions.
5. Suffering enforces the missionary command to go.
6. The supremacy of Christ is manifest in suffering.

10. *Don't preach a gospel that ignores the shift from a come-see religion in the Old Testament to a go-tell religion in the New Testament.*

A fundamental change happened with the coming of Christ into the world. Until that time, God had focused his redemptive work on Israel with occasional works among the nations. Paul said, "In past generations [God] allowed all the nations to walk in their own ways" (Acts 14:16). He called them "times of ignorance." "The times of ignorance God overlooked, but now he commands all people everywhere to repent" (Acts 17:30). Now the focus has shifted from Israel to the nations. Jesus said, "The kingdom of God will be taken away from you [Israel] and given to a people producing its fruits [followers of the Messiah]" (Matt. 21:43). A hardening has come upon Israel until the full number of the nations comes in (Rom. 11:25).

One of the main differences between these two eras is that in the Old Testament, God glorified himself largely by blessing Israel so that the nations could see and know that the Lord is God. "May [the LORD] maintain the cause of . . . his people Israel, as each day requires, *that all the peoples of the earth may know that the LORD is God*; there is no other" (1 Kings 8:59–60). Israel was not yet sent on a "Great Commission" to gather the nations; rather, she was glorified so that the nations would see her greatness and come to her.

24. See pp. 108–25.

So when Solomon built the temple of the Lord it was spectacularly lavish with overlaid gold.

> The inner sanctuary was twenty cubits long, twenty cubits wide, and twenty
> cubits high, and he overlaid it with *pure gold*. He also overlaid an altar of
> cedar. And Solomon overlaid the inside of the house with *pure gold*, and
> he drew chains of *gold* across, in front of the inner sanctuary, and overlaid
> it with *gold*. *And he overlaid the whole house with gold*, until all the house
> was finished. Also the whole altar that belonged to the inner sanctuary he
> overlaid with *gold*.
>
> 1 Kings 6:20–22

And when he furnished it, the gold was again just as abundant.

> So Solomon made all the vessels that were in the house of the LORD: the
> *golden* altar, the *golden* table for the bread of the Presence, the lampstands
> of *pure gold*, five on the south side and five on the north, before the inner
> sanctuary; the flowers, the lamps, and the tongs, of *gold*; the cups, snuffers,
> basins, dishes for incense, and fire pans, of *pure gold*; and the sockets of
> *gold*, for the doors of the innermost part of the house.
>
> 1 Kings 7:48–50

It took Solomon seven years to build the house of the Lord. Then he
took thirteen years to build his own house (1 Kings 6:38–7:1). It too was
lavish with gold and costly stones (1 Kings 7, 10).

Then, when all was built, the point of this opulence is seen in 1 Kings
10 as the queen of Sheba, representing the Gentile nations, comes to see
the glory of the house of God and of Solomon. When she saw it, "there
was no more breath in her" (1 Kings 10:5). She said, "Blessed be the LORD
your God, who has delighted in you and set you on the throne of Israel!
Because the LORD loved Israel forever, he has made you king" (1 Kings
10:9).

In other words, the pattern in the Old Testament is *a come-see religion*.
There is a geographic center of the people of God. There is a physical
temple, an earthly king, a political regime, an ethnic identity, an army to
fight God's earthly battles, and a band of priests to make animal sacrifices
for sins.

With the coming of Christ all of this changed. There is no geographic
center for Christianity (John 4:20–24); Jesus has replaced the temple, the
priests, and the sacrifices (John 2:19; Heb. 9:25–26); there is no Chris-

tian political regime because Christ's kingdom is not of this world (John 18:36); and we do not fight earthly battles with chariots and horses or bombs and bullets, but spiritual ones with the word and the Spirit (Eph. 6:12–18; 2 Cor. 10:3–5).

All of this supports the great change in mission. The New Testament does not present a come-see religion, but a go-tell religion. "And Jesus came and said to them, 'All authority in heaven and on earth has been given to me. Go therefore and make disciples of all nations, baptizing them in the name of the Father and of the Son and of the Holy Spirit, teaching them to observe all that I have commanded you. And behold, I am with you always, to the end of the age'" (Matt. 28:18–20).

The implications of this are huge for the way we live and the way we think about money and lifestyle. One of the main implications is that we are "sojourners and exiles" (1 Peter 2:11) on the earth. We do not use this world as though it were our primary home. "Our citizenship is in heaven, and from it we await a Savior, the Lord Jesus Christ" (Phil. 3:20).

This leads to a wartime lifestyle. That means we don't amass wealth to show the world how rich our God can make us. We work hard and seek a wartime austerity for the cause of spreading the gospel to the ends of the earth. We maximize giving to the war effort, not comforts at home. We raise our children with a view to helping them embrace the suffering that it will cost to finish the mission.

So if a prosperity preacher asks me about all the promises of wealth for faithful people in the Old Testament, my response is: Read your New Testament carefully and see if you see the same emphasis. You won't find it. And the reason is that things have dramatically changed.

"We brought nothing into the world, and we cannot take anything out of the world. But if we have food and clothing, with these we will be content" (1 Tim. 6:7–8). Why? Because the call to Christ is a call to "share in suffering as a good soldier of Christ Jesus" (2 Tim. 2:3). The emphasis of the New Testament is not riches to lure us in to sin, but sacrifice to carry us out.

One providential confirmation that God intended this distinction between a come-see orientation in the Old Testament and a go-tell orientation in the New Testament is the difference between the language of the Old Testament and the language of the New. Hebrew, the language of the Old Testament, was shared by no other peoples of the ancient world. It was unique to Israel. This is an astonishing contrast with Greek, the language of the New Testament, which was the trade language of the Roman world. So the very languages of the Old and New Testaments signal the difference in mission. Hebrew was not well-suited for missions to the ancient world. Greek was ideally suited for missions to the Roman world.

11. *Don't preach a gospel that minimizes the sin of making godliness a means of gain.*

The apostle Paul set us an example by how vigilant he was not to give the impression that he was in the ministry for money. He said that ministers of the world have a right to make a living from the ministry. But then to show us the danger in that he refuses to fully use that right.

> It is written in the Law of Moses, "You shall not muzzle an ox when it treads out the grain." . . . It was written for our sake, because the plowman should plow in hope and the thresher thresh in hope of sharing in the crop. If we have sown spiritual things among you, is it too much if we reap material things from you? If others share this rightful claim on you, do not we even more? Nevertheless, we have not made use of this right, but we endure anything rather than put an obstacle in the way of the gospel of Christ."
>
> 1 Corinthians 9:9–12

In other words, he renounced a legitimate right in order not to give anyone the impression that money was the motivation of his ministry. He did not want the money of his converts: "We never came with words of flattery, as you know, nor with a pretext for greed—God is witness" (1 Thess. 2:5).

He preferred to work with his hands rather than give the impression that he was peddling the gospel: "I coveted no one's silver or gold or apparel. You yourselves know that these hands ministered to my necessities and to those who were with me. In all things I have shown you that by working hard in this way we must help the weak and remember the words of the Lord Jesus, how he himself said, 'It is more blessed to give than to receive'" (Acts 20:33–35).

He knew that there were peddlers of God's word who thought "godliness is a means of gain" (1 Tim. 6:5–6). But he refused to do anything that would put him in that category: "We are not, like so many, *peddlers of God's word*, but as men of sincerity, as commissioned by God, in the sight of God we speak in Christ" (2 Cor. 2:17).

Too many prosperity preachers not only give the impression that they "peddle God's word" and make "godliness a means of gain" but actually develop a bogus theology to justify their extravagant displays of wealth. Paul did just the opposite.

12. Don't preach a gospel that obscures the biblical truth that God himself is the greatest treasure.

My biggest concern about the effects of the prosperity movement is that it diminishes Christ by making him less central and less satisfying than his gifts. Christ is not magnified most by being the giver of wealth. He is magnified most by satisfying the soul of those who sacrifice to love others in the ministry of the gospel.

When we commend Christ as the one who makes us rich, we glorify riches, and Christ becomes a means to the end of what we really want—namely, health, wealth, and prosperity. But when we commend Christ as the one who satisfies our soul forever—even when there is no health, wealth, and prosperity—then Christ is magnified as more precious than all those gifts.

We see this in Philippians 1:20–21. Paul says, "It is my eager expectation and hope that . . . Christ will be honored in my body, whether by life or by death. For to me to live is Christ, and to die is gain." Honoring Christ happens when we treasure him so much that dying is *gain*. Because dying means "to depart and be with Christ" (Phil. 1:23).

This is the missing note in prosperity preaching. The New Testament aims at the glory of Christ, not the glory of his gifts. To make that clear, it puts the entire Christian life under the banner of joyful self-denial. "If anyone would come after me, let him *deny himself* and take up his cross and follow me" (Mark 8:34). "I have been crucified with Christ" (Gal. 2:20).

But even though self-denial is a hard road that leads to life (Matt. 7:14), it is the most joyful of all roads. "The kingdom of heaven is like treasure hidden in a field, which a man found and covered up. Then *in his joy* he goes and sells all that he has and buys that field" (Matt. 13:44). Jesus says that finding Christ as our treasure makes all other possessions *joyfully* dispensable. "*In his joy* he goes and sells all that he has and buys that field."

I do not want prosperity preachers to stop calling people to maximum joy. On the contrary, I appeal to them to stop encouraging people to seek their joy in material things. The joy Christ offers is so great and so durable that it enables us to lose prosperity and still rejoice. "You joyfully accepted the plundering of your property, *since you knew that you yourselves had a better possession and an abiding one*" (Heb. 10:34). The grace to be joyful in the loss of prosperity—that is the miracle prosperity preachers should seek. That would be the salt of the earth and the light of the world. That would magnify Christ as supremely valuable.

Jesus Will Build His Church

God is sovereign over the world and over the mission of his church. All authority belongs to him in heaven and on earth (Matt. 28:18). The new configuration of world Christianity is his doing. He is building his church (Matt. 16:18). Both its blessings and its blemishes are under his sovereign sway. The gospel of the kingdom *will* be preached as a testimony to all the unreached peoples of the world (Matt. 24:14). The Lord of the harvest will see to it that the workers are sent and that the harvest is gathered in (Matt. 9:38). The good shepherd has other sheep outside the fold and he *must* bring them also. They will listen to his voice and there will be one flock and one shepherd (John 10:16).

The fundamental task of world missions remains the same—as it has for two thousand years. The aim is still captured in the words of Psalm 67:4: "Let the nations be glad and sing for joy." The gladness of the nations through faith in Christ for the glory of God—that is the great aim of missions. Declaring his glory—the glory of grace in the saving death and resurrection of Jesus—is the great task among all the unreached peoples of the world. "Declare his glory among the nations, his marvelous works among all the peoples!" (Ps. 96:3).

God is infinitely passionate for his glory and for its praise among the nations. He has been, is now, and always will be supreme in missions, until the Lord Jesus himself returns and brings history as we know it to a close. The price of finishing this mission will be much sacrifice and many lives (Col. 1:24; Rev. 6:11). The fuel of that sacrifice will not be the love of money or a passion for prosperity; it will be a love for Christ and a passion for his glory. May the Lord purify his church. May he refine like gold the growing faith of the Global South. And may he remember mercy and grant Europe and America a great awakening for the glory of his name and the gladness of the nations.

PART 1

MAKING GOD SUPREME IN MISSIONS

THE PURPOSE, THE POWER, AND THE PRICE

1

The Supremacy of God
in Missions through Worship

Missions is not the ultimate goal of the church. Worship is. Missions exists because worship doesn't. Worship is ultimate, not missions, because God is ultimate, not man. When this age is over, and the countless millions of the redeemed fall on their faces before the throne of God, missions will be no more. It is a temporary necessity. But worship abides forever.[1]

Worship, therefore, is the fuel and goal of missions. It's the goal of missions because in missions we simply aim to bring the nations into the white-hot enjoyment of God's glory. The goal of missions is the gladness of the peoples in the greatness of God. "The LORD reigns, let the earth *rejoice*; let the many coastlands *be glad*!" (Ps. 97:1). "Let the peoples praise you, O God; let all the peoples praise you! Let the nations *be glad and sing for joy*!" (Ps. 67:3–4).

1. In the 2003 edition of this book, I added a chapter to clarify in great detail and application what I mean by "worship" and how it relates to "worship services" and the worship of practical obedience (Rom. 12:1–2). It is titled "The Inner Simplicity and Outer Freedom of Worldwide Worship." The thesis is that the New Testament is stunningly silent about the outward forms of worship and radically focused on the inner experience of treasuring God, because it is a book of vision for missions in all cultures, not a worship manual for how to "do worship" in our culture.

But worship is also the fuel of missions. Passion for God in worship precedes the offer of God in preaching. You can't commend what you don't cherish. Missionaries will never call out, "Let the nations *be glad!*" if they cannot say from the heart, "*I rejoice* in the LORD. . . . *I will be glad and exult in you*, I will sing praise to your name, O Most High" (Pss. 104:34; 9:2). Missions begins and ends in worship.

If the pursuit of God's glory is not ordered above the pursuit of man's good in the affections of the heart and the priorities of the church, man will not be well served, and God will not be duly honored. I am not pleading for a diminishing of missions but for a magnifying of God. When the flame of worship burns with the heat of God's true worth, the light of missions will shine to the darkest peoples on earth. And I long for that day to come!

Where passion for God is weak, zeal for missions will be weak. Churches that are not centered on the exaltation of the majesty and beauty of God will scarcely kindle a fervent desire to "declare *his glory* among the nations" (Ps. 96:3). Even outsiders feel the disparity between the boldness of our claim upon the nations and the blandness of our engagement with God.

Albert Einstein's Indictment

For example, Charles Misner, a scientific specialist in general relativity theory, expressed Albert Einstein's skepticism over the church with words that should waken us to the shallowness of our experience with God in worship:

> The design of the universe . . . is very magnificent and shouldn't be taken for granted. In fact, I believe that is why Einstein had so little use for organized religion, although he strikes me as a basically very religious man. *He must have looked at what the preachers said about God and felt that they were blaspheming. He had seen much more majesty than they had ever imagined, and they were just not talking about the real thing.* My guess is that he simply felt that religions he'd run across did not have proper respect . . . for the author of the universe.[2]

The charge of blasphemy is loaded. The point is to pack a wallop behind the charge that in our worship services God simply doesn't come through

2. Quoted in *First Things* 18 (December 1991): 63 (emphasis added).

for who he is. He is unwittingly belittled. For those who are stunned by the indescribable magnitude of what God has made, not to mention the infinite greatness of the One who made it, the steady diet on Sunday morning of practical how-to's and psychological soothing and relational therapy and tactical planning seem dramatically out of touch with Reality—the God of overwhelming greatness.

It is possible to be distracted from God in trying to serve God. Martha-like, we neglect the one thing needful and soon begin to present God as busy and fretful as we are. A. W. Tozer warned us about this:

> We commonly represent God as a busy, eager, somewhat frustrated Father hurrying about seeking help to carry out His benevolent plan to bring peace and salvation to the world. . . . Too many missionary appeals are based upon this fancied frustration of Almighty God.[3]

Scientists know that light travels at the speed of 5.87 trillion miles a year. They also know that the galaxy of which our solar system is a part is about 100,000 light-years in diameter—about 587,000 trillion miles. It is one of about a million such galaxies in the optical range of our most powerful telescopes. It has been estimated that in our galaxy there are more than 200 billion stars. The sun is one of them, a modest star burning at about 6,000 degrees centigrade on the surface and traveling in an orbit at 135 miles per second, which means it will take about 250 million years to complete a revolution around the galaxy.

Scientists know these things and are awed by them. And they say, "If there is a personal God, as the Christians say, who spoke this universe into being, then there is a certain respect and reverence and wonder and dread that would have to come through when we talk about him and when we worship him."

We who believe the Bible know this even better than the scientists because we have heard something even more amazing:

> "To whom then will you compare me, that I should be like him?" says the Holy One. Lift up your eyes on high and see: who created these [stars]? He who brings out their host by number, calling them all by name, by the greatness of his might, and because he is strong in power not one is missing."

Isaiah 40:25–26

3. Quoted in Tom Wells, *A Vision for Missions* (Carlisle, Pa.: Banner of Truth Trust, 1985), 35.

Every one of the billions of stars in the universe is there by God's specific appointment. He knows their number. And most astonishing of all, he knows them by name. They do his bidding as his personal agents. When we feel the weight of this grandeur in the heavens, we have only touched the hem of his garment. "Behold, these are but the outskirts of his ways, and how small a whisper do we hear of him!" (Job 26:14). That is why we cry, "Be exalted, O God, above the heavens!" (Ps. 57:5). God is the absolute reality that everyone in the universe must come to terms with. Everything depends utterly on his will. All other realities compare to him like a raindrop compares to the ocean or like an anthill compares to Mount Everest. To ignore him or belittle him is unintelligible and suicidal folly. How shall one ever be the emissary of this great God who has not trembled before him with joyful wonder?

The Second Greatest Activity in the World

The most crucial issue in missions is the centrality of God in the life of the church. How can people who are not stunned by the greatness of God be sent with the ringing message, "*Great* is the LORD, and *greatly* to be praised; he is to be feared above all gods" (Ps. 96:4)? Missions is not first and ultimate; God is. And these are not just words. This truth is the lifeblood of missionary inspiration and endurance. William Carey, the father of modern missions, who set sail for India from England in 1793, expressed the connection:

> When I left England, my hope of India's conversion was very strong; but amongst so many obstacles, it would die, unless upheld by God. Well, I have God, and His Word is true. Though the superstitions of the heathen were a thousand times stronger than they are, and the example of the Europeans a thousand times worse; though I were deserted by all and persecuted by all, yet my faith, fixed on the sure Word, would rise above all obstructions and overcome every trial. God's cause will triumph.[4]

Carey and thousands like him have been moved and carried by the vision of a great and triumphant God. That vision must come first. Savoring it in worship precedes spreading it in missions. All of history is moving toward one great goal, the white-hot worship of God and his

---

4. Quoted in Iain Murray, *The Puritan Hope* (Edinburgh: Banner of Truth Trust, 1971), 140. For an introduction to Carey's life, see Timothy George, *Faithful Witness: The Life and Mission of William Carey* (Birmingham, Ala.: New Hope, 1991).

Son among all the peoples of the earth. Missions is not that goal. It is the means. And for that reason it is the second greatest human activity in the world.

God's Passion for God Is the Foundation for Ours

One of the things God uses to make this truth take hold of a person and a church is the stunning realization that it is also true for God himself. Missions is not *God's* ultimate goal, worship is. And when this sinks into a person's heart everything changes. The world is often turned on its head, and everything looks different—including the missionary enterprise.

The ultimate foundation for our passion to see God glorified is his own passion to be glorified. God is central and supreme in his own affections. There are no rivals for the supremacy of God's glory in his own heart. God is not an idolater. He does not disobey the first and great commandment. With all his heart and soul and strength and mind he delights in the glory of his manifold perfections.[5] The most passionate heart for God in all the universe is God's heart.

This truth, more than any other I know, seals the conviction that worship is the fuel and goal of missions. The deepest reason why our passion for God should *fuel* missions is that God's passion for God fuels missions. Missions is the overflow of our delight in God because missions is the overflow of God's delight in being God. And the deepest reason why worship is the *goal* in missions is that worship is God's goal. We are confirmed in this goal by the biblical record of God's relentless pursuit of praise among the nations. "Praise the LORD, all nations! Extol him, all peoples!" (Ps. 117:1). If it is God's goal, it must be our goal.

The Chief End of God Is to Glorify God and Enjoy Himself Forever

All my years of preaching and teaching on the supremacy of God in the heart of God have proved that this truth hits most people like a truck laden with unknown fruit. If they survive the impact, they discover that this is the most luscious fruit on the planet. I have unpacked this truth

5. I have tried to unfold this wonderful truth of the Father's delight in himself in *The Pleasures of God: Meditations on God's Delight in Being God*, rev. and exp. ed. (Sisters, Ore.: Multnomah, 2000), chap. 1, "The Pleasure of God in His Son" (25–45).

with lengthy arguments in other places.[6] So here I will give just a brief overview of the biblical basis. What I am claiming is that the answer to the first question of the Westminster Catechism is the same when asked concerning God as it is when asked concerning man. Question: "What is the chief end of man?" Answer: "The chief end of man is to glorify God and enjoy him forever." Question: "What is the chief end of God?" Answer: "The chief end of God is to glorify God and enjoy himself forever."

Another way to say it is simply that God is righteous. The opposite of righteousness is to value and enjoy what is not truly valuable or rewarding. This is why people are called unrighteous in Romans 1:18. They suppress the truth of God's value and exchange God for created things. So they belittle God and discredit his worth. Righteousness is the opposite. It means recognizing true value for what it is and esteeming it and enjoying it in proportion to its true worth. The unrighteous in 2 Thessalonians 2:10 perish because they refuse to *love* the truth. The righteous, then, are those who welcome a *love* for the truth. Righteousness is recognizing and welcoming and loving and upholding what is truly valuable.

God is righteous. This means that he recognizes, welcomes, loves, and upholds with infinite jealousy and energy what is infinitely valuable, namely, the worth of God. God's righteous passion and delight is to display and uphold his infinitely valuable glory. This is not a vague theological conjecture. It flows inevitably from dozens of biblical texts that show God in the relentless pursuit of praise and honor from creation to consummation.

Probably no text in the Bible reveals the passion of God for his own glory more clearly and bluntly than Isaiah 48:9–11, where God says:

> For my name's sake I defer my anger, for the sake of my praise I restrain it for you, that I may not cut you off. Behold, I have refined you, but not as silver; I have tried you in the furnace of affliction. For my own sake, for my own sake, I do it, for how should my name be profaned? My glory I will not give to another.

I have found that for many people these words come like six hammer blows to a man-centered way of looking at the world:

6. See especially "Appendix 1: The Goal of God in Redemptive History," in *Desiring God: Meditations of a Christian Hedonist* (Sisters, Ore.: Multnomah, 1996), 255–66; and the entirety of *The Pleasures of God*.

For *my* name's sake!

For the sake of *my* praise!

For *my* own sake!

For *my* own sake!

How should *my* name be profaned!

My glory I will not give to another!

What this text hammers home to us is the centrality of God in his own affections. The most passionate heart for the glorification of God is God's heart. God's ultimate goal is to uphold and display the glory of his name.

Biblical Texts to Show God's Zeal for His Own Glory

God chose his people for his glory:

> He chose us in Him before the foundation of the world, that we should be holy and blameless before Him. In love He predestined us to adoption as sons through Jesus Christ to Himself, according to the kind intention of His will, to the praise of the glory of His grace.
>
> Ephesians 1:4–6 NASB; cf. vv. 12, 14

God created us for his glory:

> Bring my sons from afar and my daughters from the end of the earth, everyone who is called by my name, *whom I created for my glory.*
>
> Isaiah 43:6–7

God called Israel for his glory:

> You are my servant, Israel, in whom I will be glorified.
>
> Isaiah 49:3

> I made the whole house of Israel and the whole house of Judah cling to me, declares the LORD, *that they might be for me a people, a name, a praise, and a glory.*
>
> Jeremiah 13:11

God rescued Israel from Egypt for his glory:

Our fathers, when they were in Egypt, did not consider your wondrous works . . . but rebelled by the Sea, at the Red Sea. Yet he saved them *for his name's sake, that he might make known his mighty power.*

Psalm 106:7–8

God raised Pharaoh up to show his power and glorify his name:

For the Scripture says to Pharaoh, "For this very purpose I have raised you up, that I might show my power in you, and that my name might be proclaimed in all the earth."

Romans 9:17

God defeated Pharaoh at the Red Sea to show his glory:

And I will harden Pharaoh's heart, and he will pursue them, and *I will get glory over Pharaoh* and all his host, and the Egyptians *shall know that I am the* Lord. . . . *And the Egyptians shall know that I am the* Lord, *when I have gotten glory* over Pharaoh, his chariots, and his horsemen.

Exodus 14:4, 18; cf. v. 17

God spared Israel in the wilderness for the glory of his name:

I acted for the sake of my name, that it should not be profaned in the sight of the nations, in whose sight I had brought them out.

Ezekiel 20:14

God gave Israel victory in Canaan for the glory of his name:

Who is like your people Israel, the one nation on earth whom God went to redeem to be his people, *making himself a name* and doing for them great and awesome things by driving out before your people, whom you redeemed for yourself from Egypt, a nation and its gods?

2 Samuel 7:23

God did not cast away his people for the glory of his name:

Do not be afraid; you have done all this evil. Yet do not turn aside from following the Lord. . . . For the Lord will not forsake his people, *for his great name's sake.*

1 Samuel 12:20, 22

God saved Jerusalem from attack for the glory of his name:

For I will defend this city to save it, *for my own sake* and for the sake of my servant David.

2 Kings 19:34; cf. 20:6

God restored Israel from exile for the glory of his name:

Thus says the Lord GOD: It is not for your sake, O house of Israel, that I am about to act, but *for the sake of my holy name . . . And I will vindicate the holiness of my great name. . . .* And the nations will know that I am the LORD.

Ezekiel 36:22–23; cf. v. 32

Jesus sought the glory of his Father in all he did:

The one who speaks on his own authority seeks his own glory, but *the one who seeks the glory of him who sent him* is true, and in him there is no falsehood.

John 7:18

Jesus told us to do good works so that God gets glory:

In the same way, let your light shine before others, so that they may see your good works and *give glory to your Father who is in heaven.*

Matthew 5:16; cf. 1 Peter 2:12

Jesus warned that not seeking God's glory makes faith impossible:

How can you believe, when you receive glory from one another and do not *seek the glory that comes from the only God?*

John 5:44

Jesus said that he answers prayer that God would be glorified:

Whatever you ask in my name, this I will do, *that the Father may be glorified in the Son.*

John 14:13

Jesus endured his final hours of suffering for God's glory:

"Now is my soul troubled. And what shall I say? 'Father, save me from this hour?' *But for this purpose I have come to this hour. Father, glorify your* name.'" Then a voice came from heaven: *"I have glorified it, and I will glorify it again."*

John 12:27–28

Father, the hour has come; *glorify your Son that the Son may glorify you.*

John 17:1; cf. 13:31–32

God gave his Son to vindicate the glory of his righteousness:

God put [Christ] forward as a propitiation by his blood . . . *to show God's righteousness.* . . . It was to show his righteousness at the present time.

Romans 3:25–26

God forgives our sins for his own sake:

I, I am he who blots out your transgressions *for my own sake*, and I will not remember your sins.

Isaiah 43:25

For *your name's sake*, O LORD, pardon my guilt, for it is great.

Psalm 25:11

Jesus receives us into his fellowship for the glory of God:

Welcome one another as Christ has welcomed you, *for the glory of God.*

Romans 15:7

The ministry of the Holy Spirit is to glorify the Son of God:

He will glorify me, for he will take what is mine and declare it to you.

John 16:14

God instructs us to do everything for his glory:

So, whether you eat or drink, or whatever you do, *do all to the glory of God.*

1 Corinthians 10:31; cf. 6:20

God tells us to serve in a way that will glorify him:

Whoever serves, [let him do it] as one who serves by the strength that God supplies—*in order that in everything God may be glorified* through Jesus Christ. To him belong glory and dominion forever and ever. Amen.

1 Peter 4:11

Jesus will fill us with fruits of righteousness for God's glory:

> It is my prayer that . . . [you be] filled with the fruit of righteousness that comes through Jesus Christ, *to the glory and praise of God.*
>
> Philippians 1:9, 11

All are under judgment for dishonoring God's glory:

> They became fools, and *exchanged the glory of the immortal God for images.*
>
> Romans 1:22–23

> For all have sinned and *fall short of the glory of God.*
>
> Romans 3:23

Herod is struck dead because he did not give glory to God:

> Immediately an angel of the Lord struck him down, because *he did not give God the glory.*
>
> Acts 12:23

Jesus is coming again for the glory of God:

> They will suffer the punishment of eternal destruction, away from the presence of the Lord and from the glory of his might, when he comes on that day *to be glorified in his saints, and to be marveled at among all who have believed.*
>
> 2 Thessalonians 1:9–10

Jesus' ultimate aim for us is that we see and enjoy his glory:

> Father, I desire that they also, whom you have given me, may be with me where I am, *to see my glory* that you have given me because you loved me before the foundation of the world.
>
> John 17:24

Even in wrath God's aim is to make known the wealth of his glory:

> Desiring to show his wrath and to make known his power, [God] has endured with much patience vessels of wrath prepared for destruction, *in*

order to make known the riches of his glory for vessels of mercy, which he has prepared beforehand for glory.

Romans 9:22–23

God's plan is to fill the earth with the knowledge of his glory:

For the earth will be filled with *the knowledge of the glory of the* LORD as the waters cover the sea.

Habakkuk 2:14

Everything that happens will redound to God's glory:

From him and through him and to him are all things. *To him be glory forever.* Amen.

Romans 11:36

In the New Jerusalem, the glory of God replaces the sun:

And the city has no need of sun or moon to shine on it, for *the glory of God gives it light*, and its lamp is the Lamb.

Revelation 21:23

God's passion for God is unmistakable. God struck me with this most powerfully when I first read Jonathan Edwards's book titled *The Dissertation Concerning the End for Which God Created the World*.[7] There he piles reason upon reason and Scripture upon Scripture to show this truth:

The great end of God's works, which is so variously expressed in Scripture, is indeed but ONE; and this one end is most properly and comprehensively called, THE GLORY OF GOD.[8]

In other words, the chief end of God is to glorify God and enjoy himself forever.

7. For an introduction to the life of Edwards, the implications of his theology for evangelicalism, and the complete text of *The End for Which God Created the World*, see John Piper, *God's Passion for His Glory: Living the Vision of Jonathan Edwards* (Wheaton: Crossway, 1998).
8. Ibid., 246.

The Belittling of God's Glory and the Horrors of Hell

The condition of the human heart throws God's God-centeredness into stark relief. Man by nature does not have a heart to glorify God. "All have sinned and *fall short of the glory of God*" (Rom. 3:23). In our wickedness, we suppress the truth that God is our Sovereign and worthy of all our allegiance and affection. By nature we exchange the glory of the immortal God for dim images of it in creation (Rom. 1:18, 23). We forsake the fountain of living waters and hew out for ourselves broken cisterns that can hold no water (Jer. 2:13).

The nations "are darkened in their understanding, alienated from the life of God because of the ignorance that is in them, due to their hardness of heart" (Eph. 4:18). By nature we were all once dead in trespasses and sins, following the slave master Satan, and therefore children of wrath (Eph. 2:1–3). Our end was "eternal punishment" (Matt. 25:46), exclusion "from the presence of the Lord" (2 Thess. 1:9), and endless torments in "the lake that burns with fire and sulfur, which is the second death" (Rev. 21:8; cf. 14:11; 20:10).[9]

The infinite horrors of hell are intended by God to be a vivid demonstration of the infinite value of the glory of God. The biblical assumption of the justice of hell is a clear testimony to the infiniteness of the sin of failing to glorify God. All of us have failed. All the nations have failed. Therefore, the weight of infinite guilt rests on every human head because of our failure to cherish the glory of God. The biblical vision of God, then, is that he is supremely committed, with infinite passion, to uphold and display the glory of his name. And the biblical vision of man without grace is that he suppresses this truth and by nature finds more joy in his own glory than he does in God's. God exists to be worshiped, and man worships the work of his own hands. This twofold reality creates the critical need for missions. And the very God-centeredness of God, which creates the crisis, also creates the solution.

How Can Self-Exaltation Be Love?

For over thirty years I have tried to present to Christians in various places this central biblical truth of God's passion for the glory of God. The major objection has been that it seems to make God unloving. The merciful, kind, loving heart of God seems to disappear in the passions of an overweening

9. In defense of the reality of eternal conscious torment in hell for those who reject the truth of God, see chapter 4.

ego. Doesn't the Bible say, "Love . . . does not seek its own" (1 Cor. 13:5 NASB)? How then can God be loving and seek his own glory? It's a good question. And in answering it we will see how the supremacy of God in the heart of God is the spring of mercy and kindness and love—which means the spring of missions.

There are two ways to see harmony between God's passion for his own glory and Paul's statement "Love . . . does not seek its own." One is to say that Paul doesn't mean that every way of seeking your own is wrong. Some ways are, and some ways aren't. The other is to say that God is unique and that Paul's statement does not apply to him the way it does to us. I think both of these are true.

Love Seeks Its Own Joy in the Joy of Others

First, "Love . . . does not seek its own" was not meant by Paul to condemn every possible way of "seeking your own." He did not mean that seeking your own happiness in loving others is loveless. We know this because in Acts 20:35 Paul told the elders of the church of Ephesus to "remember" the word of the Lord Jesus: "It is more blessed to give than to receive." If it were unloving to be motivated by the blessedness of loving, then Paul would not have told the elders to "remember" this word, that is, to keep it in their minds where it could function as a conscious motive. If seeking your own blessing in giving to others ruined the act, Paul would not have told us to keep this blessing in mind.

Those who have thought most deeply about motivation realize this and have interpreted Paul's words in 1 Corinthians 13:5 with great wisdom. For example, Jonathan Edwards pointed out that what Paul is opposing in the words "Love . . . does not seek its own" is not

> the degree in which [a person] loves his own happiness, but in his placing his happiness where he ought not, and in limiting and confining his love. Some, although they love their own happiness, do not place that happiness in their own confined good, or in that good which is limited to themselves, but more in the common good—in that which is the good of others, or in the good to be enjoyed in and by others. . . . And when it is said that *Charity seeketh not her own*, we are to understand it of her own private good—good limited to herself.[10]

10. Jonathan Edwards, *Charity and Its Fruits* (1852; reprint, Edinburgh: Banner of Truth Trust, 1969), 164.

In other words, Paul did not mean to condemn every possible way of seeking your own. He had in mind the selfish attitude that finds its happiness not in helping others but in using others or ignoring others for personal gain. He did not have in mind the attitude that *seeks its own* joy precisely in doing good to others. In fact, he appeals to that motive two verses earlier when he says, "If I give away all I have, and if I deliver up my body to be burned, but have not love, I *gain nothing*" (1 Cor. 13:3). He is saying, "Surely you do not want to 'gain nothing,' do you? Well, then be sure that you love. Then you will gain much." So he actually appeals to the very motive that some say he is denouncing. But he is not appealing to low, selfish, materialistic motives. He is calling for the radical transformation of heart that finds its joy in the act of love and all the goodness that comes from it.

So the way is opened perhaps for God to "seek his own" and still be loving. But I said there are two ways to see harmony between God's passion for his own glory and Paul's statement "Love seeks not its own." We've seen one, namely, that Paul is not opposing "seeking one's own" if "one's own" is really the good of others.

The Sin of Imitating God

The other way to see this harmony is to say that God is unique and that Paul's statement does not apply to him the way it does to us. This is true. Things are forbidden to us that are not forbidden to God precisely because we are not God and he is. The reason we are not to exalt our own glory but God's is because he is God and we are not. For God to be faithful to this same principle means that he too would exalt not our glory but his. The unifying principle is not, Don't exalt your own glory. The unifying principle is, Exalt the glory of what is infinitely glorious. For us that means exalt God. And for God that means exalt God. For us it means don't seek your own glory. For God it means *do* seek your own glory.

This can be very slippery. Satan saw this and used it in the Garden of Eden. He came with the temptation to Adam and Eve: If you eat from the forbidden tree, "you will be like God, knowing good and evil" (Gen. 3:5). Now, what Adam and Eve should have said was, "We are already like God. We have been created *in his image*" (Gen. 1:27). But instead of putting this truth against Satan's temptation, they allowed the truth to make error look plausible: "If we are in the image of God, then it can't be wrong to want to be like God. So the suggestion of the serpent that we will be like God can't be bad." So they ate.

But the problem is that it is *not* right for humans to try to be like God in every way. God's God-ness makes some things right for him to do that are not right for us to do. In Adam and Eve's case, it is God's right to decide for them what is good and what is evil, what is helpful and what is harmful. They are finite and do not have the wisdom to know all the factors to take into account in living a happy life. Only God knows all that needs to be known. Therefore, humans have no right to be independent of God. Independent judgment about what is helpful and harmful is folly and rebellion. That was the temptation. And that was the essence of their disobedience.

The point is simply that even though we are created in the image of God, and even though in some ways we are to "be imitators of God" (Eph. 5:1), we are mistaken to think that God does not have some rights that we do not have. A father wants his child to imitate his manners and courtesies and integrity, but he does not want the child to imitate his authority, neither toward his parents nor toward his brothers and sisters.

Thus, it is right for God to do some things that we are forbidden to do. And one of those things is to exalt his own glory. He would be unrighteous if he did not do so, because he would not be prizing what is infinitely valuable. He would in fact be an idolater if he esteemed as his infinite treasure something less precious than his own glory.

God Is Most Glorified in Us When We Are Most Satisfied in Him

But is it loving for God to exalt his own glory? Yes, it is. And there are several ways to see this truth clearly. One is to ponder this sentence: *God is most glorified in us when we are most satisfied in him.* This is perhaps the most important sentence in my theology.[11] If it is true, then it becomes plain why God is loving when he seeks to exalt his glory in my life, for that would mean that he would seek to maximize my satisfaction in him, since he is most glorified in me when I am most satisfied in him. Therefore, God's pursuit of his own glory is not at odds with my joy, and that means it is not unkind or unmerciful or unloving of him to seek his glory. In fact, it means

11. For an extended elaboration of this thesis, see Piper, *Desiring God*, and its abbreviated version, *The Dangerous Duty of Delight: The Glorified God and the Satisfied Soul* (Sisters, Ore.: Multnomah, 2001). See also Sam Storms, *Pleasures Evermore: The Life-Changing Power of Enjoying God* (Colorado Springs: NavPress, 2000).

that the more passionate God is for his own glory, the more passionate he is for my satisfaction in that glory. And therefore, God's God-centeredness and God's love soar together.

To illustrate the truth that God is most glorified in us when we are most satisfied in him, consider what I might say on a pastoral visit when entering the hospital room of one of my people. They look up from their bed with a smile and say, "Oh, Pastor John, how good of you to come. What an encouragement." And suppose I lift my hand, as it were to deflect the words, and say matter-of-factly, "Don't mention it. It's my duty as a pastor." Now, what is wrong here? Why do we cringe at such a thoughtless pastoral statement? It is my duty. And duty is a good thing. So why does that statement do so much damage?

It damages because it does not honor the sick person. Why? Because delight confers more honor than duty does. Doing hospital visitation out of mere duty honors duty. Doing it out of delight honors the patients. And they feel that. The right pastoral response to the patient's greeting would have been, "It's a pleasure to be here. I'm glad I could come." Do you see the paradox here? Those two sentences would show that I am "seeking my own." "It's *my* pleasure to be here. *I'm* glad I could come." And yet the reason these statements are not selfish is that they confer honor on the patient, not on the pastor. When someone delights in you, you feel honored. When someone finds happiness in being around you, you feel treasured, appreciated, "glorified." Visiting the sick because you are glad to be there is a loving thing to do.

This then is the answer to why God is not unloving to magnify his glory. God is glorified precisely when we are satisfied in him—when we delight in his presence, when we like to be around him, when we treasure his fellowship. This is an utterly life-changing discovery. It frees us to pursue our joy in God and God to pursue his glory in us because they are not two different pursuits. God is most glorified in us when we are most satisfied in him.

God's Self-Exaltation: Signpost to Human Satisfaction

Therefore, when we read hundreds of texts in the Bible that show God passionately exalting his own glory, we no longer hear them as the passions of an overweening, uncaring ego. We hear them as the rightful exaltation of One who is infinitely exalted, and we hear them as God's pursuit of our deepest satisfaction in him. God is utterly unique. He is the only being in the universe worthy of worship. Therefore, when he exalts himself he directs people to true and lasting joy. "In your presence there is fullness of joy; at your right hand are pleasures forevermore" (Ps. 16:11). But when we exalt ourselves, we are distracting people from what will bring true and lasting joy. So for us to be loving we must exalt God, and for God to be loving he must exalt God. Love is helping people toward the greatest beauty, the highest value, the deepest satisfaction, the most lasting joy, the biggest reward, the most wonderful friendship, and the most overwhelming worship—love is helping people toward God. We do this by pointing to the greatness of God. And God does it by pointing to the greatness of God.

God Exalts Himself in Mercy

There is another way to see how God's passion for his own glory is loving, and here the connection between the supremacy of God and the cause of missions becomes explicit. The connection between missions and the supremacy of God is found in this sentence: *The glory God seeks to magnify is supremely the glory of his mercy.* The key text is Romans 15:8–9:

> I tell you that Christ became a servant to the circumcised [Jewish people] to show God's truthfulness, *in order to confirm the promises given to the patriarchs, and in order that the Gentiles might glorify God for his mercy.*

Notice three interlocking truths in these great missionary verses.

1. *Zeal for the glory of God motivates world missions.* Paul gives three reasons why Christ humbled himself as a servant and came into the world on that first great missionary journey from heaven to earth. First, "Christ became a servant . . . *to show God's truthfulness.*" Second, he came "in order *to confirm* [God's] *promises.*" Third, he came "in order that the [nations] *might glorify God* for his mercy."

In other words, Christ was on a mission to magnify God. He came to show that *God* is truthful. He came to show that *God* is a promise-keeper. And he came to show that *God* is glorious. Jesus came into the world for *God's sake*—to certify *God's* integrity, to vindicate *God's* Word, to magnify *God's* glory. Since God sent his Son to do all this, it is plain that the primary motive of the first great mission to unreached peoples—the mission of Jesus from heaven—was God's zeal for the glory of God. That's the first truth from Romans 15:8–9: Zeal for the glory of God motivates world missions.

2. *A servant spirit and a heart of mercy motivate world missions.* "Christ became a *servant* . . . in order that the Gentiles might glorify God for his

mercy." Christ became a servant . . . and Christ brought mercy. He was a servant not only in that he humbled himself to do what the Father wanted him to do at great cost to himself. He was also a servant in that he lived his life for the sake of extending mercy to the nations. During his lifetime, he showed the connection between compassion and missions. We see this, for example, in Matthew 9:36–38:

> When he saw the crowds, he had compassion for them, because they were harassed and helpless, like sheep without a shepherd. Then he said to his disciples, "The harvest is plentiful, but the laborers are few; therefore pray earnestly to the Lord of the harvest to send out laborers into his harvest."

Jesus' compassion came to expression in the call to pray for more missionaries. From first to last, mercy was moving missions in the life of Jesus. And not only in his life but also in his death. "You were slain, and by your *blood* you ransomed people for God from every tribe and language and people and nation" (Rev. 5:9). Mercy was the very heart of Jesus' mission. No one deserved his mission. It was all mercy and all servanthood. That's the second truth from Romans 15:8–9: A servant spirit and a heart of mercy motivate world missions.

3. *The third truth is that the first and second truths are one truth.* Zeal for the glory of God and a servant heart of mercy for the nations are one. This is plain from the wording of verse 9: Christ came "in order that the Gentiles might glorify God." Yes! That was the passion of Christ, and it should be our passion—that the nations might love the glory of God and praise the glory of God. But the verse goes on: Christ came "that the Gentiles might glorify God *for his mercy.*" The motive of mercy and the motive of God's glory are not two different motives, because the glory we want to see exalted among the nations is supremely the glory of God's mercy.

Mercy is the apex of God's glory the way the overflow of a fountain is the apex of the fountain's fullness. God is free to be merciful because he is full and utterly self-sufficient in himself. He has no deficiencies or needs or defects. He relies totally on himself for all that he is. He never had a beginning or underwent any process of improvement through some influence outside himself. The glory of his all-sufficiency overflows in the freedom of his mercy to the nations. Therefore, extending God's mercy and exalting God's glory are one.[12]

12. For a more extended treatment of how God's God-centeredness is the ground of his mercy, see *Pleasures of God*, 104–9.

A heart for the glory of God and a heart of mercy for the nations make a Christlike missionary.[13] These must be kept together. If we have no zeal for the glory of God, our mercy becomes superficial, man-centered human improvement with no eternal significance. And if our zeal for the glory of God is not a reveling in his mercy, then our so-called zeal, in spite of all its protests, is out of touch with God and hypocritical (cf. Matt. 9:13).

He Does Everything for the Praise of the Glory of His Grace

This wonderful agreement between God's passion to be glorified and his passion to be gracious is also strikingly evident in the first chapter of Ephesians. Three times Paul says that God is doing all his saving work "to the praise of His glory" (NASB). And verse 6 makes clear that this glory is "the glory of His grace." Election, predestination, adoption, redemption, sealing by the Spirit, working all things according to the counsel of his will—God does all this to elicit praise for the glory of his grace. Verses 5–6: "He predestined us to adoption as sons through Jesus Christ . . . *to the praise of the glory of His grace.*" Verses 11–12: "[God] works all things after the counsel of His will, to the end that we who were the first to hope in Christ should be *to the praise of His glory.*" Verse 14: "[The Holy Spirit] is given as a pledge of our inheritance, with a view to the redemption of God's own possession, *to the praise of His glory.*"

This is just what we saw in Romans 15:9. There the nations glorify God for his mercy. Here they praise God for his grace. In both cases, God gets the glory and humans get the joy. So the more passionate God is for his glory, the more passionate he is for meeting our need as sinners. Grace is our only hope and the only hope of the nations. Therefore, the more zealous God is for his grace to be glorified, the more hope there is that missions will succeed.

The Power of Missions Is Worship

What we have been showing is that God's supremacy in his own heart is not unloving. It is, in fact, the fountain of love. God's full delight in

13. For further reflection on the interconnectedness of mercy and magnifying God in missions, see chapter 6 of this book, "A Passion for God's Supremacy and Compassion for Man's Soul."

his own perfections overflows in his merciful will to share that delight with the nations. We may reaffirm then the earlier truth that worship is the fuel and the goal that drive us in missions because it is the fuel and the goal that drive God in missions. Missions flows from the fullness of God's passion for God, and it aims at the participation of the nations in the very passion that he has for himself (cf. Matt. 25:21, 23; John 15:11; 17:13, 26). The power of the missionary enterprise is to be caught up into God's fuel and God's goal. And that means being caught up in worship.

Only One God Works for People Who Wait for Him

This remarkable vision of God as one who "exalts himself to show mercy" (Isa. 30:18) impels world missions in more ways than one. One way we have not pondered is the sheer uniqueness of this God among all the gods of the nations. Isaiah realizes this and says, "From of old no one has heard or perceived by the ear, no eye has seen a God besides you, who acts for those who wait for him" (Isa. 64:4). In other words, Isaiah is stunned that the greatness of God has the paradoxical effect that he does not need people to work for him but rather magnifies himself by working for them, if they will renounce self-reliance and "wait for him."

Isaiah anticipated the words of Paul in Acts 17:25: "[God is not] served by human hands, as though he needed anything, since he himself gives to all mankind life and breath and everything." The uniqueness at the heart of Christianity is the glory of God manifest in the freedom of grace. God is glorious because he does not need the nations to work for him. He is free to work for them. "The Son of Man came not to be served but to serve, and to give his life as a ransom for many" (Mark 10:45). Missions is not a recruitment project for God's labor force. It is a liberation project from the heavy burdens and hard yokes of other gods (Matt. 11:28–30).

Isaiah says that such a God has not been seen or heard anywhere in the world. "From of old no one has heard or perceived by the ear, no eye has seen a God besides you, who acts for those who wait for him" (Isa. 64:4). What Isaiah sees everywhere he looks are gods who have *to be served* rather than serve. For example, the Babylonian gods Bel and Nebo: "Bel bows down; Nebo stoops; their idols are on beasts and livestock; these things you carry are borne as burdens on weary beasts. They stoop; they bow down together; they cannot save the burden, but themselves go into captivity. Listen to me, O house of Jacob, all the remnant of the house of Israel, who have been borne by me from before your birth, carried from the womb; even to your old age I am he, and to gray hairs I will carry you. I have made, and I will bear; I will carry and will save" (Isa. 46:1–4; cf. Jer. 10:5).

The difference between the true God and the gods of the nations is that the true God carries and the other gods must be carried. God serves; they must be served. God glorifies his might by showing mercy. They glorify theirs by gathering slaves. So the vision of God as one whose passion for his glory moves him to mercy impels missions because he is utterly unique among all the gods.

The Most Shareable Message in the World

There is yet another way that such a God motivates the missionary enterprise. The gospel demand that flows from such a God to the nations is an eminently shareable, doable demand, namely, to rejoice and be glad in God. "The LORD reigns; let the earth *rejoice*; let the many coastlands *be glad*!" (Ps. 97:1). "Let the peoples praise you, O God; let all the peoples praise you! Let the nations *be glad and sing for joy*!" (Ps. 67:3–4). "Let the oppressed see it and *be glad*; you who seek God, *let your hearts revive*" (Ps. 69:32 RSV). "May all who seek you *rejoice and be glad in you*! May those who love your salvation say evermore, 'God is great!'" (Ps. 70:4). What message would missionaries rather take than the message, "Be glad in God! Rejoice in God! Sing for joy in God! For God is most glorified in you when you are most satisfied in him! God loves to exalt himself by showing mercy to sinners."

The liberating fact is that the message we take to the frontiers is that people everywhere should seek their own best interest. We are summoning people to God. And those who come say, "In your presence there is fullness of joy; at your right hand are pleasures forevermore" (Ps. 16:11). God glorifies himself among the nations with the command, "Delight yourself in the LORD!" (Ps. 37:4). His first and great requirement of all men everywhere is that they repent from seeking their joy in other things and begin to seek it only in him. A God who cannot be served[14] is a God who can only be enjoyed. The great sin of the world is not that the human

14. I am aware that the Bible is replete with pictures of God's people serving him. I have dealt in some detail with the way service can be conceived biblically so as not to put God in the category of an employer who depends on wage earners. See *Desiring God*, 144–49.

race has failed to work for God so as to *increase* his glory but that we have failed to delight in God so as to *reflect* his glory, for God's glory is most reflected in us when we are most delighted in him.

The most exhilarating thought in the world is that God's inexorable purpose to display his glory in the mission of the church is virtually the same as his purpose to give his people infinite delight. The glory of a Mountain Spring is seen in how many people (and how many different peoples!) find satisfaction and life in its overflowing streams. Therefore, God is committed to the holy joy of the redeemed, gathered from every tribe and tongue and people and nation, with the same zeal that moves him to seek his own glory in all that he does. The supremacy of God in the heart of God is the driving force of his mercy and the missionary movement of his church.

Biblical Expressions of the Supremacy of God in Missions

Against the background we have developed so far, we may now be able to feel the full force of those biblical texts that emphasize the supremacy of God in the missionary impulse of the church. The motives we see will confirm the centrality of God in the missionary vision of the Bible.

We have seen some of the Old Testament texts that make the glory of God the centerpiece of missionary proclamation: "Declare his glory among the nations, his marvelous works among all the peoples!" (Ps. 96:3). "Proclaim that his name is exalted" (Isa. 12:4). There are many others.[15] But we have not yet seen the straightforward statements of Jesus, Paul, and John that say the same thing.

Leaving Family and Possessions for the Sake of the Name

When Jesus turned the rich young ruler away because he was not willing to leave his wealth to follow Jesus, the Lord said, "Only with difficulty will a rich person enter the kingdom of heaven" (Matt. 19:23). The apostles were amazed and said, "Who then can be saved?" (v. 25). Jesus answered, "With man this is impossible, but with God all things are possible" (v. 26). Then Peter, speaking as a kind of missionary who had left his home and business to follow Jesus, said, "See, we have left everything and followed you. What then will we have?" (v. 27). Jesus answered with a mild rebuke of Peter's sense of sacrifice: "Everyone who

15. See an extensive list of these texts in chapter 5.

has left houses or brothers or sisters or father or mother or children or lands, *for my name's sake,* will receive a hundredfold and will inherit eternal life" (v. 29).

The one point of focus for us here is the phrase "for my name's sake." The motive that Jesus virtually takes for granted when a missionary leaves home and family and possessions is that it is *for the sake of the name of Jesus.* That means for the sake of Jesus' reputation. God's goal is that his Son's name be exalted and honored among all the peoples of the world, for when the Son is honored, the Father is honored (Mark 9:37). When every knee bows at the name of Jesus, it will be "to the glory of God the Father" (Phil. 2:10–11). Therefore, God-centered missions exists for the sake of the name of Jesus.

A Missionary Prayer for God's Name to Be Hallowed

The first two petitions of the Lord's Prayer are perhaps the clearest statements in the teachings of Jesus that missions is driven by the passion of God to be glorified among the nations. "Hallowed be your name. Your kingdom come" (Matt. 6:9–10). Here Jesus teaches us to ask God to hallow his name and to make his kingdom come. This is a missionary prayer. Its aim is to engage the passion of God for his name among those who forget or revile the name of God (Pss. 9:17; 74:18). To hallow God's name means to put it in a class by itself and to cherish and honor it above every claim to our allegiance or affection. Jesus' primary concern—the very first petition of the prayer he teaches—is that more and more people, and more and more peoples, come to hallow God's name. This is the reason the universe exists. Missions exists because this hallowing does not.

How Much He Must Suffer for the Name

When Paul was converted on the Damascus road, Jesus Christ became the supreme treasure and joy of his life. "I count everything as loss because of the surpassing worth of knowing Christ Jesus my Lord" (Phil. 3:8). It was a costly allegiance. What Paul learned in Damascus was not only the joy of sins forgiven and fellowship with the King of the universe but also how much he would have to suffer. Jesus sent Ananias to him with this message: "I will show him how much he must suffer *for the sake of my name*" (Acts 9:16). Paul's missionary sufferings were "for the sake of the name." When he came near the end of his life and was warned not to go to Jerusalem, he answered, "What are you doing, weeping and breaking my heart? For I am ready not only to be imprisoned but even to die in Jerusalem *for the name of the Lord Jesus*" (Acts 21:13). For Paul, the glory of the name of Jesus and his reputation in the world were more important than life.

"For the Sake of His Name among All the Nations"

Paul makes crystal clear in Romans 1:5 that his mission and calling are for the name of Christ among all the nations: "We have received grace and apostleship to bring about the obedience of faith *for the sake of his name among all the nations.*"

The apostle John described the motive of early Christian missionaries in the same way. He wrote to tell one of his churches that they should send out Christian brothers in a manner "worthy of God." And the reason he gives is that "they have gone out *for the sake of the name*, accepting nothing from the Gentiles" (3 John 6–7).

John Stott comments on these two texts (Rom. 1:5; 3 John 7): "They knew that God had superexalted Jesus, enthroning him at his right hand and bestowing upon him the highest rank, in order that every tongue should confess his lordship. They longed that Jesus should receive the honor due to his name."[16] This longing is not a dream but a certainty. At the bottom of all our hope, when everything else has given way, we stand on this great reality: The everlasting, all-sufficient God is infinitely, unwaveringly, and eternally committed to the glory of his great and holy name. For the sake of his fame among the nations he will act. His name will not be profaned forever. The mission of the church will be victorious. He will vindicate his people and his cause in all the earth.

May the Blessed Redeemer See the Travail of His Soul!

David Brainerd, the missionary to the Indians in New Jersey in the 1740s, was sustained by this confidence to his death at age twenty-nine. Seven days before he died in 1747, he spoke of his longing for the glory of God in the world. These are the last words he had the strength to write with his own hand:

16. John R. W. Stott, "The Bible in World Evangelization," in *Perspectives on the World Christian Movement: A Reader*, 3d ed., ed. Ralph D. Winter and Steven C. Hawthorne (Pasadena, Calif.: William Carey Library, 1999), 22.

Friday, October 2. My soul was this day, at turns, sweetly set on God: I longed to be "with him" that I might "behold his glory." . . . Oh, that his kingdom might come in the world; that they might all love and glorify him for what he is in himself; and that the blessed Redeemer might "see of the travail of his soul, and be satisfied." Oh, "come, Lord Jesus, come quickly! Amen."[17]

The absence of Brainerd's passion for God is the great cause of missionary weakness in the churches. This was Andrew Murray's judgment a hundred years ago:

As we seek to find out why, with such millions of Christians, the real army of God that is fighting the hosts of darkness is so small, the only answer is—lack of heart. The enthusiasm of the kingdom is missing. And that is because there is so little enthusiasm for the *King*.[18]

This is still true today. Peter Beyerhaus also sees it clearly and calls us to put the glory of God at the center of our life and mission.

We are called and sent to glorify the reign of God and to manifest His saving work before the whole world. . . . Today it is extremely important to emphasize the priority of this doxological aim before all other aims of mission. Our one-sided concern with man and his society threatens to pervert mission and make it a secular or even a quasi-atheistic undertaking. We are living in an age of apostasy where man arrogantly makes himself the measuring rod of all things. Therefore, it is a part of our missionary task courageously to confess before all enemies of the cross that the earth belongs to God and to His anointed. . . . Our task in mission is to uphold the banner of the risen Lord before the whole world, because it is his own.[19]

The zeal of the church for the glory of her King will not rise until pastors and mission leaders and seminary teachers make much more of the King. When the glory of God himself saturates our preaching and teach-

17. Jonathan Edwards, *The Life of David Brainerd*, ed. Norman Pettit, vol. 7 of *The Works of Jonathan Edwards* (New Haven: Yale University Press, 1985), 474. For a more accessible version of Brainerd's diary, see Philip E. Howard Jr., *The Life and Diary of David Brainerd, ed. by Jonathan Edwards with a Biographical Sketch of the Life and Work of Jonathan Edwards* (Grand Rapids: Baker, 1989).

18. Andrew Murray, *Key to the Missionary Problem* (Fort Washington, Pa.: Christian Literature Crusade, 1979), 133.

19. Peter Beyerhaus, *Shaken Foundations: Theological Foundations for Missions* (Grand Rapids: Zondervan, 1972), 41–42.

ing and conversation and writings, and when he predominates above our talk of methods and strategies and psychological buzzwords and cultural trends, then the people might begin to feel that he is the central reality of their lives and that the spread of his glory is more important than all their possessions and all their plans.

The Power of Missions When Love for the Lost Is Weak

Compassion for the lost is a high and beautiful motive for missionary labor. Without it we lose the sweet humility of sharing a treasure we have freely received. But we have seen that compassion for people must not be detached from passion for the glory of God. John Dawson, a leader in Youth With a Mission, gives an additional reason why this is so. He points out that a strong feeling of love for "the lost" or "the world" is a very difficult experience to sustain and is not always recognizable when it comes.

> Have you ever wondered what it feels like to have a love for the lost? This is a term we use as part of our Christian jargon. Many believers search their hearts in condemnation, looking for the arrival of some feeling of benevolence that will propel them into bold evangelism. It will never happen. It is impossible to love "the lost." You can't feel deeply for an abstraction or a concept. You would find it impossible to love deeply an unfamiliar individual portrayed in a photograph, let alone a nation or a race or something as vague as "all lost people."
>
> Don't wait for a feeling of love in order to share Christ with a stranger. You already love your heavenly Father, and you know that this stranger is created by Him, but separated from Him, so take those first steps in evangelism because you love God. It is not primarily out of a compassion for humanity that we share our faith or pray for the lost; it is first of all, love for God. The Bible says in Ephesians 6:7–8: "With good will doing service, as to the Lord, and not to men, knowing that whatever good anyone does, he will receive the same from the Lord, whether he is a slave or free."
>
> Humanity does not deserve the love of God any more than you or I do. We should never be Christian humanists, taking Jesus to poor sinful people, reducing Jesus to some kind of product that will better their lot. People deserve to be damned, but Jesus, the suffering Lamb of God, deserves the reward of His suffering.[20]

20. John Dawson, *Taking Our Cities for God* (Lake Mary, Fla.: Creation House, 1989), 208–9.

The Miracle of Love

Dawson's words are a wise and encouraging warning not to limit our mission engagement to the level of compassion we feel for people we do not know. However, I don't want to minimize what the Lord is able to do in giving people a supernatural burden of love for distant peoples. For example, Wesley Duewel of OMS International tells the story of his mother's remarkable burden for China and India:

> My mother for years carried a hunger for the people of China and India. For many years practically every day as she prayed during family prayer for these two nations she would break down and weep before she finished praying. Her love was deep and constant, and she will be rewarded eternally for her years of love-burden for those lands. This is the love of Jesus reaching out and mediated through Christians by the Holy Spirit.[21]

I emphasize again that the motive of compassion and the motive of zeal for the glory of God are not separate. The weeping of compassion is the weeping of joy in God impeded in the extension of itself to another.[22]

The Call of God

God is calling us above all else to be the kind of people whose theme and passion is the supremacy of God in all of life. No one will be able to rise to the magnificence of the missionary cause who does not feel the magnificence of Christ. There will be no big world vision without a big God. There will be no passion to draw others into our worship where there is no passion for worship.

God is pursuing with omnipotent passion a worldwide purpose of gathering joyful worshipers for himself from every tribe and tongue and people and nation. He has an inexhaustible enthusiasm for the supremacy of his name among the nations. Therefore, let us bring our affections into line with his, and, for the sake of his name, let us renounce the quest for worldly comforts and join his global purpose. If we do this, God's omnipotent commitment to his name will be over us like a banner, and we will not lose, in spite of many tribulations (Acts 9:16; Rom. 8:35–39). Missions is

---

21. Wesley Duewel, *Ablaze for God* (Grand Rapids: Zondervan, 1989), 115–16.
22. On this theme, see chapter 6 of this book, "A Passion for God's Supremacy and Compassion for Man's Soul."

not the ultimate goal of the church. Worship is. Missions exists because worship doesn't. The Great Commission is first to "delight yourself in the LORD" (Ps. 37:4) and then to declare, "Let the nations *be glad and sing for joy*" (Ps. 67:4). In this way, God will be glorified from beginning to end, and worship will empower the missionary enterprise until the coming of the Lord.

> Great and amazing are your deeds,
>   O Lord God the Almighty!
> Just and true are your ways,
>   O King of the nations!
> Who will not fear, O Lord,
>   and glorify your name?
> For you alone are holy.
>   All nations will come
>   and worship you,
> for your righteous acts have been revealed.
>
>   Revelation 15:3–4

2

The Supremacy of God
in Missions through Prayer

We cannot know what prayer is for until we know that
life is war.

Life is war. That's not all it is. But it is always that. Our weakness in prayer is owing largely to our neglect of this truth. Prayer is primarily a wartime walkie-talkie for the mission of the church as it advances against the powers of darkness and unbelief. It is not surprising that prayer malfunctions when we try to make it a domestic intercom to call upstairs for more comforts in the den. God has given us prayer as a wartime walkie-talkie so that we can call headquarters for everything we need as the kingdom of Christ advances in the world. Prayer gives *us* the significance of frontline forces and gives *God* the glory of a limitless Provider. The one who gives the power gets the glory. Thus, prayer safeguards the supremacy of God in missions while linking us with endless grace for every need.

Life Is War

When Paul came to the end of his life, he said in 2 Timothy 4:7, "I have fought *the good fight*, I have finished the race, I have kept the faith." In

65

1 Timothy 6:12, he tells Timothy, "*Fight the good fight* of the faith. Take hold of the eternal life to which you were called." For Paul, all of life was war. Yes, he used other images as well—farming, athletics, family, building, shepherding, and so on. And yes, he was a man who loved peace. But the pervasiveness of war is seen precisely in the fact that one of the weapons of war is the gospel of peace! (Eph. 6:15). Yes, he was a man of tremendous joy. But this joy was usually a "rejoicing in the sufferings" of his embattled mission (Rom. 5:3; 12:12; 2 Cor. 6:10; Phil. 2:17; Col. 1:24; cf. 1 Peter 1:6; 4:13).

Life is war because the maintenance of our faith and the laying hold on eternal life is a constant fight. Paul makes clear in 1 Thessalonians 3:5 that Satan targets our faith for destruction. "I sent to learn about your *faith*, for fear that somehow the tempter had tempted you and *our labor would be in vain*." Satan's attack in Thessalonica was against the Christians' faith. His aim was to make Paul's work there "vain"—empty, destroyed.

It's true that Paul believed in the eternal security of the elect ("Those whom [God] justified he also glorified" [Rom. 8:30]). But the only people who are eternally secure are those who "make their calling and election sure" by fighting the good fight of faith and laying hold on eternal life (1 Tim. 6:12; 2 Peter 1:10). Jesus said, "The one who endures to the end will be saved" (Mark 13:13). And Satan is fighting always to bring us to ruin by destroying our faith.

The word for "fight" in 1 Timothy, *agōnizesthai*, is used repeatedly in describing the Christian life. Jesus said, "*Strive* to enter through the narrow door. For many, I tell you, will seek to enter and will not be able" (Luke 13:24). Hebrews 4:11 says, "Let us therefore *strive* to enter that rest, so that no one may fall by the same sort of disobedience." Paul compares the Christian life to a race and says, "Every athlete *strives* and uses self-control in all things. They do it to obtain a perishable crown, but we do it to obtain an imperishable one" (1 Cor. 9:25, author's translation). He describes his ministry of proclamation and teaching in these terms: "For this I toil, *struggling* with all his energy that he powerfully works within me" (Col. 1:29). And he says that prayer is part of this fight: "Epaphras, who is one of you, a servant of Christ Jesus, greets you, always *struggling* on your behalf in his prayers" (Col. 4:12). "*Strive* together with me in your prayers to God on my behalf" (Rom. 15:30). It's the same word each time: the word for "fight."

Paul is even more graphic at times with other warfare language. Concerning his own life of warfare he said, "I do not run aimlessly; I do not *box* as one beating the air. But I discipline my body and keep it under control, lest after preaching to others I myself should be disqualified" (1 Cor. 9:26–27). He runs a race, he fights a boxing match, and he strives against the forces of his own body. Concerning his ministry he said, "Though we walk in the flesh, we are not waging *war* according to the flesh. For the *weapons of our warfare* are not of the flesh but have divine power to destroy strongholds. We destroy arguments and every lofty opinion raised against the knowledge of God, and take every thought captive to obey Christ" (2 Cor. 10:3–5).

Paul encouraged Timothy to see his whole ministry as war: "This charge I entrust to you, Timothy, my child, in accordance with the prophecies previously made about you, that by them you may *wage the good warfare*" (1 Tim. 1:18). "No *soldier* gets entangled in civilian pursuits" (2 Tim. 2:4). In other words, missions and ministry are war.

Probably the most familiar passage on our daily warfare is Ephesians 6:12–18, where Paul lists the pieces of the "whole armor of God." We must not miss the forest for the trees here. The simple assumption of this familiar passage is this: Life is war. Paul simply assumes this and then tells us what kind of war it is: not "against flesh and blood, but against the rulers, against the authorities, against the cosmic powers over this present darkness, against the spiritual forces of evil in the heavenly places. Therefore take up the whole armor of God" (vv. 12–13).

Then all the precious blessings of life that could be thought of in contexts other than war are drafted for the battle. If we know *truth*, it is for a belt in the armor. If we have *righteousness*, we must wear it as a breastplate. If we cherish *the gospel of peace*, it must become a soldier's footwear. If we love *resting* in the promises of God, that faith must be fastened on our left arm as a shield against flaming arrows. If we delight in our *salvation*, we must fit it securely on our head as a helmet. If we love *the Word of God* as sweeter than honey, we must make the honey a sword. Virtually every "civilian" blessing in the Christian life is conscripted for the war. There is not a warfare part of life and a non-warfare part. Life is war.[1]

The Absence of Austerity

But most people do not believe this in their heart. Most people show by their priorities and their casual approach to spiritual things that they believe we are in peacetime, not wartime.

1. There are other texts we could look at besides those cited, for example, Rev. 6:2; 12:17; 17:14.

In wartime, the newspapers carry headlines about how the troops are doing. In wartime, families talk about the sons and daughters on the front lines and write to them and pray for them with heart-wrenching concern for their safety. In wartime, we are on the alert. We are armed. We are vigilant. In wartime, we spend money differently—there is austerity, not for its own sake but because there are more strategic ways to spend money than on new tires at home. The war effort touches everybody. We all cut back. The luxury liner becomes a troop carrier.

Very few people think that we are in a war that is greater than World War II or any imaginable nuclear war. Few reckon that Satan is a much worse enemy than any earthly foe or realize that the conflict is not restricted to any one global theater but is in every town and city in the world. Who considers that the casualties of this war do not merely lose an arm or an eye or an earthly life but lose everything—even their own soul—and enter a hell of everlasting torment?

In the *Screwtape Letters* by C. S. Lewis, Screwtape (the devil) tells Wormwood (a subordinate evil spirit) "not to hope for too much from a war." He was referring to the agonies of the Second World War. He explains that war will not destroy the faith of real believers and will, thanks to God's high-handed ways, produce a good deal of unwanted seriousness about life, death, and the issues of eternity. "How disastrous for us," the devil complains, "is the continual remembrance of death which war enforces. One of our best weapons, contented worldliness, is rendered useless. In wartime not even a human can believe that he is going to live forever."[2] So it may even take a lesser war—such as a World War III or a war of sheer terrorism—to waken us to the more serious war that rages daily for the soul.

Prayer Is for Wielding the Word

Until we feel the force of this, we will not pray as we ought. We will not even know what prayer is. In Ephesians 6:17–18, Paul makes the connection between the life of war and the work of prayer: "Take . . . the sword of the Spirit, which is the word of God, praying at all times in the Spirit, with all prayer and supplication. To that end keep alert with all perseverance, making supplication for all the saints." Notice that, true to the original Greek, verse 18 does not begin a new sentence. It connects with verse 17

2. C. S. Lewis, *Screwtape Letters* (London: Geoffrey Bles: The Centenary Press, 1942), 32.

like this: "Take the sword of the Spirit, which is the word of God, praying at all times in the Spirit, with all prayer and supplication." Take the sword . . . praying! This is how we are to wield the word—by prayer.

Prayer is the communication with headquarters by which the weapons of warfare are deployed according to the will of God. That's the connection between the weapons and prayer in Ephesians 6. Prayer is for war.

Missions Is Given as a Field for Prayer

The connection between prayer and missions can be seen in a passage that doesn't use warfare words but deals with the same reality, namely, John 15:16. Jesus said, "You did not choose me, but I chose you and appointed you that you should go and bear fruit and that your fruit should abide, *so that* whatever you ask the Father in my name, he may give it to you."

The logic of this sentence is crucial. Why is the Father going to give the disciples what they ask in Jesus' name? Answer: Because they have been sent to bear fruit. The reason the Father gives the disciples the instrument of prayer is because Jesus has given them a mission. In fact, the grammar of John 15:16 implies that the reason Jesus gives them their mission is so that they will be able to use the power of prayer. "I appointed you that you should go and bear fruit . . . *so that* whatever you ask the Father in my name, he may give it to you." This is just another way of saying that prayer is a wartime walkie-talkie. God designed it and gave it to us for use on a mission. You can say the mission is to "bear fruit," or you can say the mission is to "set the captives free." The point stays the same: Prayer is designed to extend the kingdom into fruitless enemy territory.

Why Prayer Malfunctions

Probably the number one reason prayer malfunctions in the hands of believers is that we try to turn a wartime walkie-talkie into a domestic intercom. Until you know that life is war, you cannot know what prayer is for. Prayer is for the accomplishment of a wartime mission. It is as though the field commander (Jesus) called in the troops, gave them a crucial mission (go and bear fruit), handed each of them a personal transmitter coded to the frequency of the General's headquarters, and said, "Comrades, the General has a mission for you. He aims to see it accomplished. And to that end he has authorized me to give each of you personal access to him through these transmitters. If you stay true to his mission and seek his victory first, he will always be as close as your transmitter, to give tactical advice and to send air cover when you need it."

But what have millions of Christians done? We have stopped believing that we are in a war. No urgency, no watching, no vigilance. No strategic planning. Just easy peace and prosperity. And what did we do with the walkie-talkie? We tried to rig it up as an intercom in our houses and cabins and boats and cars—not to call in firepower for conflict with a mortal enemy but to ask for more comforts in the den.

Times of Great Distress

In Luke 21:34–35, Jesus warned his disciples that times of great distress and opposition were coming. Then he said, "But stay awake at all times, *praying* that you may have strength to escape all these things that are going to take place, and to stand before the Son of Man" (v. 36). In other words, following Jesus will lead us into severe conflict with evil. It will mean war. Evil will surround us and attack us and threaten to destroy our faith. But God has given us a transmitter. If we go to sleep, it will do us no good. But if we are alert, as Jesus says, and call for help in the conflict, the help will come and the Commander will not let his faithful soldiers be denied their crown of victory before the Son of Man. Thus, repeatedly we see the same truth: We cannot know what prayer is for until we know that life is war.

Praying for Peace Is Part of the War

But 1 Timothy 2:1–4 looks as though it might conflict with this battlefield image of prayer. Paul says that he wants us to pray for kings and for all who are in high positions "that we may lead a peaceful and quiet life, godly and dignified in every way" (v. 2). Now, that sounds very domestic and civilian and peaceful.

But read on. The reason for praying this way is highly strategic. Verses 3–4 say, "This [praying for peace] is good, and it is pleasing in the sight of God our Savior, who desires all people to be saved and to come to the knowledge of the truth." God aims to save people from every tribe and tongue and people and nation. But one of the great obstacles to victory is when people are swept up into social, political, and militaristic conflicts that draw away their attention, time, energy, and creativity from the real battle of the universe.

Satan's aim is that no one be saved and come to a knowledge of the truth. And one of his key strategies is to start battles in the world that draw our attention away from the real battle for the salvation of the lost and the perseverance of the saints. He knows that the real battle, as Paul says, is not against flesh and blood. So the more wars and conflicts and revolutions of "flesh and blood" he can start, the better, as far as he is concerned.

So when Paul tells us to pray for peace precisely because God desires all men to be saved and to come to a knowledge of the truth, he is not picturing prayer as a kind of harmless domestic intercom for increasing our civilian conveniences. He is picturing it as a strategic appeal to headquarters to ask that the enemy not be allowed to draw any firepower away to decoy conflicts of flesh and blood.

The Crying Need of the Hour

So the truth is reaffirmed: God has given us prayer because Jesus has given us a mission. We are on this earth to press back the forces of darkness, and we are given access to headquarters by prayer to advance this cause. When we try to turn it into a civilian intercom to increase our conveniences, it stops working, and our faith begins to falter. We have so domesticated prayer that for many of us it is no longer what it was designed to be—a wartime walkie-talkie for the accomplishment of Christ's mission.

We simply must seek for ourselves and for our people a wartime mentality. Otherwise the biblical teaching about the urgency of prayer and the vigilance of prayer and the watching in prayer and the perseverance of prayer and the danger of abandoning prayer will make no sense and find no resonance in our hearts. Until we feel the desperation of a bombing raid or the thrill of a new strategic offensive for the gospel, we will not pray in the spirit of Jesus.

The crying need of the hour is to put the churches on a wartime footing. Mission leaders are crying out, "Where is the church's concept of militancy, of a mighty army willing to suffer, moving ahead with exultant determination to take the world by storm? Where is the risk-taking, the launching out on God alone?"[3] The answer is that it has been swallowed up in a peacetime mentality.

We are a "third soil century." In the parable of the soils, Jesus says that the seed is the Word. He sows his urgent Word of kingdom power. But

3. James Reapsome, "What's Holding Up World Evangelization?" *Evangelical Missions Quarterly* 24, no. 2 (April 1988): 118.

instead of taking it up as our sword (or bearing fruit), we "are those who hear the word, but the cares of the world and the deceitfulness of riches and the desires for other things enter in and choke the word, and it proves unfruitful" (Mark 4:18–19).

This is why Paul says that *all* of life is war—every moment. Before we can even engage in the mission of the church, we have to fight against "the deceitfulness of riches" and "desires for other things." We must fight to cherish the kingdom above all "other things"—that is our first and most constant battle. That is the fight of faith. Then, when we have some experience in that basic battle, we join the fight to commend the kingdom to all the nations.

God Will Win the War

Now, into this warfare God asserts himself for the triumph of his cause. He does this in an unmistakable way so that the victory will redound to his glory. His purpose in all of history is to uphold and display his glory for the enjoyment of his redeemed people from all the nations. Therefore, God engages in the battle so that the triumphs are manifestly his. As we saw in chapter 1, the chief end of God is to glorify God and enjoy his excellence forever. This is what guarantees the victory of his cause. In order to magnify his glory, he will exert his sovereign power and complete the mission he has commanded.

Power of the Puritan Hope

This confidence in the sovereignty of God and the triumph of his cause is essential in the prayers of God's people and the mission of the church. It has proven to be a powerful force in the history of missions. The first missionary endeavor of the Protestants in England burst forth from the soil of Puritan hope. The Puritans were those pastors and teachers in England (and then New England), roughly between the years 1560 and 1660, who wanted to purify the Church of England and bring it into theological and practical alignment with the teachings of the Reformation.[4]

4. For introductions to Puritanism, see Leland Ryken, *Worldly Saints: The Puritans as They Really Were* (Grand Rapids: Zondervan, 1991); J. I. Packer, *A Quest for Godliness: The Puritan Vision of the Godly Life* (Wheaton: Crossway, 1994); Peter Lewis, *The Genius of Puritanism* (Morgan, Pa.: Soli Deo Gloria, 1998); and Erroll Hulse, *Who Are the Puritans, and What Do They Teach?* (Darlington, England: Evangelical Press, 2000).

They had a view of God's sovereignty that produced an undaunted hope in the victory of God over all the world. They were deeply stirred by a passion for the coming of God's kingdom over all the nations. Their hearts really believed the truth of the promises that Christ's cause would triumph. "I will build my church, and the gates of hell shall not prevail against it" (Matt. 16:18). "This gospel of the kingdom will be proclaimed throughout the whole world as a testimony to all the nations, and then the end will come" (Matt. 24:14). "All the nations you have made shall come and worship before you, O Lord, and shall glorify your name" (Ps. 86:9). "In you all the families of the earth shall be blessed" (Gen. 12:3). "I will make the nations your heritage" (Ps. 2:8). "All the ends of the world shall remember and turn to the LORD, and all the families of the nations shall worship before you" (Ps. 22:27). "All the earth will worship You, And will sing praises to You; They will sing praises to Your name" (Ps. 66:4 NASB). "To him shall be the obedience of the peoples" (Gen. 49:10).[5]

This tremendous confidence that Christ would one day conquer hearts in every nation and be glorified by every people on earth gave birth to the first Protestant missionary endeavor in the English-speaking world, and it happened 150 years before the modern missionary movement began with William Carey in 1793.

Between 1627 and 1640, 15,000 people emigrated from England to America, most of them Puritans, carrying this great confidence in the worldwide reign of Christ. In fact, the seal of the colonists of Massachusetts Bay had on it a North American Indian with these words coming out of his mouth: "Come over into Macedonia and help us," which was taken from Acts 16:9. What this shows is that in general the Puritans saw their emigration to America as part of God's missionary strategy to extend his kingdom among the nations.

The Prayers and Pain of John Eliot

One of those hope-filled Puritans who crossed the Atlantic in 1631 was John Eliot. He was twenty-seven years old and a year later became the pastor of a new church in Roxbury, Massachusetts, about a mile from Boston. But something happened that made him much more than a pastor.

5. For additional texts concerning the promise of Christ's victory over the nations and their eventual turning to him, see chapter 5.

According to Cotton Mather, there were twenty tribes of Indians in that vicinity. John Eliot could not avoid the practical implications of his theology: If the infallible Scriptures promise that all nations will one day bow down to Christ, and if Christ is sovereign and able by his Spirit through prayer to subdue all opposition to his promised reign, then there is good hope that a person who goes as an ambassador of Christ to one of these nations will be the chosen instrument of God to open the eyes of the blind and to set up an outpost of the kingdom of Christ.

And so when he was slightly over forty (not twenty but forty!) years old, Eliot set himself to study Algonquin. He deciphered the vocabulary, grammar, and syntax and eventually translated the entire Bible as well as books that he valued such as Richard Baxter's *Call to the Unconverted*. By the time Eliot was eighty-four years old, there were numerous Indian churches, some with their own Indian pastors. It is an amazing story of a man who once said, "Prayers and pains through faith in Christ Jesus will do any thing!"[6]

The reason I tell this story is to highlight the tremendous importance of solid biblical *hope* on the basis of which we pray in the cause of world missions. God has promised and God is sovereign: "*All the nations . . . shall come and worship before you, O Lord, and shall glorify your name*" (Ps. 86:9).

This is what gripped the Puritan mind and eventually gave birth to the modern missionary movement in 1793. William Carey was nourished on this tradition, as were David Brainerd[7] and Adoniram Judson, Alexander Duff and David Livingstone, John Paton[8] and a host of others who gave their lives to reach the unreached peoples of the world. The modern missionary movement did not arise in a theological vacuum. It grew out of a great Reformation tradition that put the sovereignty of God square in

6. Cotton Mather, *The Great Works of Christ in America*, vol. 1 (1702; reprint, Edinburgh: Banner of Truth Trust, 1979), 562.

7. For a brief overview of Brainerd's life and ministry, refer to John Piper, "'Oh, That I May Never Loiter on My Heavenly Journey!' Misery and Mission in the Life of David Brainerd," in John Piper, *The Hidden Smile of God: The Fruit of Affliction in the Lives of John Bunyan, William Cowper, and David Brainerd* (Wheaton: Crossway, 2001), 123–59. An earlier version of this biographical sketch may be found at www.DesiringGod.org. Also see Jonathan Edwards, *The Life of David Brainerd*, ed. Norman Pettit, vol. 7 of *The Works of Jonathan Edwards* (1749; reprint, New Haven: Yale University Press, 1985).

8. For a brief overview of Paton's life and ministry, refer to John Piper, "'You Will Be Eaten By Cannibals!' Courage in the Cause of World Missions: Lessons from the Life of John G. Paton" at www.DesiringGod.org. Also see *John G. Paton: Missionary to the New Hebredes, An Autobiography Edited by His Brother* (1889, 1891; reprint, Edinburgh: Banner of Truth Trust, 1965).

the center of human life. In the warfare of world missions, God bares his arm and triumphs for his own glory.[9]

Missions Is Supremely the Work of God

It is even more important to see how God triumphs for his own glory in Scripture than in the faith of great missionaries. The New Testament makes clear that God has not left his Great Commission to the uncertainties of the human will. The Lord said from the beginning, "I will build my church" (Matt. 16:18). World missions is supremely the work of the risen Lord Jesus.

"I Have Other Sheep . . . I Must Bring Them Also"

In the Gospel of John, Jesus put it like this: "I have other sheep that are not of this fold. I must bring them also, and they will listen to my voice" (John 10:16). This is the great missionary text in the Gospel of John. It is full of hope and power. It means that Christ has people besides those already converted. "I have *other sheep* that are not of this fold." This is a reference to the doctrine of election.[10] God chooses who will belong to his sheep, and they are already his before Jesus calls them. "All that the Father gives me will come to me, and whoever comes to me I *will* never cast out" (John 6:37; cf. 6:44–45; 8:47; 10:26–27; 17:6; 18:37). These sovereign "wills" of the Lord Jesus guarantee his invincible engagement in world missions.

There will always be people who argue that the doctrine of election makes missions unnecessary. But they are wrong. It does not make missions unnecessary; it makes missions hopeful. John Alexander, a former

9. Whether one is a postmillennialist, as were most of the Puritans (though not all, e.g., William Twisse, Thomas Goodwin, William Bridge, and Jeremiah Burroughs, who were all premillennial Westminster divines in the seventeenth century), or whether one is a pre- or amillennialist, my point remains the same. Hope for the unstoppable success of Christ's mission (whether you see it as a golden age of gospel sway on earth or as an ingathering of the elect from every people group on earth) is a crucial element in motivation and power for missions. Iain Murray's book, *The Puritan Hope* (Edinburgh: Banner of Truth Trust, 1971), is an inspiring and compelling account of this truth. Its thesis is: "We believe it can be conclusively shown that the inspiration which gave rise to the first missionary societies of the modern era was nothing other than the doctrine and outlook which, revitalized by the eighteenth-century revival, had come down from the Puritans" (135).

10. I have given an extensive biblical defense of this truth in "The Pleasure of God in Election," in *The Pleasures of God* (Sisters, Ore.: Multnomah, 2000), 121–55.

president of InterVarsity Christian Fellowship, said in a message at Urbana '67 (a decisive event in my own life), "At the beginning of my missionary career I said that if predestination were true I could not be a missionary. Now after twenty some years of struggling with the hardness of the human heart, I say I could never be a missionary *unless I believed in the doctrine of predestination*."[11] It gives hope that Christ most certainly has "other sheep" among the nations.[12]

When Jesus says, "I must bring them also," he does not mean that he will do it without missionaries. That's plain from the fact that salvation comes through faith (John 1:12; 3:16; 6:35), and faith comes through the word of his disciples (John 17:20). Jesus brings his sheep into the fold through the preaching of those whom he sends, just as the Father sent him (John 20:21). So it is just as true today as in that day, "My sheep hear my voice, and I know them, and they follow me" (John 10:27). It is *Christ* who calls in the gospel. *Christ* gathers his sheep in world missions. That is why there is complete assurance that they will come.

Clothed with Power for Missions

When Jesus ascended to heaven, he told the disciples, "All authority in heaven and on earth has been given to me. . . . I am with you always, to the end of the age" (Matt. 28:18, 20). That's the authority with which he calls his sheep.

Then to make it plain that it would be his authority and his presence that would give success to the mission, he told his disciples to wait in Jerusalem until they were clothed with his power from on high (Luke 24:49). He said that the coming of that power through the Holy Spirit would enable them to be his witnesses "in Jerusalem and in all Judea and Samaria, and to the end of the earth" (Acts 1:8). When the Spirit comes, it is the Lord himself fulfilling the promise to build his church. Accordingly, Luke says, "The *Lord* added to their number day by day those who were being saved" (Acts 2:47). The Lord did it. And he continued to do it by converting the greatest missionary of all time (Acts 26:16–18) and directing the

---

11. This is a paraphrase of a sentence that is emblazoned on my memory because of the effect it had on my life at the time.

12. It was precisely this truth that encouraged the apostle Paul when he was downcast in Corinth. "And the Lord said to Paul one night in a vision, 'Do not be afraid, but go on speaking and do not be silent, for I am with you, and no one will attack you to harm you, for I have many in this city who are my people" (Acts 18:9–10). In other words, there are sheep here, and Jesus will call them through you, and they *will* come. Take heart.

missionaries in their travels (Acts 8:26, 29; 16:7, 10) and giving them the words that they needed (Mark 13:11; Acts 6:10).

"Not I, but the Grace of God That Is with Me"

Paul was deeply aware that the success of his mission was the Lord's work and not his own. He said, "I will not venture to speak of anything except *what Christ has accomplished through me* to bring the Gentiles to obedience—by word and deed, by the power of signs and wonders, *by the power of the Spirit of God*" (Rom. 15:18–19). Paul's passion, as always, was to focus all glory on the supremacy of Christ in the mission of the church. The Lord was building his church.

How did Paul then speak of his own labors? He said, "By the grace of God I am what I am, and his grace toward me was not in vain. On the contrary, I worked harder than any of them, *though it was not I, but the grace of God that is with me*" (1 Cor. 15:10). Paul worked. Paul fought the fight and ran the race. But he did so, as he said in Philippians 2:13, because beneath and within his willing, God was at work to will and to do his good pleasure. Using a farming image, Paul put it like this: "I planted, Apollos watered, but God gave the growth. So neither he who plants nor he who waters is anything, but only God who gives the growth" (1 Cor. 3:6–7). Paul was jealous to uphold the supremacy of God in the mission of the church.

This jealousy for the glory of God in the mission of the church drove the apostles to minister in a way that would always magnify God and not themselves. For example, Peter taught the young churches, "Whoever serves [should do so] as one who serves by the strength that God supplies—in order that in everything God may be glorified through Jesus Christ" (1 Peter 4:11; cf. Heb. 13:20–21). The one who gives the strength gets the glory. So Peter drove home the absolute necessity of serving in the strength that God supplies and not our own. If God did not build his church, he would not get the glory, and all would be in vain, no matter how "successful" the work may look to the world.

New Covenant Confidence in the Sovereignty of God

The apostles knew that what was happening in their mission was the fulfillment of the promises of the new covenant. "[God] has made us competent to be ministers of a new covenant" (2 Cor. 3:6). And the new covenant promises were that God would overcome hardness of heart and make people new on the inside. "And I will give you a new heart, and a new spirit I will put within you. And I will remove the heart of stone from your flesh and give you a heart of flesh. And I will put my Spirit within you, and cause you to walk in my statutes and be careful to obey my rules" (Ezek. 36:26–27).

So as Luke tells how the Christian movement spread, he repeatedly records God's sovereign initiative in the growth of the church. When Cornelius and his household are converted, it is described as God's doing. "Then to the Gentiles also *God has granted repentance* that leads to life" (Acts 11:18). "God first visited the Gentiles, to take from them a people for his name" (Acts 15:14). When the gospel broke loose on European soil in Philippi beginning with Lydia, it was God who did it: "*The Lord opened her heart* to pay attention to what was said by Paul" (Acts 16:14).

In all these ways the supremacy of God in the mission of the church is clear. God does not put his gospel and his people in the world and leave them to wage war on their own. He is the main combatant, and the battle is to be fought in a way that gives him the glory.

Prayer Proves the Supremacy of God in Missions

This is why God has ordained prayer to have such a crucial place in the mission of the church. The purpose of prayer is to make clear to all the participants in this war that the victory belongs to the Lord. Prayer is God's appointed means of bringing grace to us and glory to himself. This is crystal clear in Psalm 50:15. God says, "Call upon me in the day of trouble; I will deliver you, and you shall glorify me." Charles Spurgeon makes the point unavoidable:

> God and the praying man take shares. . . . First, here is your share: "Call upon me in the day of trouble." Secondly, here is God's share: "I will deliver thee." Again, you take a share—for you shall be delivered. And then again it is the Lord's turn—"Thou shalt glorify me." Here is a compact, a covenant that God enters into with you who pray to Him, and whom He helps. He says, "You shall have the deliverance, but I must have the glory. . . ." Here is a delightful partnership: we obtain that which we so greatly need, and all that God getteth is the glory which is due unto His name.[13]

13. Charles Spurgeon, *Twelve Sermons on Prayer* (Grand Rapids: Baker, 1971), 105.

Prayer puts God in the place of the all-sufficient Benefactor and puts us in the place of the needy beneficiaries. So when the mission of the church moves forward by prayer, the supremacy of God is manifest and the needs of the Christian troops are met.

Prayer Is for the Glory of the Father

Jesus had taught this to his disciples before he left. He had told them, "Whatever you ask in my name, this I will do, *that the Father may be glorified in the Son*" (John 14:13). In other words, the ultimate purpose of prayer is that the Father be glorified. The other side of the purpose comes out in John 16:24. Jesus says, "Until now you have asked nothing in my name. Ask, and you will receive, *that your joy may be full*." The purpose of prayer is that our joy may be full. The unity of these two goals—the glory of God and the joy of his people—is preserved in the act of prayer.

The zeal that the apostles had for the exaltation of God's supreme influence in all their missionary work was built into them by Jesus. In John 15:5, Jesus says, "I am the vine; you are the branches. Whoever abides in me and I in him, he it is that bears much fruit, *for apart from me you can do nothing*." So we really are totally ineffective as missionaries in ourselves. We may have many human strategies and plans and efforts, but the spiritual effect for the glory of Christ will be nothing. But according to John 15:5, God does not intend for us to be fruitless but to "bear much fruit." So he promises to do for us and through us what we can't do in and of ourselves.

How then do we glorify him? Jesus gives the answer in John 15:7: "If you abide in me, and my words abide in you, *ask* whatever you wish, and it will be done for you." We *pray*. We *ask* God to do for us through Christ what we can't do for ourselves—bear fruit. Then verse 8 gives the result: "*By this my Father is glorified*, that you bear much fruit." So how is God glorified by prayer? Prayer is the open admission that without Christ we can do nothing. And prayer is the turning away from ourselves to God in the confidence that he will provide the help we need. Prayer humbles *us* as needy and exalts *God* as all-sufficient.

This is why the missionary enterprise advances by prayer. The chief end of God is to glorify God. He will do this in the sovereign triumph of his missionary purpose that the nations worship him. He will secure this triumph by entering into the warfare and becoming the main combatant. And he will make that engagement plain to all the participants *through prayer*, because prayer shows that the power is from the Lord. The range of his powerful engagement in the warfare of missions becomes evident from the range of things that the church prays for in her missionary enterprise. Consider the amazing scope of prayer in the vibrant missionary life of the early church. How greatly was God glorified in the breadth of his provision!

God Was Sought in Everything

They called on God to exalt his name in the world: "Pray then like this: 'Our Father in heaven, hallowed be your name'" (Matt. 6:9).

They called on God to extend his kingdom in the world: "Your kingdom come, your will be done, on earth as it is in heaven" (Matt. 6:10).

They called on God that the gospel would speed ahead and be honored: "Finally, brothers, pray for us, that the word of the Lord may speed ahead and be honored, as happened among you" (2 Thess. 3:1).

They called on God for the fullness of the Holy Spirit: "If you then, who are evil, know how to give good gifts to your children, how much more will the heavenly Father give the Holy Spirit to those who ask him!" (Luke 11:13; cf. Eph. 3:19).

They called on God to vindicate his people in their cause: "And will not God vindicate his elect, who cry to him day and night?" (Luke 18:7 RSV).

They called on God to save unbelievers: "Brothers, my heart's desire and prayer to God for them is that they may be saved" (Rom. 10:1).

They called on God to direct the use of the sword: "Take . . . the sword of the Spirit, which is the word of God, praying at all times in the Spirit, with all prayer and supplication" (Eph. 6:17–18).

They called on God for boldness in proclamation: "Praying at all times in the Spirit . . . and also for me, that words may be given to me in opening my mouth boldly to proclaim the mystery of the gospel" (Eph. 6:18–19). "And now, Lord, look upon their threats and grant to your servants to continue to speak your word with all boldness" (Acts 4:29).

They called on God for signs and wonders: "And now, Lord, . . . grant to your servants to continue to speak your word with all boldness, while you stretch out your hand to heal, and signs and wonders are performed through the name of your holy servant Jesus" (Acts 4:29–30).

"Elijah was a man with a nature like ours, and he prayed fervently that it might not rain, and for three years and six months it did not rain on the earth. Then he prayed again, and heaven gave rain, and the earth bore its fruit" (James 5:17–18).

They called on God for the healing of wounded comrades: "Let them pray over him, anointing him with oil in the name of the Lord. And the prayer of faith will save the one who is sick, and the Lord will raise him up" (James 5:14–15).

They called on God for the healing of unbelievers: "It happened that the father of Publius lay sick with fever and dysentery. And Paul visited him and prayed, and putting his hands on him healed him" (Acts 28:8).

They called on God for the casting out of demons: "And he said to them, 'This kind cannot be driven out by anything but prayer'" (Mark 9:29).

They called on God for miraculous deliverances: "So Peter was kept in prison, but earnest prayer for him was made to God by the church. . . . When he realized [he had been freed], he went to the house of Mary, the mother of John whose other name was Mark, where many were gathered together and were praying" (Acts 12:5, 12). "About midnight Paul and Silas were praying and singing hymns to God, and the prisoners were listening to them, and suddenly there was a great earthquake" (Acts 16:25–26).

They called on God for the raising of the dead: "But Peter put them all outside, and knelt down and prayed; and turning to the body he said, 'Tabitha, arise.' And she opened her eyes, and when she saw Peter she sat up" (Acts 9:40).

They called on God to supply his troops with necessities: "Give us this day our daily bread" (Matt. 6:11).

They called on God for strategic wisdom: "If any of you lacks wisdom, let him ask God, who gives generously to all without reproach, and it will be given him" (James 1:5).

They called on God to establish leadership in the outposts: "And when they had appointed elders for them in every church, with prayer and fasting they committed them to the Lord in whom they had believed" (Acts 14:23).

They called on God to send out reinforcements: "Therefore pray earnestly to the Lord of the harvest to send out laborers into his harvest"

(Matt. 9:38). "While they were worshiping the Lord and fasting, the Holy Spirit said, 'Set apart for me Barnabas and Saul for the work to which I have called them.' Then after fasting and praying they laid their hands on them and sent them off" (Acts 13:2–3).

They called on God for the success of other missionaries: "I appeal to you, brothers, by our Lord Jesus Christ and by the love of the Spirit, to strive together with me in your prayers to God on my behalf, that I may be delivered from the unbelievers in Judea, and that my service for Jerusalem may be acceptable to the saints" (Rom. 15:30–31).

They called on God for unity and harmony in the ranks: "I do not ask for these only, but also for those who will believe in me through their word, that they may all be one, just as you, Father, are in me, and I in you, that they also may be in us, so that the world may believe that you have sent me" (John 17:20–21).

They called on God for the encouragement of togetherness: "We pray most earnestly night and day that we may see you face to face and supply what is lacking in your faith" (1 Thess. 3:10).

They called on God for a mind of discernment: "And it is my prayer that your love may abound more and more, with knowledge and all discernment, so that you may approve what is excellent, and so be pure and blameless for the day of Christ" (Phil. 1:9–10).

They called on God for a knowledge of his will: "And so, from the day we heard, we have not ceased to pray for you, asking that you may be filled with the knowledge of his will in all spiritual wisdom and understanding" (Col. 1:9).

They called on God to know him better: "[We have not ceased to pray for you to be] increasing in the knowledge of God" (Col. 1:10; cf. Eph. 1:17).

They called on God for power to comprehend the love of Christ: "I bow my knees before the Father . . . [that you] may have strength to comprehend with all the saints what is the breadth and length and height and depth, and to know the love of Christ that surpasses knowledge" (Eph. 3:14, 18–19).

They called on God for a deeper sense of assured hope: "I do not cease to give thanks for you, remembering you in my prayers . . . that you may know what is the hope to which he has called you, what are the riches of his glorious inheritance in the saints" (Eph. 1:16, 18).

They called on God for strength and endurance: "[We have not ceased to pray for you to be] strengthened with all power, according to his glorious might, for all endurance and patience with joy" (Col. 1:11; cf. Eph. 3:16).

They called on God for a deeper sense of his power within them: "I do not cease to give thanks for you, remembering you in my prayers . . . that you may know . . . what is the immeasurable greatness of his power toward us who believe" (Eph. 1:16, 18–19).

They called on God that their faith not be destroyed: "I have prayed for you that your faith may not fail. And when you have turned again, strengthen your brothers" (Luke 22:32). "But stay awake at all times, praying that you may have strength to escape all these things that are going to take place, and to stand before the Son of Man" (Luke 21:36).

They called on God for greater faith: "Immediately the father of the child cried out and said, 'I believe; help my unbelief!'" (Mark 9:24; cf. Eph. 3:17).

They called on God that they might not fall into temptation: "Lead us not into temptation" (Matt. 6:13). "Watch and pray that you may not enter into temptation. The spirit indeed is willing, but the flesh is weak" (Matt. 26:41).

They called on God that he would complete their resolves: "To this end we always pray for you, that our God may make you worthy of his calling and may fulfill every resolve for good and every work of faith by his power" (2 Thess. 1:11).

They called on God that they would do good works: "[We have not ceased to pray for you that you] walk in a manner worthy of the Lord, fully pleasing to him, bearing fruit in every good work" (Col. 1:10).

They called on God for forgiveness of their sins: "Forgive us our debts, as we also have forgiven our debtors" (Matt. 6:12).

They called on God for protection from the evil one: "Deliver us from evil" (Matt. 6:13).

Since the Giver gets the glory, what all this prayer shows is that the early church meant to make God supreme in the mission of the church. She would not live on her own strength or her own wisdom or even her own faith. She would live on God. God would be the one who would give the power and the wisdom and the faith. And therefore God would get the glory.

God's Ultimate Goal Will Come Only through Prayer

This crucial place of prayer reaffirms the great goal of God to uphold and display his glory for the enjoyment of the redeemed from all the nations. God has made it the ground of his oath: "All the earth shall be filled with the glory of the LORD" just as surely as that the Lord lives (Num. 14:21). The missionary purpose of God is as invincible as the fact that he is God. He will achieve this purpose by creating white-hot worshipers from every people, tongue, tribe, and nation (Rev. 5:9; 7:9). And he will be engaged to do it through prayer.

But *the* Work of Missions Is Not Prayer

Therefore, it is almost impossible to overemphasize the awesome place of prayer in the purposes of God for the world. But a caution is needed here. I sense the danger of overstating the role of prayer in relation to the Word of God and the preaching of the gospel. I am not comfortable, for example, with calling prayer "*the* work of missions." We will not jeopardize its awesome indispensability if we deny this claim. I do not deny it because of any desire to minimize the place of prayer but out of a zeal for the place of the Word of God in world missions. So let me say loud and clear that I believe the proclamation of the gospel in Word and deed is *the* work of missions. Prayer is the power that wields the weapon of the Word, and the Word is the weapon by which the nations will be brought to faith and obedience.

The frontline work of missions is the preaching of the Word of God, the gospel. If this public act is displaced by prayer, the supremacy of Christ in the mission of the church will be compromised. Jesus said, "When the Spirit of truth comes . . . he will glorify me" (John 16:13–14). This is why the Spirit becomes active to save people precisely where the gospel of Jesus is preached. His mission is to glorify Jesus. Where Jesus and his saving work are not proclaimed, there is no truth for the Holy Spirit to empower and no knowledge of Christ for him to exalt. Therefore, it is vain to pray that the hearts of people will be opened where there is no gospel portrait of Christ to see.

> "Everyone who calls on the name of the Lord will be saved." But how are they to call on him in whom they have not believed? And how are they to believe in him of whom they have never heard? And how are they to *hear*

without *someone preaching*. . . . Faith comes from *hearing*, and hearing through the word of Christ.

Romans 10:13–14, 17

God has ordained that saving faith comes by hearing the Word of Christ because faith is a response to Christ. If Christ is to be glorified in the mission of the church, he must be heard and known.[14] This happens only through the Word. No prayer can replace it. Prayer can only empower it. The New Testament pattern is: "Take . . . the sword of the Spirit, which is the word of God, *praying* . . ." (Eph. 6:17–18). "When they had *prayed* . . . they were all filled with the Holy Spirit and continued to *speak the word of God with boldness*" (Acts 4:31).

Prayer Releases the Power of the Gospel

But even the power that comes from the Holy Spirit through prayer is in some sense the unique power of the Word of God itself: "*The gospel . . . is the power of God* for salvation" (Rom. 1:16). Perhaps we should speak of prayer as God's instrument to *release* the power of the gospel, for it is clear that the Word of God is the immediate regenerating instrument of the Spirit: "You have been born again, not of perishable seed but of imperishable, through the living and abiding *word of God*" (1 Peter 1:23). "[God] brought us forth by the *word of truth,* that we should be a kind of firstfruits of his creation" (James 1:18).

The central promise of world missions in the teaching of Jesus concerns the spreading of the *Word*: "This *gospel of the kingdom* will be *proclaimed* throughout the whole world as a *testimony* to all nations, and then the end will come" (Matt. 24:14). In his parable about sowing, Jesus said, "The seed is *the word of God*" (Luke 8:11). When he prayed for the future mission of his disciples, he said, "I do not ask for these only, but also for those who will believe in me *through their word*" (John 17:20). And after his resurrection in his risen lordship over the mission of his church, he continued to exalt the Word: "The Lord . . . bore witness to the word of his grace, granting signs and wonders to be done by [the apostles'] hands" (Acts 14:3).

As the Christian movement spread, Luke repeatedly described its growth as the growth of the Word of God. "And *the word of God* continued to

14. This is what I argue for in chapter 4.

increase, and the number of disciples multiplied greatly in Jerusalem" (Acts 6:7). "*The word of God* increased and multiplied" (Acts 12:24). "*The word of the Lord* was spreading throughout the whole region" (Acts 13:49). "*The word of the Lord continued to increase* and prevail mightily" (Acts 19:20).

This is why I am jealous to say that the proclamation of the gospel is "*the* work of missions." It is the weapon that God designed to use in penetrating the kingdom of darkness and gathering the children of light from all the nations (Acts 26:16–18). His whole redemptive plan for the universe hangs on the success of his Word. If the proclamation of the Word aborts, the purposes of God fail.

The Word of God Cannot Fail

But that cannot happen:

> For as the rain and the snow come down from heaven and do not return there but water the earth, making it bring forth and sprout, giving seed to the sower and bread to the eater, *so shall my word be that goes out from my mouth*; it shall not return to me empty, but it shall accomplish that which I purpose, and shall succeed in the thing for which I sent it.
>
> Isaiah 55:10–11

God is sovereign. Yes, he has made all his plans hang on the success of his Word proclaimed by frail and sinful men and women; nevertheless, his purposes cannot fail. This is the essence of the new covenant oath: "I will put my Spirit within you, and cause you to walk in my statutes" (Ezek. 36:27). "The LORD your God will circumcise your heart and the heart of your offspring, so that you will love the LORD your God with all your heart and with all your soul" (Deut. 30:6). The Lord will work in his church "to will and to work for his good pleasure" (Phil. 2:13). A generation may be passed over in their disobedience, but none can undermine the plan of God. Job learned this long ago: "I know that you can do all things, and that no purpose of yours can be thwarted" (Job 42:2). Whenever God wills, his Word stands, and none can stay his hand.[15]

15. I have tried to argue extensively for the sovereignty of God in this irresistible sense in "The Pleasure of God in All He Does," in *The Pleasures of God*, 47–75.

Victory Even from Inside the Tomb

It will often look as though Christ is defeated. That's the way it looked on Good Friday. He *let* himself be libeled and harassed and scorned and shoved around and killed. But in it all he was in control. "No one takes [my life] from me" (John 10:18). So it will always be. If China was closed for forty years to the Western missionaries, it was not as though Jesus accidentally slipped and fell into the tomb. He *stepped* in. And when it was sealed over, he saved fifty million Chinese from inside—without Western missionaries. And when it was time, he pushed the stone away so we could see what he had done.[16]

When it looks as though he is buried for good, Jesus is doing something awesome in the dark. "The kingdom of God is as if a man should scatter seed on the ground. He sleeps and rises night and day, and the seed sprouts and grows; he knows not how" (Mark 4:26–27). The world thinks Jesus is done for—out of the way. They think his Word is buried and his plans have failed.

But Jesus is at work in the dark places: "Unless a grain of wheat falls into the earth and dies, it remains alone; but if it dies, it bears much fruit" (John 12:24). He lets himself be buried, and he comes out in power when and where he pleases. And his hands are full of fruit made in the dark. "God raised him up, loosing the pangs of death, because *it was not possible for him to be held by it*" (Acts 2:24). Jesus goes about his invincible missionary plan "by the power of an *indestructible life*" (Heb. 7:16).

For twenty centuries, the world has given it their best shot to hold him in. They can't bury him. They can't hold him in. They can't silence him or limit him. Jesus is alive and utterly free to go and come wherever he pleases. All authority in heaven is his. All things were made through him and for him, and he is absolutely supreme over all other powers (Col. 1:16–17). "He upholds the universe by the word of his power" (Heb. 1:3). And the preaching of his Word is *the* work of missions that cannot fail.

16. "The growth of the Church in China since 1977 has no parallels in history. . . . Mao Zedong unwittingly became the greatest evangelist in history. . . . [He] sought to destroy all religious 'superstition' but in the process cleared spiritual roadblocks for the advancement of Christianity. Deng [Xiaoping] reversed the horrors inflicted by Mao and in freeing up the economy, gave more freedom to the Christians. . . . [Today] the Church of the Lord Jesus is larger than the Communist Party of China." Patrick Johnstone and Jason Mandryk, *Operation World: When We Pray God Works* (Carlisle, U.K.: Paternoster, 2001), 161. The second sentence is from the 1993 edition of *Operation World*, 164.

The Truly Awesome Place of Prayer in the Purpose of God

Now we can say again, safely and stunningly, what the awesome place of prayer is in the purpose of God to fill the earth with his glory. Not only has God made the accomplishment of his purposes hang on the preaching of the Word, but he has also made the success of that preaching hang on prayer. God's goal to be glorified will not succeed without the powerful proclamation of the gospel. And that gospel will not be proclaimed in power to all the nations without the prevailing, earnest, faith-filled prayers of God's people. This is the awesome place of prayer in the purpose of God for the world. That purpose won't happen without prayer.

This accounts for Paul's repeated call for prayer in support of the Word. "Finally, brothers, *pray* for us, that the word of the Lord may speed ahead and be honored" (2 Thess. 3:1). *Pray* "also for me, that *words* may be given to me in opening my mouth boldly to proclaim the mystery of the *gospel*" (Eph. 6:19). "*Pray* also for us, that God may open to us a door for the *word*" (Col. 4:3). "[God] will deliver us [to go on preaching the Word, if you] help us by *prayer*" (2 Cor. 1:10–11; cf. Phil. 1:19).

Prayer is the walkie-talkie of the church on the battlefield of the world in the service of the Word. It is not a domestic intercom to increase the temporal comforts of the saints. It malfunctions in the hands of soldiers who have gone AWOL. It is for those on active duty. And in their hands it proves the supremacy of God in the pursuit of the nations. When missions moves forward by prayer, it magnifies the power of God. When it moves by human management, it magnifies man.

The Return to Prayer in Our Day

The return to prayer at the beginning of the twenty-first century is a remarkable work of God. It is full of hope for the awakening of the church and the finishing of the Great Commission. Looking back on the way God aroused and honored seasons of prayer in the past should enlarge our expectation that wonderful works of power are on the horizon. A hundred years ago, A. T. Pierson made this point exactly the way I would like to make it, namely, by highlighting the connection between prayer and the supremacy of God. He said:

> Every new Pentecost has had its preparatory period of supplication. . . . God has compelled his saints to seek Him at the throne of grace, so that every

new advance might be so plainly due to His power that even the unbeliever might be constrained to confess: "Surely this is the finger of God!"[17]

More recently, there were movements in the twentieth century that kindled expectation of significant breakthroughs in missions. Thousands of us have been stirred deeply by the missionary credo of Jim Elliot: "He is no fool who gives what he cannot keep to gain what he cannot lose." But not as many of us know the atmosphere of prayer from which the missionary passions in the late 1940s and 1950s came. David Howard, the General Director of the World Evangelical Fellowship, was in that atmosphere and tells part of the story of what God was doing to magnify himself in the prayers of students in those days.

I still have a small, faded World Evangelism Decision Card dated 1946, with my signature. Unfortunately, I did not record the day, but it is quite possible that I signed this card at the close of the first student missionary convention at the University of Toronto.

The card used to be green. I can tell by the small green circle where a thumb tack used to hold this card above my desk throughout the rest of my college days. It served as a daily prayer reminder that I had committed myself to serve God overseas unless he were clearly to direct otherwise. The fact that I had 15 years of exciting service in Latin America is attributable in large measure to prayer—much of it stimulated by that little card.

Upon returning to college after the Toronto convention students began to meet regularly to pray for missions. My closest friend in college was Jim Elliot. Jim was only to live for a few years beyond college, but in that short life he would leave a mark for eternity on my life and the lives of hundreds of others. Exactly 10 years to the week when the Toronto convention ended, Jim and his four companions were speared to death by the Huaorani Indians on the Curaray River in Ecuador. In his death he would speak to multiplied thousands, although we did not know that in our college days. Jim encouraged a small group of us to meet every day at 6:30 a.m. to pray for ourselves and our fellow students on behalf of missions. This became a regular part of my college life.

Jim Elliot also organized a round-the-clock cycle, asking students to sign up for a 15 minute slot each day when he or she would promise to pray for missions and for mission recruitment on our campus. The entire 24 hours were filled in this way. Thus, every 15 minutes throughout the day and night at least one student was on his knees interceding for missions at Wheaton College.

17. A. T. Pierson, *The New Acts of the Apostles* (New York: Baker and Taylor, 1894), 352ff.

Art Wiens was a war veteran who had served in Italy and planned to return as a missionary. He decided to pray systematically through the college directory, praying for 10 students by name every day. Art followed this faithfully through his college years.

I did not see Art again until we met in 1974 at the Lausanne Congress on World Evangelization in Switzerland. As we renewed fellowship and reminisced about old times, he said, "Dave, do you remember those prayer meetings we used to have at Wheaton?"

"I certainly do," I replied.

Then Art said, "You know, Dave, I am still praying for 500 of our college contemporaries who are now on the mission field." "How do you know that many are overseas?" I asked. "I kept in touch with the alumni office and found out who was going as a missionary, and I still pray for them."

Astounded, I asked Art if I could see his prayer list. The next day he brought it to me, a battered old notebook he had started in college days with the names of hundreds of our classmates and fellow students.[18]

When I first read that account of prevailing prayer and the remarkable fruit that has come of it to the glory of Christ through the lives of radical, Spirit-empowered missionaries, I felt a surge of longing to set my hand to the plow and never take it off. I long to be like George Mueller in the tenacity of prayer and missions. Mueller wrote in his *Autobiography*:

I am now, in 1864, waiting upon God for certain blessings, for which I have daily besought Him for 19 years and 6 months, without one day's intermission. Still the full answer is not yet given concerning the conversion of certain individuals. In the meantime, I have received many thousands of answers to prayer. I have also prayed daily, without intermission, for the conversion of other individuals about ten years, for others six or seven years, for others four, three, and two years, for others about eighteen months; and still the answer is not yet granted, concerning these persons [whom I have prayed for nineteen years and six months]. . . . Yet I am daily continuing in prayer and expecting the answer. . . . Be encouraged, dear Christian reader, with fresh earnestness to give yourself to prayer, if you can only be sure that you ask for things which are for the glory of God.[19]

The call of Jesus is for prevailing prayer: "Always . . . pray and [do] not lose heart" (Luke 18:1). By this his Father will be glorified (John 14:13). The supremacy of God in the mission of the church is proved and prized

18. David Howard, "The Road to Urbana and Beyond," *Evangelical Missions Quarterly* 21, no. 1 (January 1985): 115–16.

19. George Mueller, *Autobiography*, comp. G. Fred Bergin (London: J. Nisbet, 1906), 296.

in prevailing prayer. I believe Christ's word to his church at the beginning of the twenty-first century is a question: "Will not God give justice to his elect, who cry to him day and night? Will he delay long over them? I tell you, he will give justice to them speedily" (Luke 18:7–8).

Do you ever cry out to the Lord, "How long, O Lord? How long till you vindicate your cause in the earth? How long till you rend the heavens and come down with power on your church? How long till you bring forth victory among all the peoples of the world?"

Is not his answer plain: "When my people cry to me *day and night*, I will vindicate them, and my cause will prosper among the nations." The war will be won by God. He will win it through the gospel of Jesus Christ. This gospel will run and triumph through prevailing prayer—so that in everything God might be glorified through Jesus Christ.

3

The Supremacy of God
in Missions through Suffering

We measure the worth of a hidden treasure by what we will gladly sell to buy it. If we will sell all, then we measure the worth as supreme. If we will not, what we have is treasured more. "The kingdom of heaven is like treasure hidden in a field, which a man found and covered up. Then *in his joy* he goes and sells *all that he has* and buys that field" (Matt. 13:44). The extent of his *sacrifice* and the depth of his *joy* display the worth he puts on the treasure of God. Loss and suffering, joyfully accepted for the kingdom of God, show the supremacy of God's worth more clearly in the world than all worship and prayer.

This is why the stories of missionaries who gladly gave their all have made God more real and precious to many of us. The life of Henry Martyn has had this remarkable effect for almost two hundred years.

Henry Martyn Submits to God

Martyn was born in England on February 18, 1781. His father was well-to-do and sent his son to a fine grammar school, as they called them in those days, and then to Cambridge in 1797, when he was sixteen. Four years later Martyn took highest honors in mathematics, and the year after that first prize in Latin prose composition.

He had turned his back on God as a youth, and during these days of academic achievement, he became disillusioned with his dream. "I obtained my highest wishes, but was surprised to find that I had grasped a shadow." The treasure of the world rusted in his hands. The death of his father, the prayers of his sister, the counsel of a godly minister, and the diary of David Brainerd brought him to his knees in submission to God. In 1802, he resolved to forsake a life of academic prestige and ease and become a missionary. That was the first measure of the kingdom's worth in his life.

Martyn served as the assistant to Charles Simeon, the great evangelical preacher at Trinity Church in Cambridge, until he departed for India on July 17, 1805. His ministry was to be a chaplain with the East India Company. He arrived in Calcutta on May 16, 1806, and the first day ashore found William Carey.

Martyn was an evangelical Anglican; Carey was a Baptist. And there was some tension over the use of liturgy. But Carey wrote that year, "A young clergyman, Mr. Martyn, is lately arrived, who is possessed of a truly missionary spirit. . . . We take sweet counsel together, and go to the house of God as friends."

Alongside his chaplain's duties, Martyn's main work was translation. Within two years, by March 1808, he had translated part of the Book of Common Prayer, a commentary on the parables, and the entire New Testament into "Hindostanee." He was then assigned to supervise the Persian version of the New Testament. It was not as well received as the other, and his health gave way in the process. So he decided to return to England for recovery and to go by land through Persia in the hope of revising his translation on the way.

He became so sick, however, that he could barely press on. He died among strangers in the city of Tocat in Asiatic Turkey on October 16, 1812. He was thirty-one years old.

Martyn's Hidden Pain

What you can't see in this overview of Martyn's life are the inner flights and plunges of spirit that make his achievement so real and so helpful to real people. I am persuaded that the reason David Brainerd's *Life and Diary* and Henry Martyn's *Journal and Letters* have such abiding and deep power for the cause of missions is that they portray the life of the missionary as a life of constant warfare in the soul, not a life of uninterrupted calm. The suffering and struggle make us feel the supremacy of God in their lives all the more.

Listen to how he felt on the boat on the way to India:

I found it hard to realize divine things. I was more tried with desires after the world, than for two years past. . . . The sea-sickness, and the smell of the ship, made me feel very miserable, and the prospect of leaving all the comforts and communion of saints in England, to go forth to an unknown land, to endure such illness and misery with ungodly men for so many months, weighed heavy on my spirits. My heart was almost ready to break.

On top of this there is a love story to tell. Martyn was in love with Lydia Grenfell. He didn't feel right taking her along without going before her and proving his own reliance on God alone. But two months after he arrived in India on July 30, 1806, he wrote and proposed and asked her to come.

He waited fifteen months (!) for the reply. His journal entry on October 24, 1807, reads:

An unhappy day; received at last a letter from Lydia, in which she refuses to come, because her mother will not consent to it. Grief and disappointment threw my soul into confusion at first; but gradually, as my disorder subsided, my eyes were opened, and reason resumed its office. I could not but agree with her, that it would not be for the glory of God, nor could we expect his blessing, if she acted in disobedience to her mother.

He took up his pen and wrote her that same day:

Though my heart is bursting with grief and disappointment, I write not to blame you. The rectitude of all your conduct secures you from censure. . . . Alas my rebellious heart—what a tempest agitates me! I knew not that I had made so little progress in a spirit of resignation to the Divine will.

For five years he held out hope that things might change. A steady stream of letters covered the thousands of miles between India and England. His last known letter, written two months before his death (August 28, 1812), was addressed as usual to "My dearest Lydia." It closed:

Soon we shall have occasion for pen and ink no more; but I trust I shall shortly see thee face to face. Love to all the saints.

> Believe me to be yours ever,
> most faithfully and affectionately,
> H. Martyn

Martyn never saw her again on this earth. But dying was not what he feared most, nor seeing Lydia what he desired most. His passion was to make known the supremacy of Christ in all of life. Near the very end he wrote, "Whether life or death be mine, may Christ be magnified in me! If he has work for me to do, I cannot die." Christ's work for Martyn was done. And he had done it well. His losses and pain made the supremacy of God in his life powerful for all time.[1]

"He Bids Him Come and Die"

Some suffering is the calling of every believer but especially of those God calls to bear the gospel to the unreached. Dietrich Bonhoeffer's famous lines are biblical: "The cross is not the terrible end to an otherwise God-fearing and happy life, but it meets us at the beginning of our communion with Christ. When Christ calls a man, he bids him come and die."[2] This is simply a paraphrase of Mark 8:34: "If anyone would come after me, let him deny himself and *take up his cross* and follow me." To take up a cross and follow Jesus means to join Jesus on the Calvary road with a resolve to suffer and die with him. The cross is not a burden to bear; it is an instrument of pain and execution. It would be like saying, "Pick up your electric chair and follow me to the execution room." Or "Pick up this sword and carry it to the place of beheading." Or "Take up this rope and carry it to the gallows."

The domestication of cross-bearing into coughs and cranky spouses takes the radical thrust out of Christ's call. He is calling every believer to "renounce all that he has," to "hate his own life" (Luke 14:33, 26), and to take the road of obedience joyfully, no matter the loss on this earth. Following Jesus means that wherever obedience requires it, we will accept betrayal and rejection and beating and mockery and crucifixion and death. Jesus gives us the assurance that if we will follow him to Golgotha during all the Good Fridays of this life, we will also rise with him on the last Easter day of the resurrection. "Whoever loses his life for my sake and the gospel's will save it" (Mark 8:35). "Whoever hates his life in this world will keep it for eternal life" (John 12:25).

1. All the quotes in this account are from Henry Martyn, *Journal and Letters of Henry Martyn* (New York: Protestant Episcopal Society for the Promotion of Evangelical Knowledge, 1851).

2. Dietrich Bonhoeffer, *The Cost of Discipleship* (New York: Macmillan, 1963), 99.

Do We Need Martyr Models?

The question about martyrdom is dangerous given the new rise of terrorism in the twenty-first century. There is a fundamental difference between
Christian martyrs and those who have gained notoriety through terrorism.
First, the life of a Christian martyr is taken by those whom he wants to
save. He does not fall on his own sword, and he does not use it against his
adversary. Second, Christian martyrs do not pursue death; they pursue love.
Christians do not advance the cause of the gospel of Christ by the use of
the sword: "For all who take the sword will perish by the sword" (Matt.
26:52). Jesus said, "My kingdom is not of this world. If my kingdom were
of this world, my servants would have been fighting. . . . But my kingdom
is not from the world" (John 18:36). Christianity advances not by shedding
the blood of others, even if it is mingled with ours. It advances by suffering
to bring life, not suffering to cause death (Mark 10:45; Col. 1:24).

One of the most stunning and sobering words spoken at the second
Lausanne Congress on World Evangelization in Manila in 1989 was spoken
by George Otis concerning the call to martyrdom. He asked, "Is our failure
to thrive in Muslim countries the absence of martyrs? Can a covert church
grow in strength? Does a young church need martyr models?" Many places
in the world today feel the words of Jesus with all their radical impact:
To choose Christ is to choose death, or the very high risk of death. David
Barrett has estimated that in 2002 approximately 164,000 Christians will
die as martyrs and that the average number of Christian martyrs each year
will grow to 210,000 by the year 2025.[3] In the 2001 edition of *World Christian Encyclopedia*, he says there were 45,400,000 martyrs in the twentieth
century.[4]

"I Am Crucified with Christ"

It's true that taking up our cross involves a spiritual transaction by which
our "old nature" or "the flesh" dies with Christ and a "new creature" comes

3. David Barrett, "Annual Statistical Table on Global Mission: 2002," *International Bulletin of Missionary Research* 26, no. 1 (January 2002): 23.

4. David Barrett, George T. Kurian, and Todd M. Johnson, *World Christian Encyclopedia: A Comparative Survey of Churches and Religions—AD 30 to 2200*, vol. 1 (Oxford: Oxford University Press, 2001), 11. Lest we think Christians are the only ones who endure martyrdom in huge numbers, Barrett compares Islam to Christianity: 80 million Muslim martyrs, 70 million Christian martyrs over the history of their two religions. He observes that there are 210 countries that have lengthy histories of martyrdom and are now fully evangelized (11).

into being. This is one way the apostle applies the call of Jesus to take up our cross. "Those who belong to Christ Jesus have *crucified the flesh* with its passions and desires" (Gal. 5:24). "*I have been crucified with Christ*. It is no longer I who live, but Christ who lives in me. And the life I now live in the flesh I live by faith in the Son of God, who loved me and gave himself for me" (Gal. 2:19–20). "Our old self *was crucified with him* in order that the body of sin might be brought to nothing, so that we would no longer be enslaved to sin" (Rom. 6:6). "Set your minds on things that are above, not on things that are on earth. For *you have died*, and your life is hidden with Christ in God" (Col. 3:2–3).

But the point of this spiritual death is not that it takes the place of a real, practical application of Jesus' teaching to physical suffering and death but that it makes that application possible. Precisely because our old, selfish, worldly, unloving, fearful, proud self has died with Christ and a new, trusting, loving, heaven-bent, hope-filled self has come into being—precisely because of this inner death and new life, we are able to take risks, and suffer the pain, and even die without despair but full of hope.

"If They Persecuted Me, They Will Persecute You"

So we must not water down the call to suffer. We must not domesticate the New Testament teaching on affliction and persecution just because our lives are so smooth. It may be that we have not chosen to live in all the radical ways of love that God wants us to. It may be that our time of suffering is just around the corner. But it will not do to take our own comfortable lives and make them the measure of what we allow the Bible to mean.

Jesus came into the world to give his life as a ransom for many (Mark 10:45). There was a divine necessity upon him to suffer: "The Son of Man *must* suffer many things" (Mark 8:31; cf. Luke 17:25). Because this was his vocation, suffering also becomes the vocation of those who follow him. It is implied in the words, "As the Father has sent me, even so I am sending you" (John 20:21). And Jesus made it explicit when he said, "Remember the word that I said to you: 'A servant is not greater than his master.' If they persecuted me, they will also persecute you" (John 15:20). "If they have called the master of the house Beelzebul, how much more will they malign those of his household?" (Matt. 10:25).

Does His Suffering for Us Mean We Escape Suffering?

It would be easy to make a superficial mistake about the death of Christ as a substitutionary atonement. The mistake would be to say that since Christ died for me, I don't need to die for others. Since he suffered for me, I don't need to suffer for others. In other words, if his death is really substitutionary, shouldn't I escape what he bore for me? How can his death be a call for my death if his death took the place of my death?

The answer is that Christ died for us so that we would not have to die for sin, *not* so that we would not have to die for others. Christ bore the punishment of our sin so that our death and suffering are never punishment from God. The call to suffer with Christ is not a call to bear our sins the way he bore them but to love the way he loved. The death of Christ for the sin of my selfishness is not meant to help me escape the suffering of love but to enable it. Because he took my guilt and my punishment and reconciled me to God as my Father, I do not need to cling any longer to the comforts of earth in order to be content. I am free to let things go for the sake of making the supremacy of God's worth known.

Christ's Death: Substitution and Pattern

Peter shows us the connection between the death of Christ as a substitution to be received and a pattern to be followed. He speaks to Christian slaves who may be mistreated by their unbelieving masters:

> For what credit is it if, when you sin and are beaten for it, you endure? But if when you do good and suffer for it you endure, this is a gracious thing in the sight of God. *For to this you have been called, because Christ also suffered for you, leaving you an example, so that you might follow in his steps.*
>
> 1 Peter 2:20–21

Notice the all-important little phrase "for you." Christ suffered "for you." This is the substitutionary atonement. He took our place and did for us what we could not do for ourselves. "He himself bore our sins in his body on the tree" (1 Peter 2:24). This is a work nobody else but the Son of God could do for us (Rom. 8:3). It cannot be imitated or duplicated. It happened once for all. "He has appeared *once for all* at the end of the ages to put away sin by the sacrifice of himself" (Heb. 9:26). This is the foundation of all our hope and joy and freedom and love. Our sins are forgiven, and we have eternal life (John 3:16; Eph. 1:7). God is for us, and nothing can separate us from him (Rom. 8:31, 35–39).

Therefore, when Peter says that Jesus "left you an example that you should follow in his steps," he did not mean that you are called to make atonement for sin. He meant that you are called to love as Jesus did and be willing to suffer for doing right as he did. The pattern we follow is not the atonement but the love and the pain. The relationship between the two is crucial. The substitution is the foundation of the imitation, not vice versa. We do not earn our forgiveness by suffering as Jesus did. We are freed to love as Jesus did because our sins are forgiven. Because he suffered *for* us, we can suffer *like* him.

In fact, Peter says, "To this [way of suffering] you have been *called*." It is our vocation. Don't make the mistake of saying, "Oh, that was addressed to slaves with cruel masters and does not apply to us." That is a mistake because 1 Peter 3:8–9 is addressed to all believers but makes the same point: "Finally, *all of you* . . . do not repay evil for evil or reviling for reviling, but on the contrary, bless, *for to this you were called*, that you may obtain a blessing." This is not the calling of slaves only. It is the calling of all Christians. The way Christ lived and suffered and died places a calling on us to show with our lives the supremacy of his love by living in the same way.

So Peter goes on to describe how Jesus handled unjust suffering. We are called to do it the way he did it: "He committed no sin, neither was deceit found in his mouth. When he was reviled, he did not revile in return; when he suffered, he did not threaten, but continued entrusting himself to him who judges justly" (1 Peter 2:22–23).

Arm Yourselves with This "Thought"

Then to make the call even more clear, Peter says later on, "Since therefore Christ suffered in the flesh, arm yourselves with the same thought" (1 Peter 4:1 RSV). The suffering of Christ is a call for a certain mind-set toward suffering, namely, that it is normal and that the path of love and missions will often require it. Thus, Peter says, "Beloved, do not be surprised at the fiery trial when it comes upon you to test you, as though something strange were happening to you" (1 Peter 4:12). Suffering with Christ is not strange; it is your calling, your vocation. The "same kinds of suffering are being experienced by your brotherhood throughout the world" (1 Peter

5:9). This is the "thought" that we need to put on like armor, lest we be vulnerable to suffering as something strange.

Preparing for Suffering—Now!

Richard Wurmbrand endured fourteen years of imprisonment and torture in his homeland of Romania between 1948 and 1964. He had been leading a secret underground ministry when the Communists seized Romania and tried to control the church for their purposes. Wurmbrand, like the apostle Peter, stressed the tremendous need to get spiritually ready to suffer.

> What shall we do about these tortures? Will we be able to bear them? If I do not bear them I put in prison another fifty or sixty men whom I know, because that is what the Communists wish from me, to betray those around me. And here comes the great need for the role of preparation for suffering which must start now. *It is too difficult* to prepare yourself for it when the Communists have put you in prison.
>
> I remember my last Confirmation class before I left Romania. I took a group of ten to fifteen boys and girls on a Sunday morning, not to a church, but to the zoo. Before the cage of lions I told them, "Your forefathers in faith were thrown before such wild beasts for their faith. Know that you also will have to suffer. You will not be thrown before lions, but you will have to do with men who would be much worse than lions. Decide here and now if you wish to pledge allegiance to Christ." They had tears in their eyes when they said yes.
>
> We have to make the preparation now, before we are imprisoned. In prison you lose everything. You are undressed and given a prisoner's suit. No more nice furniture, nice carpets, or nice curtains. You do not have a wife any more and you do not have your children. You do not have your library and you never see a flower. Nothing of what makes life pleasant remains. Nobody resists who has not renounced the pleasures of life beforehand.[5]

Paul tried to prepare his converts for suffering. Like Peter he armed them with this "thought"—that suffering is our calling. He said to the newer believers in Thessalonica, "We sent Timothy . . . to . . . exhort you in your faith that no one be moved by these afflictions. For you

5. Richard Wurmbrand, "Preparing the Underground Church," *Epiphany Journal* 5, no. 4 (Summer 1985): 46–48.

yourselves know that *we are destined for this*" (1 Thess. 3:2–3). That is, it is our calling.

Similarly, as Paul returned from his first missionary journey, he stopped at the young churches and encouraged them with this "thought." He was "strengthening the souls of the disciples, encouraging them to continue in the faith, and saying that *through many tribulations we must enter the kingdom of God*" (Acts 14:22). It was important for the new believers to be "armed with this thought": that the road to the kingdom is the Calvary road; there are many tribulations. There is a divine necessity: "We *must* enter" this way. It is our calling. "All who desire to live a godly life in Christ Jesus *will* be persecuted" (2 Tim. 3:12).

"Let Us Go to Him Outside the Camp"

The writer to the Hebrews connects the atoning work of Christ and the pattern of his suffering the same way Peter does, only with vividly different words.

> So Jesus also suffered outside the gate in order to sanctify the people through his own blood. Therefore let us go to him outside the camp and bear the reproach he endured. For here we have no lasting city, but we seek the city that is to come.
>
> Hebrews 13:12–14

Jesus suffered first in a way that we cannot: "to sanctify the people through his own blood." The death of the Son of God is absolutely unique in its effect. But then notice the word "therefore." Because Jesus died for us in this way, *therefore* let us go forth with him outside the camp and bear the abuse he endured. It does not say, since he suffered for us, *therefore* we can have an easy life free from suffering and abuse and danger. Just the opposite. Jesus' suffering is the *basis* of our going with him and bearing the same abuse he bore.

This is above all a missionary text. Outside the camp means outside the borders of safety and comfort. Outside the camp are the "other sheep" that are not of this fold. Outside the camp are the unreached nations. Outside the camp are the places and the people who will be costly to reach and will require no small sacrifice. But to this we are called: "Let us go and bear the reproach he endured." It is our vocation.

Bearing the Abuse He Endured in Sudan

The abuse may range from the slightest ostracism to agony of torture and death. Both are probably happening every day in our world. We hear only a tiny fraction of the "reproach he endured." For example, *Mission Frontiers* carried this report in 1988.

> In 1983, the Sudan was declared an Islamic republic. At that time, Islamic Sharia law was imposed on all the country's citizens. Since then, dozens of Christian pastors have been killed and countless Christian churches burned. . . .
>
> This past March 27 and 28 [1987], according to a 33 page report filed by Khartoum University professors Drs. Ushari Ahmad Mahmud and Suleyman Ali Baldo (both Muslims), more than 1,000 Dinka men, women, and children were slaughtered and burned to death in the western Sudan town of Diein.
>
> The massacre erupted when 25 Christian Dinka worshipers were driven from their evening prayer service by a mob of Rizeigat Muslims wielding sticks, spears, axes, and Soviet-made Klasmnikov guns. That evening, five to seven Dinkas were murdered, and dozens of homes were burned.
>
> Early the next morning, as many Dinkas were being loaded into rail boxcars for safe evacuation from the troubled town, hundreds of armed Rizeigats converged on the train station and began attacking the defenseless Dinkas. Burning mattresses were heaped on the top of huddled Dinkas. Others were shot, mutilated, and clubbed to death. By nightfall, more than one thousand Dinkas were dead.[6]

As horrible as this is, Peter said that when the fiery ordeal comes, we should not be surprised as though something strange were happening to us. We live in such relative ease that such thinking seems incomprehensible to us. But I believe God is calling us to arm ourselves with this very thought: Christ suffered outside the gate brutally and without justice, leaving us an example that we should follow in his steps.

May We Spend the Night on Death Row?

Charles Wesley gives us an example of how one might obey Hebrews 13:13 and go "outside the camp" and bear the abuse he endured. On July 18, 1738, two months after his conversion, Charles Wesley did an amazing thing. He

6. *Mission Frontiers* 10, no. 1 (January 1988): 29.

had spent the week witnessing to inmates at the Newgate prison with a friend named "Bray," whom he described as "a poor ignorant mechanic." One of the men they spoke to was "a black [slave] that had robbed his master." He was sick with a fever and was condemned to die.

On Tuesday, Wesley and Bray asked if they could be locked in overnight with the prisoners who were to be executed the next day [this is outside the camp!]. That night they spoke the gospel. They told the men that "One came down from heaven to save lost sinners." They described the sufferings of the Son of God, his sorrows, agony, and death.

The next day the men were loaded onto a cart and taken to Tyburn. Wesley went with them. Ropes were fastened around their necks so that the cart could be driven off, leaving them swinging in the air to choke to death.

The fruit of Wesley and Bray's nightlong labor was astonishing. Here is what Wesley wrote:

> They were all cheerful; full of comfort, peace and triumph; assuredly persuaded Christ had died for them, and waited to receive them into paradise.... The black [slave] ... saluted me with his looks. As often as his eyes met mine, he smiled with the most composed, delightful countenance I ever saw.
>
> We left them going to meet their Lord, ready for the Bridegroom. When the cart drew off, not one stirred, or struggled for life, but meekly gave up their spirits. Exactly at twelve they were turned off. I spoke a few suitable words to the crowd; and returned, full of peace and confidence in our friends' happiness. That hour under the gallows was the most blessed hour of my life.[7]

Two things in this story amaze and inspire me. One is the astonishing power of Wesley's message about the truth and love of Christ. All the condemned prisoners were converted, and they were so deeply converted that they could look death in the face (without a long period of "follow up" or "discipling") and give up their lives with confidence that Christ would receive them. Their suffering was not for righteousness' sake, but the same dynamics were at work to sustain them. They looked on their suffering as something they must pass through on the way to heaven, and the hope of glory was so real that they died in peace. Oh, for such power in witness!

The other thing that amazes me is the sheer fact that Wesley went to the prison and asked to be locked up all night with condemned criminals

7. Charles Wesley, *Journal*, vol. 1 (Grand Rapids: Baker, 1980), 120–23.

who had nothing more to lose if they killed another person. Wesley had no supervisor telling him that this was his job. He was not a professional prison minister. It would have been comfortable and pleasant to spend the evening at home conversing with friends. Then why did he go?

God put it in his heart to go. And Wesley yielded. There are hundreds of strange and radical things God is calling his people to do in the cause of world missions. Not everyone will hear the same call. Yours will be unique. It may be something you never dreamed of doing. It may be something you have only dreamed of doing. But I urge you to listen to the leading of the Spirit to see where "outside the camp" he may be taking you "to bear the reproach he endured."

"I Will Show Him How Much He Must Suffer"

Afflictions are our vocation, whether we are missionaries or not. But this is especially the calling of those appointed to reach the unreached peoples of the world. Paul is the prototype of such missionaries. When the Lord sent Ananias to Paul in Damascus, he sent him with the armor of this "thought" mentioned in 1 Peter 4:1. Only it was intensified for Paul. The Lord said, "Go, for he is a chosen instrument of mine to carry my name before the Gentiles and kings and the children of Israel. For *I will show him how much he must suffer for the sake of my name*" (Acts 9:15–16). Then God kept on pressing this "thought" on Paul: "The Holy Spirit testifies to me in every city that *imprisonment and afflictions await me*" (Acts 20:23).

Suffering was part of Paul's calling. It became so much a part of his identity and ministry that he took it as a badge of his apostolic authenticity. It was like part of his visa papers to prove his right to do what God had called him to do.

> As servants of God we commend ourselves in every way: by great endurance, in afflictions, hardships, calamities, beatings, imprisonments, riots, labors, sleepless nights, hunger; by purity, knowledge, patience, kindness, the Holy Spirit, genuine love, by truthful speech, and the power of God; with the weapons of righteousness for the right hand and for the left; through honor and dishonor, through slander and praise. We are treated as impostors, and yet are true; as unknown, and yet well known; as dying, and behold, we live; as punished, and yet not killed; as sorrowful, yet always rejoicing; as poor, yet making many rich; as having nothing, yet possessing everything.
>
> 2 Corinthians 6:4–10

The extraordinary suffering of the apostle Paul staggers the mind. The litany of 2 Corinthians 11:23–28 is overwhelming, especially if we think of the pain of each part and the multiplied pain upon pain as the parts mount up. It is a rare glimpse into the cumulative pain and sorrow of Paul's missionary life:

> . . . with far greater labors, far more imprisonments, with countless beatings, and often near death. Five times I received at the hands of the Jews the forty lashes less one. Three times I was beaten with rods. Once I was stoned. Three times I was shipwrecked; a night and a day I was adrift at sea; on frequent journeys, in danger from rivers, danger from robbers, danger from my own people, danger from Gentiles, danger in the city, danger in the wilderness, danger at sea, danger from false brothers; in toil and hardship, through many a sleepless night, in hunger and thirst, often without food, in cold and exposure. And, apart from other things, there is the daily pressure on me of my anxiety for all the churches.

Lest we pass over this too quickly, without having the breath knocked out of us, consider what it meant to receive "forty lashes less one." It meant that he was stripped and tied to some kind of stake so that he could not run or fall. Then a person trained in flogging would take a whip, maybe with or without shards in the leather, and lash Paul's back thirty-nine times. Halfway through, or earlier perhaps, the skin would begin to break and tear. By the end, parts of Paul's back would be like jelly. The lacerations would not be clean, as with a razor blade. The skin would be torn and shredded, so that healing would be slow and perhaps complicated by infection. They knew nothing of sterilization in those days and had no antiseptics. It would take perhaps months before his garments could hang on his back without pain.

Now, with that in view, consider that this happened a second time on the same back, opening all the scars. It healed more slowly the second time. Then consider that some months later it happened a third time. Imagine what his back must have looked like. Then it happened again. And finally it happened a fifth time. And this was just one of Paul's sufferings.

Does God Allow or Appoint the Suffering of His Messengers?

Why does God allow this? No, that is not quite the right question. We have to ask, Why does God *appoint* this? These things are part of God's plan for his people just as the suffering and death of Jesus were part of God's plan for salvation (Isa. 53:10; Acts 4:27–28). It is true that Satan can be the more immediate agent of suffering, but even he may do nothing without God's permission.[8]

Paul describes suffering as a gift of God: "It has been granted to you that for the sake of Christ you should not only believe in him but also *suffer for his sake*" (Phil. 1:29). Twice Peter spoke of suffering as being God's will: "It is better to suffer for doing good, *if that should be God's will*, than for doing evil. . . . Let those who suffer *according to God's will* entrust their souls to a faithful Creator while doing good" (1 Peter 3:17; 4:19).[9]

James placed all of life, including the seemingly accidental hindrances to our plans, under the sovereign will of God: "Come now, you who say, 'Today or tomorrow we will go into such and such a town and spend a year there and trade and make a profit. . . .' Instead you ought to say, '*If the Lord wills*, we will live and do this or that'" (James 4:13, 15). Flat tires, car accidents, road construction—whatever can keep you from doing your plan—are the will of God. *If God wills*, you will live and do this or that.

The writer to the Hebrews puts all our suffering under the banner of God's loving discipline. It is not an accident that he permits; it is a plan for our holiness.

8. Demons cannot even speak without the permission of Jesus: "He would not permit the demons to speak" (Mark 1:34). How much less may they do anything more harmful without permission, as Job 1:12, 21; 2:6–7, 10 makes plain. Nevertheless, Satan does persecute the church. "Behold, the devil is about to throw some of you into prison, that you may be tested" (Rev. 2:10). For a more extensive treatment of this problem of how God's sovereignty relates to the evil things men do, see John Piper, *The Pleasures of God* (Portland, Ore.: Multnomah, 2000), 66–75.

9. For a discussion of two different ways of talking about God's will (his will of decree and his will of command), see John Piper, "Are There Two Wills in God? Divine Election and God's Desire for All to Be Saved," in *The Pleasures of God: Meditations on God's Delight in Being God* (Sisters, Ore.: Multnomah, 2000), 313–40. (This essay is also found in Thomas R. Schreiner and Bruce A. Ware, eds., *Still Sovereign: Contemporary Perspectives on Election, Foreknowledge, and Grace* [Grand Rapids: Baker, 2000], 107–31.) The point is that when we think about the will of God, we must distinguish between actions that he commands to be done, such as "You shall not murder" (Exod. 20:13), and actions that he ordains in his sovereignty to come to pass, such as the death of his Son at the hands of murderers (Acts 2:23; 4:27–28). In other words, God sometimes ordains that things happen according to his *will of decree* that are against his *will of command*. That is surely the case in the crucifixion of his Son, which was planned from of old and yet necessarily involved the sins of men in the act of crucifixion. But most Christians have always believed that it is not sin in God to will that sin be. This is a difficult issue, and I only mention it here because it may trouble some readers that suffering is described as God's will. It *is* in one sense, and it may *not be* in another. And yet man always remains responsible for it. I hope the troubled reader will seek help in the essay referred to above and in other parts of that same book, for example, chapter 2, "The Pleasure of God in All That He Does," 47–75.

In your struggle against sin you have not yet resisted to the point of shedding your blood. And have you forgotten the exhortation that addresses you as sons? "My son, do not regard lightly the discipline of the Lord, nor be weary when reproved by him. For the Lord disciplines the one he loves, and chastises every son whom he receives."

Hebrews 12:4–6

The suffering that missionaries meet is not something unforeseen by the Lord. He saw it clearly, embraced it for himself, and sent his disciples into the same danger. "Behold, I am sending you out as sheep in the midst of wolves" (Matt. 10:16). "I will send them prophets and apostles, some of whom they will kill and persecute" (Luke 11:49). As Paul says in 1 Thessalonians 3:3, we are "destined" or "appointed" for these things.

Six Reasons God Appoints Suffering for His Servants

So our question is Why? Why did God appoint for Paul to suffer so much as the prototype of the frontier missionary? God is sovereign. As every child knows, he could toss Satan into the pit today if he wanted to, and all his terrorizing of the church would be over. But God wills that the mission of the church advance through storm and suffering. What are the reasons? I will mention six.

1. Suffering Deepens Faith and Holiness

As we have just seen in Hebrews 12, God disciplines his children through suffering. His aim is deeper faith and deeper holiness. "He disciplines us for our good, that we may share his holiness" (v. 10). Jesus experienced the same thing. "Although he was a son, he learned obedience through what he suffered" (Heb. 5:8). This does not mean that Jesus grew from disobedience to obedience. The same writer says Jesus never sinned (Heb. 4:15). Rather, the process through which he grew in deeper and deeper obedience was the process of suffering. For us there is the need not only to have our obedience tested and proven but also to be purified of all remnants of self-reliance and entanglement with the world.

Paul described this experience in his own life like this:

For we do not want you to be ignorant, brothers, of the affliction we experienced in Asia. For we were so utterly burdened beyond our strength that we despaired of life itself. Indeed, we felt that we had received the sentence of death. But *that was to make us rely not on ourselves but on God who raises the dead.*

2 Corinthians 1:8–9

Paul does not concede his suffering to the hand of Satan but says that God ordained it for the increase of his faith. God knocked the props of life out from under Paul's heart so that he would have no choice but to fall on God and receive his hope from the promise of the resurrection. This is the first purpose of missionary suffering: to wean us from the world and set our hope fully in God alone (cf. Rom. 5:3–4). Since the freedom to love flows from this kind of radical hope (Col. 1:4–5), suffering is a primary means of building compassion into the lives of God's servants.

Thousands of missionaries throughout the centuries have found that the sufferings of life have been the school of Christ where lessons of faith were taught that could not be learned anywhere else. For example, John G. Paton, who was born in 1824 in Scotland, was a missionary to the New Hebrides (today's Vanuatu) in the South Seas from 1858 almost until his death in 1907. He lost his wife four months after he landed on the island of Tanna at the age of thirty-four. Two weeks later his newborn son died. He buried them alone with his own hands. "But for Jesus, and the fellowship he vouchsafed to me there, I must have gone mad and died beside the lonely grave!"[10] He stayed on the island for a harrowing four years of dangers. Finally, an uprising was mounted against him, and he believed it was right to try to escape. He sought help from the one person he could trust on the island, his friend Nowar. His escape was an unforgettable discovery of grace that left a lifelong spiritual mark. Nowar told Paton to flee the village and hide in a tree that Nowar's son would show him and to stay there till the moon rose.

> Being entirely at the mercy of such doubtful and vacillating friends, I, though perplexed, felt it best to obey. I climbed into the tree and was left there alone in the bush. The hours I spent there live all before me as if it were but of yesterday. I heard the frequent discharging of muskets, and the yells of the Savages. Yet I sat there among the branches, as safe in the arms of Jesus. Never, in all my sorrows, did my Lord draw nearer to me, and speak more soothingly in my soul, than when the moonlight flickered among these chestnut leaves, and the night air played on my throbbing brow, as I told all my heart to Jesus. Alone, yet not alone! If it be to glorify my God, I will not

10. James Paton, ed., *John G. Paton: Missionary to the New Hebrides, an Autobiography* (1889, 1898; reprint, Edinburgh: Banner of Truth Trust, 1965), 80.

grudge to spend many nights alone in such a tree, to feel again my Savior's spiritual presence, to enjoy His consoling fellowship. If thus thrown back upon your own soul, alone, all alone, in the midnight, in the bush, in the very embrace of death itself, have you a Friend that will not fail you then?[11]

2. Suffering Makes Your Cup Increase

By enduring suffering with patience, the reward of our experience of God's glory in heaven increases. This is part of Paul's meaning in 2 Corinthians 4:17–18:

> For this slight momentary affliction is preparing for us an eternal weight of glory beyond all comparison, as we look not to the things that are seen but to the things that are unseen. For the things that are seen are transient, but the things that are unseen are eternal.

Paul's affliction is "preparing" or "effecting" or "bringing about" a weight of glory beyond all comparison. We must take seriously Paul's words here. He is not merely saying that he has a great hope in heaven that enables him to endure suffering. That is true. But he also says that the suffering has an effect on the weight of glory. There seems to be a connection between the suffering endured and the degree of glory enjoyed. Of course the glory outstrips the suffering infinitely, as Paul says in Romans 8:18: "I consider that the sufferings of this present time are *not worth comparing with the glory* that is to be revealed to us." Nevertheless, the weight of that glory, or the experience of that glory, seems to be more or less dependent in part on the affliction we have endured with patient faith.

Jesus pointed in the same direction when he said, "Blessed are you when others revile you and persecute you and utter all kinds of evil against you falsely on my account. Rejoice and be glad, for *your reward is great in heaven*" (Matt. 5:11–12). This would carry the greatest encouragement to rejoice if Jesus meant that the more we endure suffering in faith, the greater will be our reward. If a Christian who suffers much for Jesus and one who does not suffer much experience God's final glory in exactly the same way and degree, it would seem strange to tell the suffering Christian to rejoice and be glad (in that very day; cf. Luke 6:23) because of the reward he would receive even if he did not suffer. The reward promised seems to be in response to the suffering and a specific recompense for it. If this is

11. Ibid., 200. For a brief overview of Paton's life and ministry, refer to John Piper, "'You Will Be Eaten by Cannibals!' Courage in the Cause of World Missions: Lessons from the Life of John G. Paton" at www.DesiringGod.org.

not explicit and certain here, it does seem to be implied in other passages of the New Testament. I will let Jonathan Edwards bring them out as we listen to one of the most profound reflections on this problem I have ever read. Here Edwards deals, in a breathtaking way, with the issue of how there can be degrees of happiness in a world of perfect joy.

> There are different degrees of happiness and glory in heaven. . . . The glory of the saints above will be in some proportion to their eminency in holiness and good works here [and patience through suffering is one of the foremost good works, cf. Rom. 2:7]. Christ will reward all according to their works. He that gained ten pounds was made ruler over ten cities, and he that gained five pounds over five cities (Luke 19:17–19). "He that soweth sparingly, shall reap sparingly; and he that soweth bountifully shall reap also bountifully" (2 Cor. 9:6). And the apostle Paul tells us that, as one star differs from another star in glory, so also it shall be in the resurrection of the dead (1 Cor. 15:41). Christ tells us that he who gives a cup of cold water unto a disciple in the name of a disciple, shall in no wise lose his reward. But this could not be true, if a person should have no greater reward for doing many good works than if he did but few.
>
> It will be no damp to the happiness of those who have lower degrees of happiness and glory, that there are others advanced in glory above them: for all shall be perfectly happy, every one shall be perfectly satisfied. Every vessel that is cast into this ocean of happiness is full, though there are some vessels far larger than others; and there shall be no such thing as envy in heaven, but perfect love shall reign through the whole society. Those who are not so high in glory as others, will not envy those that are higher, but they will have so great, and strong, and pure love to them, that they will rejoice in their superior happiness; their love to them will be such that they will rejoice that they are happier than themselves; so that instead of having a damp to their own happiness, it will add to it.
>
> And so, on the other hand, those that are highest in glory, as they will be the most lovely, so they will proportionally excel in divine benevolence and love to others, and will have more love to God and to the saints than those that are lower in holiness and happiness. And besides, those that will excel in glory will also excel in humility. Here in this world, those that are above others are the objects of envy, because . . . others conceive of them as being lifted up with it; but in heaven it will not be so, but those saints in heaven who excel in happiness will also [excel] in holiness, and consequently in humility. . . . The exaltation of some in heaven above the rest will be so far from diminishing the perfect happiness and joy of the rest who are inferior, that they will be the happier for it; such will be the union in their society that they will be partakers of each other's happiness. Then will be fulfilled

in its perfections that which is declared in 1 Corinthians 12:22: "If one of the members be honored all the members rejoice with it."[12]

Thus, one of the aims of God in the suffering of the saints is to enlarge their capacity to enjoy his glory both here and in the age to come. When their cup is picked up, as it were, from the "refuse of the world" (1 Cor. 4:13) and tossed into the ocean of heaven's happiness, it will hold more happiness if they have been long weaned from the world and made to live on God alone.

3. Suffering Is the Price of Making Others Bold

God uses the suffering of his missionaries to awaken others out of their slumbers of indifference and make them bold. When Paul was imprisoned in Rome, he wrote of this to the church at Philippi. "Most of the brothers, having become confident in the Lord by my imprisonment, are much more bold to speak the word without fear" (Phil. 1:14). If he must, God will use the suffering of his devoted emissaries to make a sleeping church wake up and take risks for God.

The sufferings and dedication of young David Brainerd has had this effect on thousands. Henry Martyn recorded Brainerd's impact on his life again and again in his *Journal*.

September 11, 1805: "What a quickening example has he often been to me, especially on this account, that he was of a weak and sickly constitution!"

May 8, 1806: "Blessed be the memory of that holy man! I feel happy that I shall have his book with me in India, and thus enjoy, in a manner, the benefit of his company and example."

May 12, 1806: "My soul was revived today through God's never-ceasing compassion, so that I found the refreshing presence of God in secret duties; especially was I most abundantly encouraged by reading D. Brainerd's

---

12. Jonathan Edwards, *The Works of Jonathan Edwards*, vol. 2 (Edinburgh: Banner of Truth Trust, 1974), 902. The parable of the workers in the vineyard who all made the same wage (Matt. 20:1–16) need not be in conflict with what Edwards (and the texts he cites!) teaches here. What that text may imply is that all of us are thrown into the same ocean of happiness. Another point of that parable is that God is free to give anyone any degree of blessing more than he deserves, and if there is anyone who is self-pitying or proud about his endurance, God is indeed free to exalt a person even above him so as to humble him and make him realize all of heaven is all of grace. I think Jonathan Edwards effectively answers Craig Blomberg's question: "Is it not fundamentally self-contradictory to speak of degrees of perfection?" "Degrees of Reward in the Kingdom of Heaven," *Journal of the Evangelical Theological Society* 35, no. 2 (June 1992): 162–63. I do, however, want to side with Blomberg over against those who speak of "earning" rewards and who distort the conditional promises of heaven into promises of levels of reward in heaven.

account of the difficulties attending a mission to the heathen. Oh, blessed be the memory of that beloved saint! No uninspired writer ever did me so much good. I felt most sweetly joyful to labor amongst the poor natives here; and my willingness was, I think, more divested of those romantic notions, which have sometimes inflated me with false spirits."[13]

FIVE INSPIRING WIVES

In our own time, it is difficult to overstate the impact that the martyrdom of Jim Elliot, Nate Saint, Ed McCully, Pete Fleming, and Roger Youderian has had on generations of students.[14] The word that appeared again and again in the testimonies of those who heard the Huaorani[15] story was "dedication." But more than is often realized, it was the strength of the wives of these men that made many of us feel a surge of desire to be dedicated like that.

Barbara Youderian, the wife of Roger, wrote in her diary that night in January 1956:

Tonight the Captain told us of his finding four bodies in the river. One had tee-shirt and blue-jeans. Roj was the only one who wore them. . . . God gave me this verse two days ago, Psalm 48:14, "For this God is our God for ever and ever; He will be our Guide even unto death." As I came face to face with the news of Roj's death, my heart was filled with praise. He was worthy of his homegoing. Help me, Lord, to be both mummy and daddy.[16]

It is not difficult to feel the biblical point Paul was making. The suffering of the servants of God, borne with faith and even praise, is a shattering experience to apathetic saints whose lives are empty in the midst of countless comforts.

APPLICATIONS DOUBLED AT HIS DEATH

The execution of Wycliffe missionary Chet Bitterman by the Colombian guerrilla group M-19 on March 6, 1981, unleashed an amazing zeal for

13. *Journal and Letters of Henry Martyn*, 240, 326–28.
14. For their remarkable story, see the following resources: Elisabeth Elliot, *Through Gates of Splendor*, 40th ann. ed. (Wheaton: Tyndale, 1986); Elisabeth Elliot, *Shadow of the Almighty: The Life and Testament of Jim Elliot* (San Francisco: HarperSanFrancisco, 1989); Elisabeth Elliot, *The Savage My Kinsmen*, 40th ann. ed. (Ann Arbor, Mich.: Servant, 1996); Steve Saint, "Did They Have to Die?" *Christianity Today* 40, no. 10 (16 September 1996): 20–27; and Russell T. Hitt, *Jungle Pilot: The Gripping Story of the Life and Witness of Nate Saint, Martyred Missionary to Ecuador* (Grand Rapids: Discovery House, 1997).
15. This is the name of the tribe formerly known as "Auca" ["savage"] by outsiders.
16. Quoted in Elisabeth Elliot, *Through Gates of Splendor* (New York: Harper & Row, 1957), 235–36.

the cause of Christ. Chet had been in captivity for seven weeks while his wife, Brenda, and little daughters, Anna and Esther, waited in Bogotá. The demand of M-19 was that Wycliffe get out of Colombia.

They shot him just before dawn—a single bullet to the chest. Police found his body in the bus where he died, in a parking lot in the south of town. He was clean and shaven, his face relaxed. A guerrilla banner wrapped his remains. There were no signs of torture.

In the year following Chet's death, "applications for overseas service with Wycliffe Bible Translators doubled. This trend was continued."[17] It is not the kind of missionary mobilization that any of us would choose. But it is God's way. "Unless a grain of wheat falls into the earth and dies, it remains alone; but if it dies, it bears much fruit" (John 12:24).

4. Suffering Fills Up What Is Lacking in Christ's Afflictions

The suffering of Christ's messengers ministers to those they are trying to reach and may open them to the gospel. This was one of the ways Paul brought the gospel to bear on the people in Thessalonica. "You know what kind of men we proved to be among you *for your sake*. And *you became imitators of us* and of the Lord, for *you received the word in much affliction*, with the joy of the Holy Spirit" (1 Thess. 1:5–6). The Thessalonians had imitated Paul by enduring much affliction with joy. And that is the kind of man Paul had proven to be among them. So it was his suffering that moved them and drew them to his authentic love and truth.

This is the kind of ministry Paul had in mind when he said, "As we share abundantly in Christ's sufferings, so through Christ we share abundantly in comfort too. If we are afflicted, it is for your comfort and salvation" (2 Cor. 1:5–6). His sufferings were the means God was using to bring salvation to the Corinthian church. They could see the suffering love of Christ in Paul. He was actually sharing in Christ's sufferings and making them real for the church.

This is part of what Paul meant in that amazing statement in Colossians 1:24: "I rejoice in my sufferings for your sake, and in my flesh I am *filling up what is lacking in Christ's afflictions for the sake of his body*, that is, the church." Christ's afflictions are not lacking in their atoning sufficiency. They are lacking in that they are not known and felt by people who were not at the cross. Paul dedicates himself not only to carry the message of those sufferings to the nations but also to suffer with Christ

17. Steve Estes, *Called to Die* (Grand Rapids: Zondervan, 1986), 252.

and for Christ in such a way so that what people see are "Christ's sufferings." In this way he follows the pattern of Christ by laying down his life
for the life of the church. "I endure everything for the sake of the elect,
that they also may obtain the salvation that is in Christ Jesus with eternal
glory" (2 Tim. 2:10).

"When We Saw Your Blistered Feet"

In 1992, I had an opportunity to hear J. Oswald Sanders speak. His
message touched deeply on suffering. He was eighty-nine years old at
the time and still traveled and spoke around the world. He had written a
book a year since turning seventy! I mention that only to exult in the utter
dedication of a life poured out for the gospel without thought of coasting
in self-indulgence from sixty-five to the grave.[18]

He told the story of an indigenous missionary who walked barefoot
from village to village preaching the gospel in India. After a long day of
many miles and much discouragement, he came to a certain village and
tried to speak the gospel but was spurned. So he went to the edge of the
village dejected and lay down under a tree and slept from exhaustion.

When he awoke, the whole town was gathered to hear him. The head
man of the village explained that they had looked him over while he was
sleeping. When they saw his blistered feet, they concluded that he must
be a holy man and that they had been evil to reject him. They were sorry
and wanted to hear the message for which he was willing to suffer so much
to bring them.

At the Third Beating the Women Wept

One of the unlikeliest men to attend the Itinerant Evangelists' Confer-
ence in Amsterdam sponsored by the Billy Graham Association was a
Masai Warrior named Joseph. But his story won him a hearing with Dr.
Graham himself. The story is told by Michael Card.

One day Joseph, who was walking along one of these hot, dirty African
roads, met someone who shared the gospel of Jesus Christ with him. Then
and there he accepted Jesus as his Lord and Savior. The power of the Spirit
began transforming his life; he was filled with such excitement and joy that
the first thing he wanted to do was return to his own village and share that
same Good News with the members of his local tribe.

18. See note 25 on the development of the Finishers Project devoted to helping people nearing
retirement give their energy, skill, and heart to the cause of Christ. Part of their vision statement
says, "We can either give them to Jesus to lay up as treasure in Heaven or lose them."

Joseph began going from door-to-door, telling everyone he met about the Cross of Jesus and the salvation it offered, expecting to see their faces light up the way his had. To his amazement the villagers not only didn't care, they became violent. The men of the village seized him and held him to the ground while the women beat him with strands of barbed wire. He was dragged from the village and left to die alone in the bush.

Joseph somehow managed to crawl to a waterhole, and there, after days of passing in and out of consciousness, found the strength to get up. He wondered about the hostile reception he had received from people he had known all his life. He decided he must have left something out or told the story of Jesus incorrectly. After rehearsing the message he had first heard, he decided to go back and share his faith once more.

Joseph limped into the circle of huts and began to proclaim Jesus. "He died for you, so that you might find forgiveness and come to know the living God," he pleaded. Again he was grabbed by the men of the village and held while the women beat him, reopening wounds that had just begun to heal. Once more they dragged him unconscious from the village and left him to die.

To have survived the first beating was truly remarkable. To live through the second was a miracle. Again, days later, Joseph awoke in the wilderness, bruised, scarred—and determined to go back.

He returned to the small village and this time, they attacked him before he had a chance to open his mouth. As they flogged him for the third and probably the last time, he again spoke to them of Jesus Christ, the Lord. Before he passed out, the last thing he saw was that the women who were beating him began to weep.

This time he awoke in his own bed. The ones who had so severely beaten him were now trying to save his life and nurse him back to health. The entire village had come to Christ.[19]

Surely this is something of what Paul meant when he said, "I fill up what is lacking in Christ's afflictions, for the sake of his body" (Col. 1:24).

5. Suffering Enforces the Missionary Command to Go

The suffering of the church is used by God to reposition the missionary troops in places they might not have otherwise gone. This is clearly the effect that Luke wants us to see in the story of the martyrdom of Stephen and the persecution that came after it. God spurs the church into missionary service by the suffering she endures. Therefore, we must not judge too

19. Michael Card, "Wounded in the House of Friends," *Virtue* (March/April 1991): 28–29, 69.

quickly the apparent setbacks and tactical defeats of the church. If you see things with the eyes of God, the Master strategist, what you see in every setback is the positioning of troops for a greater advance and a greater display of his wisdom, power, and love.

Acts 8:1 charts the divine strategy for the persecution: "There arose on that day [the day of Stephen's murder] a great persecution against the church in Jerusalem, and they were all scattered throughout the regions of *Judea and Samaria*, except the apostles." Up until now no one had moved out to Judea and Samaria in spite of what Jesus had said in Acts 1:8: "You will receive power when the Holy Spirit has come upon you, and you will be my witnesses in Jerusalem and in all Judea and Samaria." It is no accident that these were the very two regions to which the persecution sent the church. What obedience will not achieve, persecution will.

To confirm this divine missionary purpose of the persecution, Luke refers to it in Acts 11:19: "Now those who were scattered because of the persecution that arose over Stephen traveled as far as Phoenicia and Cyprus and Antioch, speaking the word to no one except Jews." But in Antioch some spoke to Greeks also. In other words, the persecution sent the church not only to Judea and Samaria (Acts 8:1) but also beyond to the nations (Acts 11:19).

The Inertia of Ease, the Apathy of Abundance

The lesson here is not just that God is sovereign and turns setbacks into triumphs. The lesson is also that comfort and ease and affluence and prosperity and safety and freedom often cause a tremendous inertia in the church. The very things that we think would produce personnel, energy, and creative investment of time and money for the missionary cause instead produce the exact opposite: weakness, apathy, lethargy, self-centeredness, preoccupation with security.

Studies have shown that the richer we are the smaller the percentage of our income we give to the church and its mission. The poorest fifth of the church gives 3.4 percent of its income to the church, and the richest fifth gives 1.6 percent—half as much as the poorer church members.[20] It is a strange principle that probably goes right to the heart of our sinfulness and Christ's sufficiency: Hard times, like persecution, often produce more personnel, more prayer, more power, and more open purses than do easy times.

20. The *Minneapolis Star Tribune* carried an article on Friday, 3 May 1991, from which these data are taken.

It is difficult for a rich man to enter the kingdom of heaven, Jesus said (Matt. 19:23). It is also difficult for rich people to help others enter. Jesus said as much in the parable of the soils. "The cares of the world and *the deceitfulness of riches* and *the desires for other things* enter in and choke the word, and it proves unfruitful" (Mark 4:19)—unfruitful for missions and most every other good work.

Persecution can have harmful effects on the church, but prosperity it seems is even more devastating to the mission God calls us to. My point here is not that we should seek persecution. That would be presumption—like jumping off the temple. The point is that we should be wary of prosperity, excessive ease, comfort, and affluence. And we should not be disheartened but filled with hope if we are persecuted for righteousness' sake, because the point of Acts 8:1 is that God makes persecution serve the mission of the church.

We must not be glib about this. The price of missionary advance is immense. Stephen paid for it with his life. And Stephen was one of the brightest stars in the Jerusalem sky. His enemies "could not withstand the wisdom and the Spirit with which he was speaking" (Acts 6:10). Surely he was more valuable alive than dead, we would all reason. He was needed! There was no one like Stephen! But God saw it another way.

How Joseph Stalin Served the Cause

The way God brought entire Uzbek villages to Christ in the twentieth century is a great illustration of God's strange use of upheaval and displacement. Bill and Amy Stearns tell the story in their hope-filled book, *Catch the Vision 2000*.[21] The key player was Joseph Stalin.

Thousands of Koreans fled what is now North Korea in the 30s as the Japanese invaded. Many of these settled around Vladivostok. When Stalin in the late 30s and early 40s began developing Vladivostok as a weapons manufacturing center, he deemed the Koreans a security risk. So he relocated them in five areas around the Soviet Union. One of those areas was Tashkent, hub of the staunchly Muslim people called the Uzbeks. Twenty million strong, the Uzbeks had for hundreds of years violently resisted any Western efforts to introduce Christianity.

As the Koreans settled around Tashkent, the Uzbeks welcomed their industry and kindness. Within a few decades, the Koreans were included in nearly every facet of Uzbek cultural life.

21. Bill and Amy Stearns, *Catch the Vision 2000* (Minneapolis: Bethany, 1991), 12–13.

As usual in God's orchestration of global events, He had planted within the relocated Koreans strong pockets of believers. Little did Stalin suspect that these Koreans would not only begin enjoying a wildfire revival among their own people, they would also begin bringing their Muslim, Uzbek and Kazak friends to Christ.

The first public sign of the Korean revival and its breakthrough effects on the Uzbeks and Kazaks came on June 2, 1990, when in the first open air Christian meeting in the history of Soviet Central Asia, a young Korean from America preached to a swelling crowd in the streets of Alma-Ata, capital of Kazakhstan.

The result of these roundabout, decade-long maneuverings by God to position his people in inaccessible places is that Muslims, who would not receive missionaries, are confessing that Isa (Jesus) is the way, the truth, and the life. This was a costly strategy for many believers. Being uprooted from their homeland in Korea, and then again from their new home near Vladivostok, must have been a severe test of the Koreans' faith that God is good and had a loving plan for their lives. The truth was that God did have a loving plan, and not only for them but also for many unreached Muslims among the Uzbek and Kazak peoples.

GOING FORWARD BY GETTING ARRESTED

God's strange ways of guiding the missionary enterprise are also seen in the way Jesus told the disciples to expect arrest and imprisonment as God's deployment tactic to put them with people they would never otherwise reach. "They will lay their hands on you and persecute you, delivering you up to the synagogues and prisons, and you will be brought before kings and governors for my name's sake. *This will be your opportunity to bear witness*" (Luke 21:12–13; cf. Mark 13:9).

The June/July 1989 issue of *Mission Frontiers* carried an article signed with the pseudonym Frank Marshall. This missionary in a politically sensitive Latin American country told the story of his recent imprisonment. He and his coworkers had been beaten numerous times and thrown in jail before. This time federal agents accused him of fraud and bribery because they assumed he could not have gotten his official documents without lying. They did not believe that he had been born in the country.

In prison, the Lord spared him from sexual assault by a huge man wrapped in a towel with four gold chains around his neck and a ring on every finger. When put in the cell with this man, Frank began sharing the gospel with him and praying in his heart, "Lord, deliver me from this evil." The man changed color, shouted at Frank to shut up, and told him to leave him alone.

Frank began to tell others about Christ when the men had free time in the courtyard. One Muslim named Satawa confessed Christ within the first week and invited Frank to answer questions from a group of fifteen other Muslims. In two weeks, Frank finally was able to get a lawyer. He also asked for a box of Bibles. The next Sunday forty-five men gathered in the courtyard to hear Frank preach. He spoke about how difficult it was for him to be away from his family and about how much God loved his Son and yet gave him up for sinners so that we could believe and live. Thirty of these men stayed afterward to pray and ask the Lord to lead them and forgive them. Frank was soon released and deported to the United States, but he now knows firsthand the meaning of Jesus' words, "This will be your opportunity to bear witness."

MIRACLES IN MOZAMBIQUE

During the 1960s, the Lord raised up an indigenous leader named Martinho Campos in the church in Mozambique. The story of his ministry, *Life out of Death in Mozambique*, is a remarkable testimony to God's strange ways of missionary blessing.

Martinho was leading a series of meetings in the administrative area of Gurue sixty miles from his own area of Nauela. The police arrested him and put him in jail without a trial. The police chief, a European, assumed that the gatherings were related to the emerging guerrilla group Frelimo. But even when the Catholic priest told him that these men were just "a gathering of heretics," he took no concern for justice, though he wondered why the common people brought so much food to the prisoner, as though he were someone important.

One night he was driving his truck with half a dozen prisoners in it and saw "what appeared to be a man in gleaming white, standing in the road, facing him." He swerved so sharply that the truck rolled over, and he was trapped underneath. The prisoners themselves lifted the truck so that the police chief could get out.

After brief treatment in the hospital, he returned to talk to Martinho because he knew there was some connection between this vision and the prisoner. He entered Martinho's cell and asked for forgiveness. Martinho told him about his need for God's forgiveness and how to have it. The police chief said humbly, "Please pray for me." Immediately the chief called for hot water so that the prisoner could wash, took him out of solitary confinement, and saw to it that a fair trial was held. Martinho was released.

But the most remarkable thing was what followed: "Not only did the Chief of Police make plain his respect for what Martinho stood for, but granted him official permission to travel throughout the whole area under his jurisdiction, in order to preach and hold evangelical services."[22] Such permission would never have been given through the ordinary channels. But God had made a way through suffering. The imprisonment was for the advancement of the gospel.

GOD WAS BETTER SERVED IN PRISON

On January 9, 1985, Pastor Hristo Kulichev, a Congregational pastor in Bulgaria, was arrested and put in prison. His crime was that he preached in his church even though the state had appointed another man as the pastor, whom the congregation had not elected. Kulichev's trial was a mockery of justice, and he was sentenced to eight months of imprisonment. During his time in prison, he made Christ known every way he could.

When he got out he wrote, "Both prisoners and jailers asked many questions, and it turned out that we had a more fruitful ministry there than we could have expected in church. God was better served by our presence in prison than if we had been free."[23] In many places in the world, the words of Jesus are as radically relevant as if they had been spoken yesterday. "They will lay their hands on you and persecute you, delivering you up to . . . prisons. . . . This will be your opportunity to bear witness" (Luke 21:12–13). The pain of our shattered plans is for the purpose of scattered grace.

6. *The Supremacy of Christ Is Manifest in Suffering*

The suffering of missionaries is meant by God to magnify the power and sufficiency of Christ. Suffering is finally to show the supremacy of God. When God declined to remove the suffering caused by Paul's "thorn in the flesh," he said to Paul, "My grace is sufficient for you, for *my power is made perfect in weakness.*" To this Paul responded, "I will boast all the more gladly of my weaknesses, so that the power of Christ may rest upon me. For the sake of Christ, then, I am content with weaknesses, insults, hardships, persecutions, and calamities. For when I am weak, then I am strong" (2 Cor. 12:9–10).

22. Phyllis Thompson, *Life out of Death in Mozambique* (London: Hodder & Stoughton, 1989), 111.
23. Herbert Schlossberg, *Called to Suffer, Called to Triumph* (Portland, Ore.: Multnomah, 1990), 230.

Paul was strong in persecutions because "the power of Christ" rested upon him and was made perfect in him. In other words, Christ's power was Paul's only power when his sufferings brought him to the end of his resources and cast him wholly on Jesus. This was God's purpose in Paul's thorn, and it is his purpose in all our suffering. God means for us to rely wholly on him. "That was to make us rely not on ourselves but on God who raises the dead" (2 Cor. 1:9). The reason God wants such reliance is because this kind of trust shows his supreme power and love to sustain us when we can't do anything to sustain ourselves.

We began this chapter with this claim: Loss and suffering, joyfully accepted for the kingdom of God, show the supremacy of God's worth more clearly in the world than all worship and prayer. We have seen this truth implicit in looking at six reasons why God appoints suffering for the messengers of his grace. But now we need to make explicit that the supremacy of God is the reason for suffering running through and above all the other reasons. God ordains suffering because through all the other reasons it displays to the world the supremacy of his worth above all treasures.

Jesus makes crystal clear how we can rejoice in persecution. "Blessed are you when others revile you and persecute you and utter all kinds of evil against you falsely on my account. Rejoice and be glad, *for your reward is great in heaven*" (Matt. 5:11–12). The reason we can rejoice in persecution is that the worth of our reward in heaven is so much greater than the worth of all that we lose through suffering on earth. Therefore, suffering with joy proves to the world that our treasure is in heaven, not on earth, and that this treasure is greater than anything the world has to offer. The supremacy of God's worth shines through the pain that his people will gladly bear for his name.

Gladly Will I Boast of Weakness and Calamity

I use the word "gladly" because that is the way the saints speak of it. One example is Paul saying, "I will boast all the more gladly of my weaknesses . . . insults, hardships, persecutions, and calamities" (2 Cor. 12:9–10). He says the same thing in Romans 5:3: "We rejoice in our sufferings." And the reason he gives is that it produces patience and a tested quality of life and an unfailing hope (Rom. 5:3–4). In other words, his joy flowed from his hope just the way Jesus said it should. And Paul makes clear that the reward is the glory of God. "We rejoice in hope of the glory of God" (Rom. 5:2). And so it is the supremacy of God's worth that shines through Paul's joy in affliction.

The other apostles react the same way in Acts 5:41 after being beaten for their preaching: "Then they left the presence of the council, rejoicing that they were counted worthy to suffer dishonor for the name" (Acts 5:41). This fearless joy in spite of real danger and great pain is the display of God's superiority over all that the world has to offer.

You Joyfully Accepted the Plundering of Your Property

And then there were the early Christians who visited their friends in prison, rejoicing even though it cost them their possessions. "For you had compassion on those in prison, and you joyfully accepted the plundering of your property, since you knew that you yourselves had a better possession and an abiding one" (Heb. 10:34). Joy in suffering flows from hope in a great reward. Christians are not called to live morose lives of burdensome persecution. We are called to rejoice. "Rejoice insofar as you share Christ's sufferings" (1 Peter 4:13). "Count it all joy, my brothers, when you meet trials of various kinds" (James 1:2).

The Love of God Is Better Than Life

The basis for this indomitable joy is the supremacy of God's love above life itself. The "steadfast love [of the LORD] is better than life" (Ps. 63:3). The pleasures in this life are "fleeting" (Heb. 11:25), and the afflictions are "light and momentary" (2 Cor. 4:17). But the steadfast love of the Lord is forever. All his pleasures are superior, and there will be no more pain. "In your presence there is fullness of joy; at your right hand are pleasures forevermore" (Ps. 16:11).

Glad Suffering Shines Brighter Than Gratitude

It is true that we should bear testimony to the supremacy of God's goodness by receiving his good gifts with thanksgiving (1 Tim. 4:3). But for many Christians this has become the only way they see their lifestyles glorifying God. God has been good to them to give them so much. Therefore, the way to witness to the reality of God is to take and be thankful.

But even though it is true that we should thankfully enjoy what we have, there is a relentless call in the Bible not to accumulate more and more things but to give more and more and to be deprived of things if love demands it. There are no easy rules to tell us whether the call on our lives is the call of the rich young ruler to give away all that we have or the call of Zacchaeus to give away half of what we have. What is clear from the New Testament is that suffering with joy, not gratitude in wealth, is the way the worth of Jesus shines most brightly.

Who can doubt that the supremacy of Christ's worth shines brightest in a life such as this:

> But whatever gain I had, I counted as loss for the sake of Christ. Indeed, I count everything as loss because of the surpassing worth of knowing Christ Jesus my Lord. For his sake I have suffered the loss of all things and count them as rubbish, in order that I may gain Christ.
>
> Philippians 3:7–8

You cannot show the preciousness of a person by being happy with his gifts. Ingratitude will certainly prove that the giver is not loved, but gratitude for gifts does not prove that the giver is precious. What proves that the giver is precious is the glad-hearted readiness to leave all his gifts to be with him. This is why suffering is so central in the mission of the church. The goal of our mission is that people from all the nations worship the true God. But worship means cherishing the preciousness of God above all else, including life itself. It will be difficult to bring the nations to love God from a lifestyle that communicates a love of things. Therefore, God ordains in the lives of his messengers that suffering severs our bondage to the world. When joy and love survive this severing, we are fit to say to the nations with authenticity and power: Hope in God.

How Is Hope in God Made Visible?

Peter talks about the visibility of this hope: "In your hearts regard Christ the Lord as holy, always being prepared to make a defense to anyone who asks you for a reason for the hope that is in you" (1 Peter 3:15). Why would people ask about hope? What kind of life are we to live that would make people wonder about our hope? If our security and happiness in the future were manifestly secured the way the world secures its future, no one would ask us about it. There would be no unusual hope to see. What Peter is saying is that the world should see a different hope in the lives of Christians—not a hope in the security of money or the security of power or the security of houses or lands or portfolios but in the security of "the grace that will be brought to you at the revelation of Jesus Christ" (1 Peter 1:13).

Therefore, God ordains suffering to help us release our hold on worldly hopes and put our "hope in God" (1 Peter 1:21). The fiery trials are appointed to consume the earthly dependencies and leave only the refined gold of "genuine faith" (1 Peter 1:7). "Let those who suffer according to God's will entrust their souls to a faithful Creator while doing good" (1 Peter 4:19). It's the supremacy of God's great faithfulness above all other securities that frees us to "rejoice insofar as [we] share Christ's sufferings" (1 Peter 4:13). Therefore, joy in suffering for Christ's sake makes the supremacy of God shine more clearly than all our gratitude for wealth.

Wartime Austerity for the Cause of Missions

Jesus presses us toward a wartime lifestyle that does not value simplicity for simplicity's sake but values wartime austerity for what it can produce for the cause of world evangelization. He said, "Sell your possessions, and give to the needy. Provide yourselves with moneybags that do not grow old, with a treasure in the heavens that does not fail" (Luke 12:33). "Make friends for yourselves by means of unrighteous wealth, so that when it fails they may receive you into the eternal dwellings" (Luke 16:9). "Do not seek what you are to eat and what you are to drink, nor be worried. For all the nations of the world seek after these things, and your Father knows that you need them. Instead, seek his kingdom, and these things will be added to you" (Luke 12:29–31).

The point is that an $80,000 or a $180,000 salary does not have to be accompanied by an $80,000 or a $180,000 lifestyle. God is calling us to be conduits of his grace, not cul-de-sacs. Our great danger today is thinking that the conduit should be lined with gold. It shouldn't. Copper will do. No matter how grateful we are, gold will not make the world think that our God is good; it will make people think that our god is gold. That is no honor to the supremacy of his worth.

The Deadly Desire for Wealth

The desire for riches is deadly. Gehazi, Elisha's servant, was struck with Naaman's leprosy because he could not pass up a reward (2 Kings 5:26–27). Ananias dropped dead because desire for money prompted him to lie (Acts 5:5–6). The rich young ruler could not enter the kingdom of God (Mark 10:22–23). The rich man who feasted sumptuously and neglected Lazarus was tormented in Hades (Luke 16:23). Paul said that the desire to be rich plunges men into ruin and destruction (1 Tim. 6:9).

God tells us about these tragedies not to make us hate money but to make us love him. The severity of punishment for loving money is a sign of the supremacy of God. We scorn the infinite worth of God when we covet. That is why Paul calls covetousness idolatry and says that the wrath of God is coming against it (Col. 3:5–6).

"I Had No Shirt"

It is almost impossible for Americans to come to terms with Jesus' commendation of the widow who "out of her poverty put in all she had to live on" (Luke 21:4). To see this spirit fleshed out, we may have to leave America and go elsewhere. Stanford Kelly illustrates it from Haiti.

The church was having a Thanksgiving festival, and each Christian was invited to bring a love offering. One envelope from a Haitian man named Edmund held $13. That amount was three months' income for a working man there. Kelly was as surprised as those counting a Sunday offering in the United States might be to get a $6,000 cash gift. He looked around for Edmund but could not see him.

Later Kelly met him in the village and questioned him. He pressed him for an explanation and found that Edmund had sold his horse in order to give the $13 gift to God. But why hadn't he come to the festival? He hesitated and didn't want to answer.

Finally, Edmund said, "I had no shirt to wear."[24]

Retirement and the Unreached Peoples

Two phenomena in America are emerging together: One is the challenge to give our all to do our part in finishing the task of world missions, and the other is a huge baby-boom bulge in the population reaching peak earning years and heading toward "retirement."[25] How will the Christians in this group respond to the typical American dream? Is it a biblical dream?

24. Norm Lewis, *Priority One: What God Wants* (Orange, Calif.: Promise Publishing, 1988), 120.

25. Since the first edition of this book in 1993, one of the significant advances in Christian mission strategy has been the emergence of ministries focused on mobilizing people in midlife for the cause of finishing the Great Commission. Paul's words in Acts 20:24 have come alive for thousands as they contemplate a better way to finish their earthly lives than to throw them away golfing or fishing in the unbiblical dreamworld of wasted lives called "retirement." Paul said, "But I do not account my life of any value nor as precious to myself, if only I may finish my course and the ministry that I received from the Lord Jesus, to testify to the gospel of the grace of God." For information about this movement, see the website of the Finishers Project: www .finishers.gospelcom.net/. The Finishers Project is a service designed to provide adult Christians with information and challenge for processing and discovering ministry opportunities in the missions enterprise—short term, part term, or as a second career. The vision statement (2004)

Ralph Winter asks, "Where in the Bible do they see [retirement]? Did Moses retire? Did Paul retire? Peter? John? Do military officers retire in the middle of a war?"[26] I mentioned earlier that Oswald Sanders ministered around the world until he died at ninety and that he wrote a book a year between the ages of seventy and eighty-nine.

Why Simeon's Strength Quadrupled at Sixty

Charles Simeon, the pastor of Trinity Church, Cambridge, two hundred years ago learned a very painful lesson about God's attitude toward his "retirement." In 1807, after twenty-five years of ministry at Trinity Church, his health broke. He became very weak and had to take an extended leave from his labor. Handley Moule recounts the fascinating story of what God was doing in Simeon's life.

> The broken condition lasted with variations for thirteen years, till he was just sixty, and then it passed away quite suddenly and without any evident physical cause. He was on his last visit to Scotland . . . in 1819, and found himself to his great surprise, just as he crossed the border, "almost as perceptibly renewed in strength as the woman was after she had touched the hem of our Lord's garment." He saw in this revival no miracle, in the common sense of the word, yet as a distinct providence.
>
> He says that he had been promising himself, before he began to break down, a very active life up to sixty, and then a Sabbath evening [retirement!]; and that now he seemed to hear his Master saying: "I laid you aside, because you entertained with satisfaction the thought of resting from your labour; but now you have arrived at the very period when you had promised yourself that satisfaction, and have determined instead to spend your strength for me to the latest hour of your life, I have doubled, trebled, quadrupled your strength, that you may execute your desire on a more extended plan."[27]

says, "The Finishers Project is a movement to provide information, challenge and pathways for people to join God in His passion for His glory among the nations. Boomers are and will be the healthiest and best educated generation of empty-nesters ever. This generation is skilled and resourced with a multitude of talents. We can either give them to Jesus to lay up as treasure in Heaven or lose them."

26. Ralph D. Winter, "The Retirement Booby Trap," *Missions Frontiers* 7 (July 1985): 25.

27. Handley C. G. Moule, *Charles Simeon* (1892; reprint, London: Inter-Varsity, 1948), 125. For a biographical sketch of Simeon's life, see "Charles Simeon: The Ballast of Humiliation and the Sails of Adoration," in John Piper, *The Roots of Endurance: Invincible Perseverance in the Lives of John Newton, Charles Simeon, and William Wilberforce* (Wheaton: Crossway, 2002). An earlier version of this essay is found at www.DesiringGod.org.

How many Christians set their sights on a "Sabbath evening" of life—resting, playing, traveling, and so on—the world's substitute for heaven, because they do not believe that there will be one beyond the grave. The mind-set is that we must reward ourselves in this life for our long years of labor. Eternal rest and joy after death is an irrelevant consideration. What a strange reward for a Christian to set his sights on! Twenty years of leisure while living in the midst of the last days of infinite consequence for millions of unreached people. What a tragic way to finish the last lap before entering the presence of the King who finished his so differently!

Why Not Be like Raymond Lull?

Raymond Lull was born in 1235 to an illustrious family at Palma on the island of Majorca off the coast of Spain. His life as a youth was profligate. But all that changed as a result of five visions that compelled him to a life of devotion to Christ. He first entered monastic life but later became a missionary to Muslim countries in northern Africa. He learned Arabic, which at the age of seventy-nine he was teaching in Europe.

> His pupils and friends naturally desired that he should end his days in the peaceful pursuit of learning and the comfort of companionship.
>
> Such however was not Lull's wish. His ambition was to die as a missionary and not as a teacher of philosophy. Ever his favorite "Ars Major" had to give way to that *ars maxima* expressed in Lull's own motto, "He that lives by the life cannot die." . . .
>
> In Lull's contemplations we read . . . "Men are wont to die, O Lord, from old age, the failure of natural warmth and excess of cold; but thus, if it be Thy will, Thy servant would not wish to die; he would prefer to die in the glow of love, even as Thou wast willing to die for him."
>
> The dangers and difficulties that made Lull shrink back from his journey at Genoa in 1291 only urged him forward to North Africa once more in 1314. His love had not grown cold, but burned the brighter "with the failure of natural warmth and the weakness of old age." He longed not only for the martyr's crown, but also once more to see his little band of believers [in Africa]. Animated by these sentiments he crossed over to Bugia on August 14, and for nearly a whole year labored secretly among a little circle of converts, whom on his previous visits he had won over to the Christian faith. . . .
>
> At length, weary of seclusion, and longing for martyrdom, he came forth into the open market and presented himself to the people as the same man whom they had once expelled from their town. It was Elijah showing himself to a mob of Ahabs! Lull stood before them and threatened them with divine wrath

if they still persisted in their errors. He pleaded with love, but spoke plainly the whole truth. The consequences can be easily anticipated. Filled with fanatic fury at his boldness, and unable to reply to his arguments, the populace seized him, and dragged him out of the town; there by the command, or at least the connivance, of the king, he was stoned on the 30th of June 1315.[28]

Lull was eighty years old when he gave his life for the Muslims of North Africa. As a hart longs for the flowing streams—and longs the more as the brook approaches and the smell sweetens and the thirst deepens—so longs the soul of the saint to see Christ and to glorify him in his dying (cf. John 21:19). It is beyond comprehension that soldiers of the cross would be satisfied in retiring from the battle just before the trumpet blast of victory—or just before admission to the coronation ceremony.

"Senior Discounts" Are for Missionary Travel

I am not saying that we can make professions and businesses keep us employed beyond sixty-five or seventy. I am saying that a new chapter of life opens for most people at age sixty-five. And if we have armed ourselves with the "thought" of the suffering Savior and saturated our mind with the ways of the supremacy of God, we will invest our time and energy in this final chapter very differently than if we take our cues from the American dream. Millions of "retired" people should be engaged at all levels of intensity in hundreds of assignments around the world. Talk about travel! Park the RVs and use the senior discounts and "super savers" to fly wherever the agencies have need. Let the unreached peoples of the earth reap the benefits of a lifetime of earning. "You will be repaid at the resurrection of the just" (Luke 14:14).

"You'll Be Eaten by Cannibals"

An aging Christian once objected to John G. Paton's plan to go as a missionary to the South Sea Islands with the words, "You'll be eaten by Cannibals!" Paton responded:

Mr. Dickson, you are advanced in years now, and your own prospect is soon to be laid in the grave, there to be eaten by worms; I confess to you, that

28. Samuel Zwemer, *Raymond Lull: First Missionary to the Moslems* (New York: Revell, 1902), 132–45.

if I can but live and die serving and honoring the Lord Jesus, it will make no difference to me whether I am eaten by Cannibals or worms; and in the Great Day my resurrection body will arise as fair as yours in the likeness of our risen Redeemer.[29]

When the world sees millions of "retired" Christians pouring out the last drops of their lives with joy for the sake of the unreached peoples and with a view toward heaven, then the supremacy of God will shine. He does not shine as brightly in the posh, leisure-soaked luxury condos on the outer rings of our cities.

Let There Be No Talk of Ultimate Self-Denial

From the youngest to the oldest, Christ is calling his church to a radical, wartime engagement in world missions. He is making it plain that it will not happen without pain. But let there be no Christian self-pity, no talk of ultimate self-denial. It is simply amazing how consistent are the testimonies of missionaries who have suffered for the gospel. Virtually all of them bear witness of the abundant joy and overriding compensations. Those who have suffered most often speak in the most lavish terms of the supreme blessing and joy of giving their lives away for others.

Lottie Moon said, "Surely there is no greater joy than saving souls." Sherwood Eddy said of Amy Carmichael, "Her life was the most fragrant, the most joyfully sacrificial, that I ever knew." Samuel Zwemer, after fifty years of labor (and the loss of two young children), said "The sheer joy of it all comes back. Gladly would I do it all over again." And both Hudson Taylor and David Livingstone, after lives of extraordinary hardship and loss said, "I never made a sacrifice."[30]

From this discovery I have learned that the way of love is both the way of self-denial and the way of ultimate joy. We deny ourselves the fleeting pleasures of sin and luxury and self-absorption in order to seek the kingdom above all things. In doing so we bring the greatest good to others, we magnify the worth of Christ as a treasure chest of joy, and we find our greatest satisfaction.

God is most glorified in us when we are most satisfied in him. And the supremacy of that glory shines most brightly when the satisfaction that we have in him endures in spite of suffering and pain in the mission of love.

29. Paton, *John G. Paton*, 56.
30. See John Piper, "The Battle Cry of Christian Hedonism," in *Desiring God* (Sisters, Ore.: Multnomah, 1996), 189–211.

PART 2

MAKING GOD SUPREME IN MISSIONS

THE NECESSITY AND NATURE OF THE TASK

4

The Supremacy of Christ as the Conscious Focus of All Saving Faith

The supremacy of God in missions is affirmed biblically by affirming the supremacy of his Son, Jesus Christ. It is a stunning New Testament truth that since the incarnation of the Son of God, all saving faith must henceforth fix consciously on him. This was not always true, and those times were called the "times of ignorance" (Acts 17:30). But now it is true, and Christ is the conscious center of the mission of the church. The aim of missions is to "bring about the obedience of faith *for the sake of his name* among all the nations" (Rom. 1:5). This was a new thing with the coming of Christ. God's will is to glorify his Son by making him the conscious focus of all saving faith.

Posing the Question

The general question posed in this chapter is whether the supremacy of Christ means that he is the only way to salvation. But that general question really contains three questions, and they are crucial for the missionary task of the Christian church. The three questions emerge as different people answer and qualify the main question.

Will Anyone Experience Eternal Conscious Torment under God's Wrath?

Many people today affirm that Christ is man's only hope but deny that there is eternal punishment for not believing in him.[1] Some would say that everyone is going to be saved whether they hear about Christ in this life or not. For example, even though he has been dead since 1905, the preacher-novelist George MacDonald is being published and read as never before in America and is extending the influence of his brand of universalism. He makes hell into an extended means of self-atonement and sanctification. In hell, the justice of God will eventually destroy all sin in his creatures. In this way, God will bring everyone to glory.[2] Everyone will be saved. Hell is not eternal.

Others would say that while not everyone is saved, there is still no eternal punishment because the fire of judgment annihilates those who reject Christ. Thus, unbelievers cease to exist and experience no conscious punishment. Hell is not a place of eternal punishment but an event of annihilation. This is the direction that Clark Pinnock, John Stott, Edward Fudge, and others have gone.[3]

1. For a thorough assessment of the recent departures from a historic belief in hell as eternal conscious torment of the ungodly, see Ajith Fernando, *Crucial Questions about Hell* (Wheaton: Crossway, 1994); Robert A. Peterson, *Hell on Trial: The Case for Eternal Punishment* (Phillipsburg, N.J.: Presbyterian & Reformed, 1995); D. A. Carson, *The Gagging of God: Christianity Confronts Pluralism* (Grand Rapids: Zondervan, 1996), 515–36; Larry Dixon, *The Other Side of the Good News: Confronting the Contemporary Challenges to Jesus' Teaching on Hell* (Ross-shire, Scotland: Christian Focus Publications, 2003); Robert A. Peterson and Edward William Fudge, *Two Views on Hell: A Biblical and Theological Dialogue* (Downers Grove, Ill.: InterVarsity, 2000); and Robert Peterson and Chris Morgan, eds., *Hell under Fire: Modern Scholarship Reinvents Eternal Punishment* (Grand Rapids: Zondervan, 2004).

2. See, for example, his sermon on "Justice" in *Creation in Christ,* ed. Rolland Hein (Wheaton: Shaw, 1976), 63–81, where he argues forcefully that "punishment is for the sake of amendment and atonement. God is bound by His love to punish sin in order to deliver His creature: He is bound by His justice to destroy sin in His creation" (72). I have given an extended critique of MacDonald's view of divine justice, self-atonement, and universalism in *The Pleasures of God* (Sisters, Ore.: Multnomah, 2000), 168–74.

3. Clark Pinnock and Delwin Brown, *Theological Crossfire: An Evangelical/Liberal Dialogue* (Grand Rapids: Zondervan, 1990), 226–27. "I was led to question the traditional belief in everlasting conscious torment because of moral revulsion and broader theological considerations, not first of all on scriptural grounds. It just does not make any sense to say that a God of love will torture people forever for sins done in the context of a finite life. . . . It's time for evangelicals to come out and say that the Biblical and morally appropriate doctrine of hell is annihilation, not everlasting torment." Cf. Clark H. Pinnock, "The Conditional View," in *Four Views on Hell*, ed. William Crockett (Grand Rapids: Zondervan, 1996), 135–66.

David Edwards, *Evangelical Essentials, with a Response from John Stott* (Downers Grove, Ill.: InterVarsity, 1988), 314–20. "Emotionally, I find the concept [of eternal conscious torment] intolerable and do not understand how people can live with it without either cauterizing their

Therefore, the question we must ask includes this one: Is eternal punishment at stake? That is, will anyone be eternally cut off from Christ and experience eternal conscious torment under the wrath of God?

Is the Work of Christ Necessary?

Other people today would deny that Christ is man's only hope. They may believe that Christ is the provision that God has made for Christians, but for other religions, there are other ways of getting right with God and gaining eternal bliss. The work of Christ is useful for Christians but not necessary for non-Christians.

For example, British theologian John Hick argues that different religions are "equals, though they each may have different emphases." Christianity is not superior but merely one partner in the quest for salvation. We are not to seek one world religion but rather should look to the day when "the ecumenical spirit which has so largely transformed Christianity will increasingly affect relations between the world faiths."[4]

This means that the question we are asking must include: Is the work of Christ the necessary means provided by God for eternal salvation—not just for Christians, but for all people?

---

feelings or cracking under the strain." He gives four arguments that he says suggest that "Scripture points in the direction of annihilation, and that 'eternal conscious torment' is a tradition which has to yield to the supreme authority of Scripture. . . . I do not dogmatise about the position to which I have come. I hold it tentatively. But I do plead for frank dialogue among Evangelicals on the basis of Scripture. I also believe that the ultimate annihilation of the wicked should at least be accepted as a legitimate, Biblically founded alternative to their eternal conscious torment." Edward William Fudge, *The Fire That Consumes: The Biblical Case for Conditional Immortality*, rev. ed. (Carlisle, U.K.: Paternoster, 1994).

4. John Hick, "Whatever Path Men Choose Is Mine," in *Christianity and Other Religions*, ed. John Hick and Brian Hebblethwaite (Philadelphia: Fortress, 1980), 188. Hick ends with a quote from the *Bhagavad Gita*, iv, 11: "Howsoever man may approach me, even so do I accept them; for, on all sides, whatever path they may choose is mine." For a survey of Hick's thoughts, as well as a compelling response, see Harold Netland, *Dissonant Voices: Religious Pluralism and the Question of Truth* (1991; reprint, Vancouver: Regent Publishers, 1998); Harold Netland, *Encountering Religious Pluralism: The Challenge to Christian Faith and Mission* (Downers Grove, Ill.: InterVarsity, 2001). Similarly, John Parry, the Other Faiths Secretary of the World Church and Mission Department of the United Reformed Church in London, wrote in 1985, "It is to the faith of Jesus Christ that we are called. The change of preposition from in to of is significant. It is a faith that is shown in one's trust in God, in surrender to God's purposes, in giving oneself. Such a response of faith I have witnessed among my friends of other faiths. I cannot believe they are far from the kingdom of heaven, what is more, as Dr. Starkey writes '. . . people will not be judged for correct doctrinal beliefs but for their faith. Those who will enter the kingdom on the day of judgment are those who in faith respond to God's love by loving others.'" "Exploring the Ways of God with Peoples of Faith," *International Review of Missions* 74, no. 296 (October 1985): 512.

Is Conscious Faith in Christ Necessary?

Some evangelicals say they just don't know if conscious faith in Christ is necessary.[5] Others, without denying the reality of eternal judgment or the necessity of Christ's saving work, would say, "Yes, Christ is man's only hope, but he saves some of those who never hear of him through faith that does not have Christ for its conscious object." For example, Millard Erickson represents some evangelicals[6] who argue that, similar to the saints in the Old Testament, some unevangelized persons today may "receive the benefit of Christ's death without conscious knowledge-belief in the name of Jesus."[7]

5. Edwards, *Evangelical Essentials*, 327. For example, John Stott says, "I believe the most Christian stance is to remain agnostic on this question. . . . The fact is that God, alongside the most solemn warnings about our responsibility to respond to the gospel, has not revealed how he will deal with those who have never heard it." In William V. Crockett and James G. Sigountos, eds., *Through No Fault of Their Own* (Grand Rapids: Baker, 1991); Timothy Phillips, Aida Besançon Spencer, and Tite Tienou "prefer to leave the matter in the hands of God" (259n3).

6. Crockett and Sigountos (*Through No Fault of Their Own*) include some essays by evangelicals who take the view that those who have never heard are in fact led to salvation through general revelation. Their conclusion is, "Those who hear and reject the gospel are lost. And those who do embrace the light of general revelation must be willing to turn from their dead idols to serve the living God (1 Thessalonians 1:9). General revelation, then, creates in them a desire to reject their pagan religion; it does not help them see the saving significance of their own" (260). See a good response to this in Ajith Fernando, *Sharing the Truth in Love: How to Relate to People of Other Faiths* (Grand Rapids: Discovery House, 2001), 211–33.

7. Millard Erickson argues from the revelation available in nature according to Romans 1–2 and 10:18. The essential elements in the "gospel message" in nature are: "1) The belief in one good powerful God. 2) The belief that he (man) owes this God perfect obedience to his law. 3) The consciousness that he does not meet this standard, and therefore is guilty and condemned. 4) The realization that nothing he can offer God can compensate him (or atone) for this sin and guilt. 5) The belief that God is merciful, and will forgive and accept those who cast themselves on his mercy. May it not be that if a man believes and acts on this set of tenets he is redemptively related to God and receives the benefits of Christ's death, whether he consciously knows and understands the details of that provision or not? Presumably that was the case with the Old Testament believers. . . . If this is possible, if Jews possessed salvation in the Old Testament era simply by virtue of having the form of the Christian gospel without its content, can this principle be extended? Could it be that those who ever since the time of Christ have had no opportunity to hear the gospel, as it has come through the special revelation, participate in this salvation on the same basis? On what other grounds could they fairly be held responsible for having or not having salvation (or faith)?" But here he is very tentative, for he goes on to say, "What Paul is saying in the remainder of Romans is that very few, if any, actually come to such a saving knowledge of God on the basis of natural revelation alone." Millard Erickson, "Hope for Those Who Haven't Heard? Yes, But . . ." *Evangelical Missions Quarterly* 11, no. 2 (April 1975): 124–25. He is following here A. H. Strong: "Whoever among the heathen are saved must in like manner [i.e., like the patriarchs of the Old Testament] be saved by casting themselves as helpless sinners upon God's plan of mercy, dimly shadowed forth in nature and providence." *Systematic Theology* (Westwood, N.J.: Revell, 1907), 842. This view is different from that of the older Reformed theologian Charles Hodge, who argued that only through the

So we must make clear what we are really asking: Is it necessary for people to hear of Christ in order to be eternally saved? That is, can a person today be saved by the work of Christ even if he does not have an opportunity to hear about it?

Therefore, when we ask, Is Jesus Christ humanity's only hope for salvation? we are really asking three questions:

1. Will anyone experience *eternal conscious torment* under God's wrath?
2. Is the work of Christ the *necessary* means provided by God for eternal salvation?
3. Is it necessary for people *to hear of Christ* in order to be eternally saved?

A Nerve of Urgency

Biblical answers to these three questions are crucial because in each case a negative answer would seem to cut a nerve of urgency in the missionary cause. Evangelicals such as Erickson do not intend to cut that nerve, and their view is certainly not in the same category as that of Hick or Mac-Donald. They insist that the salvation of anyone apart from the preaching of Christ is the exception rather than the rule and that preaching Christ to all is utterly important.

Nevertheless, there is a felt difference in the urgency when one believes that hearing the gospel is the only hope that anyone has of escaping the penalty of sin and living forever in happiness to the glory of God's grace. It does not ring true when William Crockett and James Sigountos argue that the existence of "implicit Christians" (saved through general revelation without hearing of Christ) actually "should increase motivation" for missions. They say that these unevangelized converts are "waiting eagerly to hear more about [God]." If we would reach them, "a strong church would spring to life, giving glory to God and evangelizing their pagan neighbors."[8] I cannot escape the impression that this is a futile attempt to make a weakness look like a strength. On the contrary, common sense presses another truth on us: The more likely it is that people can be saved without missions, the less urgency there is for missions.

Word of God heard or read does the effectual call to salvation come. *Systematic Theology*, vol. 2 (Grand Rapids: Eerdmans, 1952), 646.

8. Crockett and Sigountos, *Through No Fault of Their Own*, 260.

So with regard to all three of these questions, there is much at stake. Nevertheless, in the end, the most crucial matter is not our desire to maintain the urgency of the missionary cause but to answer, What do the Scriptures teach?

My aim here is to provide the biblical data that, in my judgment, compel a positive answer to each of these three questions. I hope to demonstrate that in the fullest sense Jesus Christ is humanity's only hope for salvation. To do this I will gather into three groups the texts that relate most directly to the three questions we have posed. Some comment will be made along the way.

A Hell of Eternal Conscious Torment

> And many of those who sleep in the dust of the earth shall awake, some to everlasting life, and some to shame and *everlasting contempt*.
>
> Daniel 12:2

It is true that the Hebrew *'olam* does not always mean "everlasting," but in this context it seems to because it points to a decisive division into joy or misery after death and resurrection. As the *life* is everlasting, so the *shame and contempt* are everlasting.

"His winnowing fork is in his hand, and he will clear his threshing floor and gather his wheat into the barn, but the chaff he will burn with *unquenchable fire*" (Matt. 3:12; cf. Luke 3:17). This is John the Baptist's prediction of the judgment that Jesus will bring in the end. He pictures a decisive separation. The term "unquenchable fire" implies a fire that will not be extinguished and therefore a punishment that will not end. This is confirmed in Mark 9:43–48:

> And if your hand causes you to sin, cut it off. It is better for you to enter life crippled than with two hands to go to hell, to the *unquenchable fire*. And if your foot causes you to sin, cut it off. It is better for you to enter life lame than with two feet to be thrown into hell. And if your eye causes you to sin, tear it out. It is better for you to enter the kingdom of God with one eye than with two eyes to be thrown into hell, "*where their worm does not die and the fire is not quenched*."

Here the "unquenchable fire" is clearly hell, and the last line shows that the point is the unending misery of those who go there ("their worm does not die"). If annihilation (the teaching that some cease to exist after death or after a limited period of conscious punishment in hell)[9] were in view, why would the verse stress the fire never being quenched and the worm never dying? John Stott struggles to escape this by saying that the worm will not die and the fire will not be quenched "until presumably their work of destruction is done."[10] That qualification is not in the text. On the contrary, the focus on eternal duration is confirmed in Matthew 18:8: "And if your hand or your foot causes you to sin, cut it off and throw it away. It is better for you to enter life crippled or lame than with two hands or two feet to be thrown into the *eternal fire*."

Here the fire is not only unquenchable but more explicitly "eternal." The fact that this fire is not merely a purifying fire of the age to come (as some take *aiōnion* to mean) is shown in the subsequent sayings of Jesus, especially the one on the unforgivable sin (Matt. 12:31–32; Luke 12:10). "And do not fear those who kill the body but cannot kill the soul. Rather fear him who can destroy both soul and body in hell" (Matt. 10:28; cf. Luke 12:4–5). The "destruction" referred to here is decisive and final, but it does not have to mean obliterate or annihilate. The word *apollymi* frequently means "ruin" or "lose" or "perish" or "get rid of" (Matt. 8:25; 9:17; 10:6; 12:14). It does not imply annihilate. It is eternal ruin (see 2 Thess. 1:9).

"Then he will say to those on his left, 'Depart from me, you cursed, into the *eternal fire* prepared for the devil and his angels.' . . . And these will go away into *eternal punishment*, but the righteous into eternal life" (Matt. 25:41, 46). The eternal fire is explicitly "punishment," and its opposite is eternal life. It does not honor the full import of "eternal life" to say that it refers only to a quality of life without eternal connotations.[11] Therefore, it would fall short of truth to say that "eternal punishment" has no reference to eternal duration. As Leon Morris says, "It is not easy

9. Clark Pinnock of McMaster Divinity College argues that "the 'fire' of God's judgment consumes the lost. . . . God does not raise the wicked in order to torture them consciously forever, but rather to declare his judgment upon the wicked and to condemn them to extinction, which is the second death." "Fire, Then Nothing," *Christianity Today* 44, no. 10 (20 March 1987): 49.

10. Edwards, *Evangelical Essentials*, 317.

11. Scot McKnight devotes extensive treatment to Matthew 25:46 in view of recent efforts (such as John Stott's) to see the eternal consequence of unrighteousness as annihilation. His conclusion is solid: "The terms for eternal in Matthew 25:46 pertain to the final age, and a distinguishing feature of the final age, in contrast to this age, is that it is eternal, endless, and temporally unlimited. It follows then that the most probable meaning of Matthew 25:46 is that just as life with God is temporally unlimited for the righteous, so punishment for sin and rejection of Christ is also temporally unlimited. . . . The final state of the wicked is conscious, eternal torment." "Eternal Consequences or Eternal Consciousness," in *Through No Fault of Their Own*, 157.

to see the fate of the wicked as anything less permanent than that of the believer."[12]

Not only that, but when we compare this text to Revelation 20:10, the case for conscious eternal torment is strengthened. Here in Matthew 25:41, the goats are sentenced to "eternal fire prepared *for the devil and his angels.*" This is precisely what is described in Revelation 20:10, namely, the final destiny of the devil. The condition is clearly one of conscious torment (see below in this text).

"The Son of Man goes as it is written of him, but woe to that man by whom the Son of Man is betrayed! *It would have been better for that man if he had not been born*" (Matt. 26:24). If Judas were destined for glory eventually (as in universalism) or even destined for extinction (as in annihilationism), it is difficult to imagine why it would have been better for him not to have been born.[13] In John 17:12, he is called the "son of destruction"—a term related to the word for "destroy" in Matthew 10:28.

"Whoever blasphemes against the Holy Spirit never has forgiveness, but is guilty of an *eternal sin*" (Mark 3:29). "And whoever speaks a word against the Son of Man will be forgiven, but whoever speaks against the Holy Spirit will not be forgiven, either in this age *or in the age to come*" (Matt. 12:32). This rules out the idea that after a time of suffering in hell, sinners will then be forgiven and admitted to heaven. Matthew says that there will be no forgiveness in the age to come for the unforgivable sin, and so Mark calls it an *eternal* sin, which shows that the word "eternal" is indeed a temporal word of endless duration and not just a word referring to a limited period in the age to come.

"And besides all this, between us and you a great chasm has been fixed, in order that those who would pass from here to you may not be able, and *none may cross from there to us*" (Luke 16:26). These are the words of Abraham in heaven speaking to the rich man in Hades. The point is that the suffering there cannot be escaped. There is no way out.

[God] will render to each one according to his works: to those who by patience in well-doing seek for glory and honor and immortality, he will give

12. Leon Morris, "The Dreadful Harvest," *Christianity Today* 35, no. 6 (27 May 1991): 36.
13. In Edwards, *Evangelical Essentials*, 314, John Stott tries to honor this text by saying, "We surely have to say that this banishment from God will be real, terrible (so that 'it would have been better for him if he had not been born,' Mark 14:21) and eternal." But he gives us no idea why a man who eats, drinks, and is merry for seventy years and then ceases to have any consciousness would have been better off not to have existed.

eternal life; but for those who are self-seeking and do not obey the truth, but obey unrighteousness, there will be wrath and fury.

Romans 2:6–8

This text is significant because wrath and fury are the alternative to "eternal life." This seems to imply that the wrath and fury are experienced instead of life "eternally"—forever.

> They will suffer the punishment of *eternal destruction*, away from the presence of the Lord and from the glory of his might, when he comes on that day to be glorified in his saints, and to be marveled at among all who have believed.

2 Thessalonians 1:9–10

The word for "destruction" (*olethros*) means "ruin" (1 Cor. 5:5; 1 Tim. 6:9). The picture is not of obliteration but of a ruin of human life out of God's presence forever.

> Let us leave the elementary doctrine of Christ and go on to maturity, not laying again a foundation of repentance from dead works and of faith toward God, and of instruction about washings, the laying on of hands, the resurrection of the dead, and *eternal judgment*.

Hebrews 6:1–2

> These are blemishes on your love feasts . . . wild waves of the sea, casting up the foam of their own shame; wandering stars, for whom the gloom of utter darkness has been reserved *forever*.

Jude 12–13

> And the smoke of their torment goes up *forever and ever*, and *they have no rest*, day or night, these worshipers of the beast and its image, and whoever receives the mark of its name.

Revelation 14:11

There is no stronger Greek expression for eternity than this one: "unto ages of ages" (*eis aiōnas aiōnōn*). "Once more they cried out, 'Hallelujah! The smoke from her goes up *forever and ever*'" (Rev. 19:3). "And the devil who had deceived them was thrown into the lake of fire and sulfur where the beast and the false prophet were, and they will be tormented *day and night forever and ever*" (Rev. 20:10). Again the strongest of expressions are used for everlasting duration: "unto the ages of the ages" (*eis tous aiōnas tōn aiōnōn*). John Stott again struggles to escape the clear intent of the eternal torments of the lake of fire. He says that Revelation 20:10 refers to the beast and false prophet who "are not individual people but symbols of the world in its varied hostility to God. In the nature of the case they cannot experience pain."[14]

But Stott fails to mention Revelation 20:15, where it says that "if anyone's name [not just that of the beast and the false prophet] was not found written in the book of life, he was thrown into the lake of fire." Similarly, Revelation 21:8 says that it is *individual sinners* whose "portion will be in the lake that burns with fire and sulfur, which is the second death." And the torment that lasts "forever and ever" in Revelation 14:11 is precisely the torment of people "with fire and sulfur"—that is, the torment of "the lake that burns with fire and sulfur" (21:8). In other words, the "lake of fire" is in view not only, as Stott suggests, when the beast, the false prophet, death, and Hades (20:13) are cast out but also when individual unbelievers are finally condemned (14:10–11; 20:15; 21:8), and that shows decisively that individual unbelieving persons will experience eternal conscious torment.[15]

Hell is a dreadful reality. To speak of it lightly proves that we do not grasp its horror. I know of no one who has overstated the terrors of hell. We can scarcely surpass the horrid images Jesus used. We are meant to shudder.

14. Ibid., 318.

15. John Stott has been gracious enough to correspond with me personally about this issue of the eternal fate of the lost. To be fair to one I count a brother and a theological and pastoral mentor for more than thirty years, I want to give his perspective on what I have written from a personal letter dated 1 March 1993. He writes: "I cannot honestly say that I think you have done justice to what I have written in *Evangelical Essentials*. . . . For example, I do strongly affirm all the 'eternal' and 'unquenchable' verses which you quote, and do believe in 'eternal punishment.' It is not the eternity but the nature of the punishment which is under discussion. You do not make this clear. I also believe in torment in the interim state (as the Dives and Lazarus story shows), and that there will be terrible 'weeping and gnashing of teeth' when the lost learn their fate. I think I believe as strongly as you do that 'it is a fearful thing to fall into the hands of the living God.' What troubles me is the way you tend to quote proof texts as knock-down arguments, when they are capable of alternative interpretations. I just find you over-dogmatic, as I wrote in my earlier letter, leaving no room for the humble agnosticism which allows that God has not revealed everything as plainly as you make out." I mentioned to Dr. Stott in an earlier letter that my less-than-positive attitude toward "agnosticism" and "tentativity" is probably influenced by the sea of relativism that I am trying to navigate, both inside and outside the church. I do not want to communicate an unwillingness to learn or to change as new light on the Scripture emerges. But my diagnosis of the sickness of our times inclines me less toward "humble agnosticism" and more toward (I hope) humble affirmation. Whether I have moved from warranted and well-grounded firmness of conviction into unwarranted and poorly argued dogmatism, I leave for others to judge.

Why? Because the infinite horrors of hell are intended by God to be a vivid demonstration of the infinite value of his glory, which sinners have belittled. The biblical assumption of the justice of hell[16] is the clearest testimony to the infiniteness of the sin of failing to glorify God. All of us have failed. All the nations have failed. Therefore, the weight of infinite guilt rests on every human head because of our failure to delight in God more than we delight in our own self-sufficiency.

The vision of God in Scripture is of a majestic and sovereign God who does all things to magnify the greatness of his glory for the everlasting

---

16. One person who has wrestled with the justice of hell and moved toward a very unusual position on annihilationism and the traditional view of conscious eternal misery is Greg Boyd, who represents the view called Open Theism. In his *Satan and the Problem of Evil* (Downers Grove, Ill.: InterVarsity, 2001), Boyd attempts to handle the texts used to argue for the eternal conscious torment of hell and the texts used to argue for annihilationism by "affirming both views as essentially correct" (336). On the one hand, he says, "When all the Biblical evidence is viewed together, it must be admitted that the case for annihilationism is quite compelling" (336). But on the other hand, he sees some texts on the other side that do not fit the simple annihilationist view (he mentions Rev. 14:10; 20:10; Matt. 25:34, 41; 2 Thess. 1:6–9 [336]). He asks, "Where does this leave us? For my part, it leaves me in a conundrum. I do not believe that either the traditional position or the annihilationists' position adequately accounts for all the Biblical evidence cited in support of the opposing side's position. Yet I do not believe that Scripture can contradict itself (John 10:35). This raises the question: Is there a logically consistent way of affirming both views as essentially correct?" (336–37). His answer is yes: "I will attempt to move beyond the impasse of the traditional and annihilationist understandings of eternal punishment and construct a model of hell that allows us to affirm the essence of both perspectives" (339). He attempts to show that "hell is the eternal suffering of agents who have been annihilated" (356). He states a crucial premise: "There can be no shared reality between those who say yes to God and those who say no, just as there can be no shared reality between the actuality that God affirms and the possibilities that God negates" (347). Here is the conclusion that follows: "Love is about relationships, and relationships are about sharing reality. Hence, when in the eschaton reality is exhaustively defined by God's love, the 'reality' of any agent who opposes love cannot be shared by anyone else and thus cannot be real to anyone else. It is experienced as real from the inside of the one who sustains it by his or her active willing it. But to all who participate in reality—that is, who are open to God and to each other through the medium of God's love—it is nothing. It is eternally willed nothingness" (350). "Hell is real only from the inside" (348). Thus, "we are able to affirm that in one sense the inhabitants of hell are annihilated, though they suffer eternally. From the perspective of all who share reality in the eschaton, the damned are no more (Obad. 16). They exist only as utter negation. . . . They continue to experience torment, but it is a torment of their own pathetic choosing in an illusory reality of their own damned imagining" (350). "As Scripture says, they are extinct, reduced to ashes, forever forgotten. . . . But we may also accept the scriptural teaching regarding the eternity of the torment of the reprobates. . . . From the inside of the rebel experience, the nothingness that they have willed is experienced as a something. To all others, it is nothing" (353). I am not persuaded that Boyd's complex and paradoxical "model" can survive close scrutiny. An extended critique of this view exceeds the bounds of this book, but I have written a partial response titled "Greg Boyd on 'The Eternal Suffering of Agents Who Have Been Annihilated,' " available from Desiring God Ministries at www.DesiringGod .org or 1-888-346-4700.

enjoyment of his people. And the view of man in Scripture is that man suppresses this truth and finds more joy in his own glory than he does in God's.

When Clark Pinnock[17] and John Stott[18] repeat the centuries-old objection that an *eternal* punishment is disproportionate to a *finite* life of sinning, they disregard the essential thing that Jonathan Edwards saw so clearly: Degrees of blameworthiness come not from how long you offend dignity but from how high the dignity is that you offend.

> The crime of one being despising and casting contempt on another, is proportionably more or less heinous, as he was under greater or less obligations to obey him. And therefore if there be any being that we are under infinite obligation to love, and honor, and obey, the contrary towards him must be infinitely faulty.
>
> Our obligation to love, honor and obey any being is in proportion to his loveliness, honorableness, and authority. . . . But God is a being infinitely lovely, because he hath infinite excellency and beauty. . . .
>
> So sin against God, being a violation of infinite obligations, must be a crime infinitely heinous, and so deserving infinite punishment. . . . The eternity of the punishment of ungodly men renders it infinite . . . and therefore renders no more than proportionable to the heinousness of what they are guilty of.[19]

One key difference between Edwards and our contemporary spokesmen who abandon the historic biblical view of hell is that Edwards was radically committed to deriving his views of God's justice and love *from God*. But more and more it seems that contemporary evangelicals are submitting to what "makes sense" to their own moral sentiments.[20] This

17. "It just does not make sense to say that a God of love will torture people forever for sins done in the context of a finite life." Pinnock and Brown, *Theological Crossfire*, 226.

18. "Would there not be serious disproportion between sins consciously committed in time and torment consciously experienced throughout eternity?" Edwards, *Evangelical Essentials*, 318.

19. Jonathan Edwards, "The Justice of God in the Damnation of Sinners," in *The Works of Jonathan Edwards*, vol. 1 (Edinburgh: Banner of Truth Trust, 1974), 669. For expositions of Edwards's view on hell, see John Gerstner, *Jonathan Edwards on Heaven and Hell* (Morgan, Pa.: Soli Deo Gloria Publishers, 1999); and Chris Morgan, *Hell and Jonathan Edwards: Toward a God-Centered Theology of Hell* (Ross-shire, Scotland: Christian Focus Publications, 2003).

20. See Pinnock's quote and Stott's quote in note 3 above. Also see my critique of the way Pinnock follows the same procedure concerning the omniscience of God in my book *Pleasures of God*, 57–59n6. Another thing overlooked is that in hell the sins of the unrepentant go on forever and ever. They do not become righteous in hell. They are given over to the corruption of their nature so that they continue rebelling and deserving eternal punishment eternally. This latter insight was suggested to me by my colleague Tom Steller.

will not strengthen the church or its mission. What is needed is a radical commitment to the supremacy of God in determining what is real and what is not.

The Necessity of Christ's Atonement for Salvation

The second question we must ask as part of our inquiry is whether Christ's work of atonement is necessary for the salvation of whoever is saved. Can people be saved any way other than by the efficacy of Christ's work? Are other religions and the provisions they offer sufficient for bringing people to eternal happiness with God?

The following biblical texts lead us to believe that Christ's atonement is necessary for the salvation of everyone who is saved. There is no salvation apart from the salvation that Christ achieved in his death and resurrection.

> If, because of one man's trespass, death reigned through that one man, much more will those who receive the abundance of grace and the free gift of righteousness reign in life through the one man Jesus Christ. Therefore, as one trespass led to condemnation for all men, so one act of righteousness leads to justification and life for all men. For as by the one man's disobedience the many were made sinners, so by the one man's obedience the many will be made righteous.
>
> Romans 5:17–19

The crucial point here is *the universality of the work of Christ*. It is not done in a corner with reference merely to Jews. The work of Christ, the second Adam, corresponds to the work of the first Adam. As the sin of Adam leads to condemnation for all humanity that are united to him as their head, so the obedience of Christ leads to righteousness for all humanity that are united to Christ as their head—"those who receive the abundance of grace" (v. 17). The work of Christ in the obedience of the cross is pictured as the divine answer to the plight of the entire human race.

> For as by a man came death, by a man has come also the resurrection of the dead. For as in Adam all die, so also in Christ shall all be made alive. But each in his own order: Christ the firstfruits, then at his coming those who belong to Christ.
>
> 1 Corinthians 15:21–23

In this text, Christ's resurrection is the answer to the universal human misery of death. Adam is the head of the old humanity marked by death. Christ is the head of the new humanity marked by resurrection. The members of this new humanity are "those who belong to Christ" (v. 23).[21] Christ is not a tribal deity relating merely to the woes of one group. He is given as God's answer to the universal problem of death. Those who attain to the resurrection of the dead attain it in Christ.

"There is one God, and there is one mediator between God and men, the man Christ Jesus, who gave himself as a ransom for all" (1 Tim. 2:5–6). The work of Christ corresponds to his role as sole Mediator in the universe between God and man.

> Worthy are you to take the scroll and to open its seals, for you were slain, and by your blood you ransomed people for God from every tribe and language and people and nation, and you have made them a kingdom and priests to our God, and they shall reign on the earth.
>
> Revelation 5:9–10

The entire Book of Revelation pictures Christ as the King of kings and Lord of lords (17:14; 19:16)—the universal ruler over all peoples and powers.

21. Note that it would be an incorrect, superficial reading of this text, as well as of Romans 5:17–19, to assume that it is teaching universalism in the sense that all human beings will be saved. The "all" who are acquitted in Romans 5 are defined in Romans 5:17 as "those who receive the abundance of grace." And the all who are made alive in 1 Corinthians 15:22 are defined as "those who belong to Christ." The term "justification and life for all men" in Romans 5:18 does not mean that every human being who is in Adam will also be justified so that no one will perish and that there is no such thing as eternal punishment for anyone. I say this for several reasons: (1) Verse 17 speaks of *receiving* the gift of righteousness as though some do and some don't. Verse 17: "For if by the transgression of the one, death reigned through the one, much more *those who receive the abundance of grace and of the gift of righteousness* will reign in life through the One, Jesus Christ." That does not sound as though everybody does receive it. (2) "Justification of life to all men" in Romans 5:18 does not mean that all humans are justified because Paul teaches in this very book that there is eternal punishment and that all humans are not justified. For example, in Romans 2:5 he says, "But because of your stubbornness and unrepentant heart you are storing up wrath for yourself in the day of wrath and revelation of the righteous judgment of God," and then in verses 7 and 8 he contrasts this wrath with "eternal life" and so shows that it is eternal wrath, not temporary wrath. So there will be some who are not justified but come under the wrath of God forever and others who have eternal life. (3) "Justification of life to all men" in Romans 5:18 does not mean that all humans are justified because in all of Romans up to this point, justification is not automatic, as if every human receives it, but it is "by faith." Romans 5:1: "Therefore, having been *justified by faith* . . ." Romans 3:28: "For we maintain that a man is *justified* by faith apart from works of the Law." Further, a universalistic reading of Paul's "all" statements renders Paul's intense grief (Rom. 9:3)—to the point of wishing he could perish, if possible, on their behalf—unintelligible.

Revelation 5:9 shows that he purchased a people for himself from all the tribes and languages of the world. His atonement is the means in every culture by which men and women become part of his kingdom. (See John 11:51–52.)

"And there is salvation in no one else, for there is no other name under heaven given among men by which we must be saved" (Acts 4:12). The work of Christ is not mentioned here explicitly, but the universality of his name as the only way to salvation would imply that whatever he did to win salvation for his people (namely, shed his blood [Acts 20:28]) has universal significance. There are no other ways that a person in another religion can be saved. If anyone would be saved, he must be saved by the name of Christ. "All have sinned and fall short of the glory of God, and are justified by his grace as a gift, through the redemption that is in Christ Jesus, whom God put forward as a propitiation by his blood, to be received by faith" (Rom. 3:23–25).

Romans 3:9–20 establishes that all humans—Jew and Gentile—are under the power of sin and are speechless before the judgment of God. Therefore, the death of Christ is set forth as an answer to this universal problem of sin. It is not one among many ways God deals with sin. It is the basis of the way God justifies any sinner.

In answer to the second question, then, the New Testament makes clear that the atoning work of Christ is not merely for Jews or merely for any one nation or tribe or language. It is the one and only way for anyone to get right with God. The problem of sin is universal, cutting people off from God. The solution to that problem is the atoning death of the Son of God offered once for all. This is the very foundation of missions. Since the work of Christ is the only basis for salvation,[22] it must be announced to all the nations, as Luke 24:46–47 says:

> Thus it is written, that the Christ should suffer and on the third day rise from the dead, and that repentance and forgiveness of sins should be proclaimed in his name to all nations, beginning from Jerusalem.

The Necessity for People to Hear of Christ in Order to Be Saved

The question that concerns us here is whether some (perhaps only a few) people are quickened by the Holy Spirit and saved by grace through faith

22. For further study of the significance of Christ's death, consider the following texts: Matt. 26:28; Mark 10:45; John 1:29; 6:51; Rom. 4:25–5:1; 5:6, 8–10; 1 Cor. 15:3; 2 Cor. 5:18–21; Gal. 1:4; 4:4; Eph. 1:7; 2:1–5, 13, 16, 18; 5:2, 25; Col. 1:20; 1 Thess. 5:9; Titus 2:14; 1 Tim. 4:10; Heb. 1:3; 9:12, 22, 26; 10:14; 12:24; 13:12; 1 Peter 1:19; 2:24; 3:18; 1 John 2:2; Rev. 1:5.

in a merciful Creator even though they never hear of Jesus in this life. In other words, are there devout people in other religions who humbly rely on the grace of the God whom they know through nature (Rom. 1:19–21) and thus receive eternal salvation?[23]

Something of immense historical significance happened with the coming of the Son of God into the world. So great was the significance of this event that the focus of saving faith was henceforth made to center on Jesus Christ alone. So fully does Christ sum up all the revelation of God and all the hopes of God's people that it would henceforth be a dishonor to him should saving faith repose on anyone but him.[24]

23. See notes 6 and 7 above for representatives of this view. Clark Pinnock embraces the idea that people from other religions will be saved without knowing Christ. "We do not need to think of the church as the ark of salvation, leaving everyone else in hell; we can rather think of it as the chosen witness to the *fullness* of salvation that has come into the world through Jesus" (emphasis added). Clark Pinnock, "Acts 4:12—No Other Name Under Heaven," in *Through No Fault of Their Own*, 113. Also see Clark H. Pinnock, *A Wideness in God's Mercy: The Finality of Jesus Christ in a World of Religions* (Grand Rapids: Zondervan, 1992); and Clark Pinnock, "An Inclusivist View," in *More Than One Way? Four Views on Salvation in a Pluralistic World*, ed. Dennis L. Okholm and Timothy R. Phillips (Grand Rapids: Zondervan, 1995), 95–123. He is following others with similar views: Charles Kraft, *Christianity in Culture* (Maryknoll, N.Y.: Orbis, 1979), 253–57; James N. D. Anderson, *Christianity and World Religions* (Downers Grove, Ill.: InterVarsity, 1984), chap. 5; John E. Sanders, "Is Belief in Christ Necessary for Salvation?" *Evangelical Quarterly* 60 (1988): 241–59; and John Sanders, *No Other Name: An Investigation into the Destiny of the Unevangelized* (Grand Rapids: Eerdmans, 1992). For a short survey of representatives on both sides of the question, see Malcolm J. McVeigh, "The Fate of Those Who've Never Heard? It Depends," *Evangelical Missions Quarterly* 21, no. 4 (October 1985): 370–79. For books with multiple views represented, see Gabriel Fackre, Ronald H. Nash, and John Sanders, *What about Those Who Have Never Heard? Three Views on the Destiny of the Unevangelized* (Grand Rapids: Zondervan, 1995); and Ockholm and Phillips, *More Than One Way?* For critiques of inclusivism, see Carson, *The Gagging of God*, 279–314; Dick Dowsett, *God, That's Not Fair!* (Sevenoaks, Kent: OMF Books, 1982); Ronald H. Nash, *Is Jesus the Only Savior?* (Grand Rapids: Zondervan, 1994); Ramesh Richard, *The Population of Heaven* (Chicago: Moody, 1994); Paul R. House and Gregory A. Thornbury, eds., *Who Will Be Saved? Defending the Biblical Understanding of God, Salvation, and Evangelism* (Wheaton: Crossway, 2000), 111–60; and the contributions of R. Douglas Geivett and W. Gary Phillips in *More Than One Way?*

24. There is a continuity between God's path to salvation in the Old Testament times and the path through faith in Jesus during the New Testament times. Even before Christ, people were not saved apart from special revelation given by God. See Fernando, *Sharing the Truth in Love*, 224–33. It is not as though general revelation through nature was effective in producing faith before Christ but ceased to be effective after Christ. According to Romans 1:18–23, general revelation through nature has always been sufficient to make people accountable to glorify and thank God, but not efficient to do so. The reason given is that people in their natural condition suppress the truth. See note 40. Thus, special revelation has always been the path to salvation, and this special revelation was centered in Israel, the promise of a Redeemer, and the foreshadowings of this salvation in the sacrificial system of the Old Testament. Jesus is now the climax and fulfillment of that special revelation so that saving faith, which was always focused on special revelation, is now focused on him.

Before his coming a grand "mystery" was kept secret for ages. With the uncovering of this mystery, the "times of ignorance" ended, and the call to repentance now sounds forth with a new specificity: Jesus Christ has been appointed Judge of all peoples by virtue of his resurrection from the dead. All appeals for mercy and acquittal must now come through him and him alone. We turn now to the texts that lay this truth open for us.

The "Mystery of Christ"

When you read this, you can perceive my insight into the *mystery of Christ*, which was not made known to the sons of men in other generations as it has now been revealed to his holy apostles and prophets by the Spirit. This mystery is that the Gentiles are fellow heirs, members of the same body, and partakers of the promise in Christ Jesus *through the gospel*.

Of this gospel I was made a minister according to the gift of God's grace, which was given me by the working of his power. To me, though I am the very least of all the saints, this grace was given, to preach to the Gentiles the unsearchable riches of Christ, and to bring to light for everyone what is the plan of the mystery hidden for ages in God who created all things, so that through the church the manifold wisdom of God might now be made known to the rulers and authorities in the heavenly places.

Ephesians 3:4–10

There was a truth that was not fully and clearly revealed before the coming of Christ. This truth, now revealed, is called the "mystery of Christ." It is the truth that *people from all the nations of the world would be full and complete partners with the chosen people of God* (Eph. 3:6). It is called the "mystery of Christ" because it is coming true "through the gospel" (3:6), which is about Christ.

Therefore, the gospel is not the revelation that the nations already belong to God. The gospel is the instrument for bringing the nations into this equal status of salvation. The mystery of Christ (drawing the nations into the inheritance of Abraham) is happening through the preaching of the gospel. Paul sees his own apostolic vocation as the means God is graciously using to declare the riches of the Messiah to the nations (3:8).

So a massive change has occurred in redemptive history. Before the coming of Christ, a truth was not fully revealed—namely, that the nations may enter with equal standing into the household of God (Eph. 2:19). The time was not "full" for this revelation because Christ had not been revealed from heaven. The glory and honor of uniting all the peoples was being reserved for him in his saving work. It is fitting then that the nations be gathered in only through the preaching of the message of Christ, whose cross is the peace that creates the worldwide church (Eph. 2:11–21).

In other words, there is a profound theological reason why salvation did not spread to the nations before the incarnation of the Son of God. The reason is that it would not have been clear that the nations were gathering for the glory of Christ. God means for his Son to be the center of worship as the nations receive the word of reconciliation. For this reason also, as we will see, the preaching of Christ is the means appointed by God for the ingathering of the nations.

(25a) Now to him who is able to strengthen you (25b) according to my gospel and the preaching of Jesus Christ, (25c) according to the revelation of the mystery that was kept secret for long ages (26a) but has now been disclosed (26b) and through the prophetic writings has been made known to all nations, (26c) according to the command of the eternal God, (26d) to bring about the obedience of faith—(27) to the only wise God be glory forevermore through Jesus Christ! Amen.

Romans 16:25–27

This is a very complex sentence. But if we patiently examine its parts and notice how they relate to one another, the crucial meaning for missions emerges.

The verses are a doxology: "Now to him who is able to strengthen you . . ." But Paul gets so caught up in God that he does not come down again to the words of the doxology until verse 27: "to the only wise God be glory forevermore through Jesus Christ! Amen."

Sandwiched between the two parts of the doxology is a massive statement about the meaning of Paul's gospel in relation to God's eternal purposes. The thought moves as follows. The strength that Paul prays will come to the Romans (25a) accords with his gospel and the preaching of Christ (25b). This means that God's power is revealed in the gospel Paul preaches, and that is the power he prays for them to be strengthened by.

Then he says that this gospel preaching is in accord with the revelation of a mystery kept secret for ages and now revealed (25c, 26a). In other words, what Paul preaches is not out of sync with God's purposes. It "accords" with them. It expresses and conforms to them. His preaching is a part of God's plan, which is now being revealed in history.

How is it being revealed? It is being disclosed through the prophetic writings (26c). This means that the mystery was not *totally* hidden in past ages. There were pointers in the prophetic writings, so much so that now these very Old Testament writings are used to make the mystery known. In Paul's preaching of the gospel, he uses the prophetic writings to help him make known the mystery. (See, for example, how Paul does this in Romans 15:9–13.)

What then is the mystery? Verses 26c–26d say that making known this mystery accords with "the command of the eternal God for the obedience of faith to all the nations" (author's translation). The most natural way to interpret this is to say that the mystery is the purpose of God to command all nations to obey him through faith.

But what makes this a mystery is that the command to the nations for the obedience of faith is specifically a command to have faith in Jesus, the Messiah of Israel, and thus become part of the people of God and heirs of Abraham (Eph. 2:19–3:6). In Romans 1:5, Paul describes his calling to the nations with these words: "We have received grace and apostleship to bring about the obedience of faith for the sake of [Christ's] name among all the nations." Here he makes plain that the aim "to bring about the "obedience of faith" in Romans 16:26d is a call for the sake of Christ's name. It is thus a call to acknowledge and trust and obey Christ. This is the mystery hidden for ages—that all the nations would be commanded to trust in Israel's Messiah and be saved through him.

The word "now" in 26a is crucial. It refers to the fullness of time in redemptive history when God put Christ forward onto the center stage of history. From "now" on things are different. The time has come for the mystery to be revealed. The time has come to command all the nations to obey God through faith in Jesus the Messiah.

God is "now" doing a new thing. With the coming of Christ, God will no longer allow "the nations to walk in their own ways" (Acts 14:16, see below). The time has come for all nations to be called to repent and for the mystery to be fully revealed that through faith in Christ the nations are "fellow heirs, members of the same body, and partakers of the promise in Christ Jesus *through the gospel*" (Eph. 3:6). Not without the gospel! But *through* the gospel. This will become increasingly obvious and crucial as we move on.

"The Times of Ignorance"

The times of ignorance God overlooked, but now he commands all people everywhere to repent, because he has fixed a day on which he will judge the world in righteousness by a man whom he has appointed; and of this he has given assurance to all by raising him from the dead.

Acts 17:30–31

This text comes from Paul's sermon to the Greeks on the Areopagus in Athens. He had noticed an "altar . . . to the unknown god." In other words, just in case there was another god in the universe whom they did not know about, they had put up an altar, hoping that this "unknowing" act of homage would be acceptable to this deity. So Paul said, "What therefore you worship as unknown, this I proclaim to you" (17:23).

It would be going too far to say that Paul means that true esteeming of the true God was going on in the building of this altar. One cannot truly esteem what one knows nothing about. The worshiping of the "unknown god" was simply a polytheistic admission that there might be another deity, unknown to them, whose favor, if he exists, they would like to have. This "ignorant" worship is one thing that makes the past generations "times of ignorance" (v. 30). And we will see that even when there is some knowledge of the true God (as in the case of Cornelius), the worship of the true God "ignorantly" is *not* a saving act.

The "times of ignorance" in Paul's sermon correspond to the ages in which the "mystery of Christ" was kept secret (Rom. 16:25; Eph. 3:4–5; Col. 1:26). These were the times in which, according to Acts 14:16, God "allowed all the nations to walk in their own ways," or as Acts 17:30 says, the times that God "overlooked."

The fact that God *overlooked* the times of ignorance does not mean that he ignored sins so as not to punish sinners. This would contradict Romans 1:18 ("The wrath of God is revealed from heaven against all ungodliness and unrighteousness of men") and Romans 2:12 ("All who have sinned without the law will also perish without the law"). Rather, God's overlooking the "times of ignorance" refers to his giving men over to their own ways. His "overlooking" was his sovereign decision to postpone an all-out pursuit of their repentance through the mission of his people. "The reason why men have wandered from the truth for so long is that God did not stretch forth his hand from heaven to lead them back to the way. . . . Ignorance was in the world, as long as it pleased God to take no notice of it."[25]

This does not mean that in the Old Testament there were no commands and instructions for Israel to bear witness to the nations of the grace of

25. John Calvin, *The Acts of the Apostles, 14–28*, trans. John W. Fraser (Grand Rapids: Eerdmans, 1973), 123.

God and invite their participation in that grace in ways appropriate to that time in redemptive history (e.g., Gen. 12:2–3; Psalm 67). It means rather that for generations God did not intervene to purify, empower, and commission his people with the incarnation, crucifixion, Great Commission, and outpouring of Pentecostal power to fulfill it. Instead, for his own wise purposes, he "allowed all the nations to walk in their own ways"—and allowed his own nation to experience extended failures of reverence and holiness and love so that other nations would come to see the full need of a Redeemer from the corruption of sin and the curse of the law and the limitations of the old covenant for world evangelization.

God's ways are not our ways. Even today we live in a similar time of "hardening"—only now the tables are turned, and it is Israel that is being passed over for a season.

> Lest you [Gentiles] be wise in your own conceits, I want you to understand this mystery, brothers: a partial hardening has come upon Israel, until the fullness of the Gentiles has come in. And in this way all Israel will be saved.
>
> Romans 11:25–26

There was a time when the Gentiles were passed over while God dealt with Israel, and now there is a time while Israel is largely passed over as God gathers the full number of his elect from the nations. This does not mean that we should neglect our mission toward Jew or Gentile "that [we] might save some" (Rom. 11:14; 1 Cor. 9:22). But God has his sovereign purposes in determining who actually hears and believes the gospel. And we may be sure that those purposes are wise and holy and will bring the greatest glory to his name.

We are given a glimpse in 1 Corinthians 1:21 of this divine wisdom: "Since, *in the wisdom of God, the world did not know God through wisdom*, it pleased God through the folly of what we preach to save those who believe." This says that it was God's wisdom that determined that men would not know him through their wisdom. In other words, this is an instance and illustration of how God overlooked (i.e., glanced over) the times of ignorance and allowed humans to go their own ways.

Why? To make crystal clear that humans on their own, by their own wisdom (religion!), will never truly know God. An extraordinary work of God would be required to bring people to a true and saving knowledge of God, namely, the preaching of Christ crucified: "It pleased God through the folly of what we preach to save those who believe." This is what Paul meant in Ephesians 3:6, when he said that the mystery of Christ is that the nations are becoming partakers of the promise *"through the gospel."* Thus, 1 Corinthians 1:21 and Ephesians 3:6 are parallel ideas and utterly crucial for seeing that in this "now" of redemptive history, knowing the gospel is the only way to become an heir of the promise.

All boasting is excluded by God's showing that man's own wisdom in all the nations—his own self-wrought religions—do not bring him to God. Rather, God saves now by means of preaching that is "a stumbling block to Jews and folly to Gentiles, but to those who are called, both Jews and Greeks, Christ the power of God and the wisdom of God" (1 Cor. 1:23–24). In this way, all boasting is excluded, for left to himself man does not come to God.

In his inspiring book, *A Vision for Missions*, Tom Wells tells the story of how William Carey illustrates this conviction in his own preaching. Carey was an English Baptist missionary who left for India in 1793. He never came home but persevered for forty years in the gospel ministry.

Once he was talking with a Brahman in 1797. The Brahman was defending idol worship, and Carey cited Acts 14:16 and 17:30. God formerly "suffered all nations to walk in their own ways," said Carey, "but now commandeth all men everywhere to repent."

"Indeed," said the native, "I think God ought to repent for not sending the Gospel sooner to us."

Carey was not without an answer. He said:

> Suppose a kingdom had been long overrun by the enemies of its true king, and he though possessed of sufficient power to conquer them, should yet suffer them to prevail, and establish themselves as much as they could desire, would not the valour and wisdom of that king be far more conspicuous in exterminating them, than it would have been if he had opposed them at first, and prevented their entering the country? Thus by the diffusion of Gospel light, the wisdom, power, and grace of God will be more conspicuous in overcoming such deep-rooted idolatries, and in destroying all that darkness and vice which have so universally prevailed in this country, than they would have been if all had not been suffered to walk in their own ways for so many ages past.[26]

Carey's answer to why God allowed nations to walk in their own ways is that in doing so the final victory of God will be all the more glorious. There is a divine wisdom in the timing of God's deliverances from darkness. We should humble ourselves to see it rather than presume to know better how God should deal with a rebellious world.

26. Tom Wells, *A Vision for Missions* (Edinburgh: Banner of Truth Trust, 1985), 12–13.

In Acts 17:30, how does Paul assess the ignorant worship of the un-known god (17:23)? He says that the time has come for repentance in view of the impending judgment of the world by Jesus Christ ("He has fixed a day on which he will judge the world in righteousness by a man whom he has appointed" [Acts 17:31]). In other words, Paul does not reveal to the worshipers in Athens that they are already prepared to meet their Judge because they render a kind of worship to the true God through their altar to the unknown god (17:23). They are not ready. They must repent.

As Jesus said in Luke 24:47, from the time of the resurrection onward, "repentance and forgiveness of sins should be proclaimed *in his name* to all nations." What is to be preached is that through confessing the name of Jesus sins can be forgiven. This was not known before, because Jesus was not here before. But now the times of ignorance are over. Jesus has brought the purposes of God to fulfillment. "All the promises of God find their Yes in [Christ]" (2 Cor. 1:20). At his throne every knee will bow (Phil. 2:10). Therefore, henceforth he is the focus of saving faith. He is now openly installed and declared as Judge, and he alone can receive the appeals for acquittal.

What then are we saying so far? We are saying that the coming of Jesus Christ into the world is an event of such stupendous proportions that a change has occurred in the necessary focus of saving faith. Before Jesus' coming, saving faith reposed in the forgiving and helping mercy of God displayed in events such as the exodus and in the sacrificial offerings and in prophetic promises such as Isaiah 53. Jesus was not known. The mystery that the nations would be fully included through the preaching of *his name* was kept secret for ages. Those were times of ignorance. God let the nations go their own way.

But "now"—a key word in the turning of God's historic work of re-demption—something new has happened. The Son of God has appeared. He has revealed the Father. He has atoned for sin. He has risen from the dead. His authority as universal Judge has been vindicated. And the message of his saving work is to be spread to all peoples. This turn in redemptive history is for the glory of Jesus Christ. Its aim is to put him at the center of all God's saving work. Therefore, it accords with this purpose that henceforth Christ be the sole and necessary focus of saving faith. Apart from a knowledge of him, none who has the physical ability to know him will be saved.[27]

27. I state it like this so as to leave open salvation for infants and the mentally handicapped who do not have the physical ability even to apprehend that there is any revelation available at

This tremendously important turn in redemptive history from the times of ignorance and the hiddenness of the mystery of Christ is not taken seriously enough by those who say people can be saved *today* who do not know Christ because people were saved *in the Old Testament* who did not know Christ. For example, Millard Erickson argues this way but does not reckon seriously enough with the tremendous significance that the New Testament sees in the historical turning point of the incarnation, which ended the times of ignorance and manifested the mystery of Christ.

> If Jews possessed salvation in the Old Testament era simply by virtue of having the form of the Christian gospel without its content, can this principle be extended? Could it be that those who ever since the time of Christ have had no opportunity to hear the gospel, as it has come through the special revelation, participate in this salvation on the same basis?[28]

This would perhaps be a valid argument if the New Testament did not teach that the coming of Christ was a decisive turn in redemptive history that henceforth makes him the focus of all saving faith.

But is this conclusion supported by other New Testament teaching? What about the case of Cornelius? Was he not a Gentile, living after the resurrection of Christ and saved through his genuine piety without focusing his faith on Christ?

The Case of Cornelius, Acts 10:1–11:18

The story of Cornelius the Gentile centurion could lead some to believe that a man can be saved today apart from knowing the gospel and just by fearing God and doing the good that he can.

Cornelius is described as a "devout man who feared God with all his household, gave alms generously to the people, and prayed continually to

---

all. The principle of accountability in Romans 1:20 (God makes knowledge available "in order that they might be without excuse") is the basis for this conviction. The Bible does not deal with this special case in any detail, and we are left to speculate that the fitness of the connection between faith in Christ and salvation will be preserved through the coming to faith of children whenever God brings them to maturity in heaven or in the age to come. For a defense of this view, see Ronald H. Nash, *When a Baby Dies: Answers to Comfort Grieving Parents* (Grand Rapids: Zondervan, 1999); and Albert Mohler, "The Salvation of the 'Little Ones': Do Infants Who Die Go to Heaven?" *Fidelitas: Commentary on Theology and Culture* (http://www.sbts.edu/mohler/fidelitas/littleones.html). Mohler points out that John Newton, Charles Spurgeon, Charles Hodge, and B. B. Warfield all held such a position. All these were strong believers in original sin, as I am, but also believed that God would provide a just way for the salvation of infants without compromising that doctrine or the doctrine of unconditional election.

28. Erickson, "Hope for Those Who Haven't Heard?" 124–25.

God" (10:2). On one occasion an angel says to him, "Cornelius, your prayer has been heard and your alms have been remembered before God. Send therefore to Joppa and ask for Simon who is called Peter" (10:31–32).

Meanwhile, the apostle Peter has had a vision from the Lord designed to teach him that the ceremonial uncleanness of the Gentiles is not a hindrance to their acceptance by God. A voice said to Peter, "What God has made clean, do not call common" (10:15).

When Peter meets Cornelius, he says, "Truly I understand that God shows no partiality, but in every nation anyone who fears him and does what is right is acceptable to him" (10:34–35). This is the sentence that might lead some to think that Cornelius was already saved from his sin even before he heard and believed the gospel. But in fact Luke's point in telling the story seems to be just the opposite.

It will be helpful to ask two questions that are really pressing in this story. One is this: Was Cornelius already saved before Peter preached Christ to him? The reason this is pressing is that verses 34–35 have led many to say that he was. These verses are the beginning of Peter's sermon: "Truly I understand that God shows no partiality, but in every nation anyone who fears him and does what is right is acceptable to him."

You can see how readers would easily conclude that Cornelius was already accepted by God since verse 2 said that he indeed feared God and prayed and gave alms. Did Peter then just inform Cornelius about the acceptance and salvation that he already had? And can we draw the conclusion for missions that there are unreached people who already have a saving relationship with God before they hear the gospel of Christ?

So the first question is, Does verse 35 mean that Cornelius and people like him are already justified and reconciled to God and saved from wrath? Is that Peter's point in saying this and Luke's point in writing it?

Was Cornelius Already Saved?

Let me give you four reasons from the text for answering no.

1. Acts 11:14 says that the message Peter brought was the means by which Cornelius was saved. In Acts 11:13–14, Peter tells the story of the angel's appearance to Cornelius: "He told us how he had seen the angel stand in his house and say, 'Send to Joppa and bring Simon who is called Peter; he will declare to you *a message by which you will be saved*, you and all your household.'"

Notice two things. First, notice that the message itself is essential. The gospel is the power of God unto salvation. Then notice that the tense of the verb is future: "a message by which you *will* be saved." In other words, the message was not simply a way of informing Cornelius that he already was saved. If he sends for Peter and hears the message and believes on the Christ of that message, then he *will* be saved. And if he does not, he won't be. This surely is why the entire story is built around God's miraculous act of getting Cornelius and Peter together. There was a message that Cornelius needed to hear to be saved (10:22, 33).

So Acts 10:35 probably does not mean that Cornelius is already saved when it says that people in unreached ethnic groups who fear God and do right are acceptable to God. Cornelius had to hear the gospel message to be saved.

2. Peter makes this point at the end of his sermon in 10:43. He brings the message to a close with these words: "To him [i.e., to Christ] all the prophets bear witness that *everyone who believes in him receives forgiveness of sins through his name.*" Forgiveness of sins is essential to salvation. No one is saved whose sins against God are not forgiven by God. And Peter says that forgiveness comes through believing in Christ, and it comes through the name of Christ.

He does not say, "I am here to announce to you that those of you who fear God and do right are already forgiven." He says, "I am here so that you may hear the gospel and receive forgiveness in the name of Christ by believing in him." So again it is unlikely that verse 35 means that Cornelius and his household were already forgiven for their sins before they heard the message of Christ.

3. Elsewhere in the Book of Acts, even those who are the most God-fearing and ethical, namely, the Jews, are told that they must repent and believe in order to be saved. The Jews at Pentecost were called "devout men" (2:5), as Cornelius was called a devout man (10:2). But Peter ended his message in Acts 2 by calling even devout Jews to repent and be baptized in the name of Jesus for the forgiveness of their sins (2:38). The same is true in Acts 3:19 and 13:38–39.

So Luke is not trying to tell us in this book that devout, God-fearing people who practice what is right the best they know how are already saved and do not need the gospel. The gospel got its start among the most devout people in the world, namely, the Jews. They had more advantages in knowing God than any of the other peoples of the earth. Yet they were told again and again that devoutness and works of righteousness and religious sincerity do not solve the problem of sin. The only hope is to believe on Jesus.

4. The fourth reason for saying that verse 35 does not mean that Cornelius and others like him are already saved is found in Acts 11:18. When the

people hear Peter tell the story about Cornelius, their initial misgivings are silenced. Luke says, "And they glorified God, saying, 'Then to the Gentiles also God has granted *repentance that leads to life.*'" In other words, they did not already have eternal life. Repentance *leads to* eternal life (literally, it is "unto eternal life"). They received eternal life when they heard the message about Christ and turned to believe and follow him.

So Acts 10:35 does not mean that Cornelius was already saved because he was in some sense a God-fearer and did many right and noble things. That is the answer to the first question.

How Was Cornelius "Acceptable" to God?

The second is simply, What then does it mean when Peter says, "In every nation anyone who fears [God] and does what is right is acceptable to him" (10:35)? And what does this have to do with our commitment to world evangelization?

In trying to answer this question, my first thought was that what Peter means in verse 35 is what God meant in the vision about the unclean animals, namely, the lesson of verse 15: "What God has made clean, do not call common." But something stopped me and made me think again.

Consider verse 28. Peter is explaining to the Gentiles why he was willing to come and says, "You yourselves know how unlawful it is for a Jew to associate with or to visit anyone of another nation, but God has shown me that I should not call *any person* common or unclean." In other words, a Christian should never look down on people from any race or ethnic group and say that that they are unfit to hear the gospel from me. Or, they are too unclean for me to go into their house to share the gospel. Or, they are not worth evangelizing. Or, they have too many offensive habits for me even to get near them.

But the phrase that makes verse 28 so powerful is the phrase "any person" or "anyone": "God has shown me that I should not call any person common or unclean." In other words, Peter learned from his vision on the housetop in Joppa that God rules no one out of his favor on the basis of race or ethnic origin or mere cultural or physical distinctives. "Common and unclean" meant rejected, despised, taboo. It was like leprosy.

Peter's point in verse 28 is that there is not one human being on the face of the earth that we should think about in that way. Not one. Our hearts should go out to every single person whatever the color, whatever the ethnic origin, whatever the physical traits, whatever the cultural distinctives. We are not to write off anybody. "God has shown me that I should not call anyone—not one—common or unclean."

Now, that is *not* what Peter says in verse 35, which is what kept me from assuming that verse 35 simply means that all people are acceptable as candidates for salvation, no matter their ethnic background. In verse 35, Peter says, "*In* every nation anyone who fears him and does what is right is acceptable to him." He is not talking about every person as he was in verse 28. Here he is talking about some *in* every nation. "*In* every nation anyone who fears him and does what is right is acceptable to him." The acceptability Peter has in mind here is something more, it seems, than merely not being common or unclean. That's everybody. Peter said, Do not "call *any person* common or unclean." Here he says that only *some* in every nation fear God and do right, and these are acceptable to God.

Now we know two things that verse 35 does not mean. (1) It does not mean that these God-fearing doers of good are saved. We saw four reasons why it can't mean that. (2) It does not mean merely that they are acceptable candidates for evangelism (not common or unclean, not taboo), because verse 28 already said that's true of everybody, not just some. But verse 35 says that only some are God-fearing, doing what is right and thus acceptable. Therefore, the meaning probably lies somewhere between these two: between being saved and being a touchable, lovable human candidate for evangelism.

My suggestion is that Cornelius represents a kind of unsaved person among an unreached people group who is seeking God in an extraordinary way. Peter is saying that God *accepts* this search as genuine (hence "acceptable" in verse 35) and works wonders to bring that person the gospel of Jesus Christ the way he did through the visions of both Peter on the housetop and Cornelius in the hour of prayer.

A Modern Cornelius

This "extraordinary searching" still happens today. Don Richardson, in his book *Eternity in Their Hearts*, tells of a conversion very similar to that of Cornelius. The Gedeo people of south-central Ethiopia were a tribe of a half-million coffee-growing people who believed in a benevolent being called *Magano*, the omnipotent Creator of all that is. Few of the Gedeo people prayed to Magano, being concerned instead to appease an evil being they called *Sheit'an*. But one Gedeo man, Warrasa Wanga, from the town of Dilla on the edge of Gedeo tribal land, prayed to Magano to reveal himself to the Gedeo people.

Then Warrasa Wanga had a vision: Two white-skinned strangers came and built flimsy shelters for themselves under the shade of a sycamore tree near Dilla. Later they built more permanent shiny-roofed structures, which eventually dotted an entire hillside. Warrasa had never seen anything like these structures, since all of the Gedeo dwellings were grass-roofed. Then Warassa heard a voice say, "These men will bring you a message from Magano, the God you seek. Wait for them." In the last scene of his vision, Warrasa saw himself remove the center pole from his own house, carry it out of the town, and set it in the ground next to one of the shiny-roofed dwellings of the men. In Gedeo symbolism, the center pole of a man's house stands for his very life.

Eight years later, in December 1948, two Canadian missionaries, Albert Brant and Glen Cain, came to Ethiopia to begin a work among the Gedeo people. They intended to ask permission from Ethiopian officials to place their new mission in the center of the Gedeo region, but they were advised by other Ethiopians that their request would be refused because of the current political climate. The advisors told them to ask permission to go only as far as Dilla, on the extreme edge of Gedeo tribal land. Permission was granted, and when they reached Dilla, the missionaries set up their tents under an old sycamore tree.

Thirty years later there were more than two hundred churches among the Gedeo people, with each church averaging more than two hundred members.[29] Almost the entire Gedeo tribe has been influenced by the gospel. Warrasa was one of the first converts and the first to be imprisoned for his faith.[30]

The Fear of God That Is Acceptable to God

The main evidence that Luke is talking about this kind of "acceptable" unsaved person who seeks the true God and his messengers is found in Acts 10:31–32, where Cornelius says that the angel said to him, "Cornelius, *your prayer has been heard* and your alms have been remembered before God. Send *therefore* to Joppa and ask for Simon who is called Peter." Notice: Your prayers have been heard . . . *therefore* send for Peter. This implies that the prayers were for God to send him what he needed in order to be saved.

So the fear of God that is acceptable to God in verse 35 is a true sense that there is a holy God, that we have to meet him someday as desperate sinners, that we cannot save ourselves and need to know God's way of salvation,

29. Don Richardson, *Eternity in Their Hearts* (Ventura, Calif.: Regal, 1981), 56–58.
30. W. Harold Fuller, *Run While the Sun Is Hot* (London: Hazell Watson and Viney Ltd., n.d.), 183–84.

and that we have to pray for it day and night and seek to act on the light we have. This is what Cornelius was doing. And God accepted his prayer and his groping for truth in his life (Acts 17:27) and worked wonders to bring the saving message of the gospel to him. Cornelius would not have been saved if no one had taken him the gospel. And no one who can apprehend revelation (see note 27) will be saved today without the gospel.

Therefore, Cornelius does not represent persons who are saved without hearing and believing the gospel; rather, he illustrates God's intention to take out a people for his name from "every nation" (Acts 10:35) through the sending of gospel messengers across cultural lines, which had once been taboo.

We should learn with the Jewish church in Jerusalem that "to the Gentiles also God has granted repentance that leads to life" (11:18). But we must be sure that we learn this the way they learned it: They inferred this from the fact that the Gentiles *believed the gospel that Peter preached* and received the Holy Spirit. They did not infer the acceptance of the Gentiles from their fear of God and their good deeds.

It appears therefore that Luke's intention in telling the Cornelius story is to show that Gentiles can become part of the chosen people of God through faith in Christ in spite of their ceremonial "uncleanness." The point is *not* that Gentiles are already part of God's chosen people because they fear God and do many good deeds. The key sentence is Acts 11:14: "He will declare to you a *message by which you will be saved*."

"No Other Name under Heaven"—Acts 4:12

The reason this message saves is that it proclaims the name that saves— the name of Jesus. Peter said that God visited the Gentiles "to take from them a people *for his name*" (Acts 15:14). It stands to reason then that the proclamation by which God takes a people for his name would be a message that hinges on the name of his Son Jesus. This is, in fact, what we saw in Peter's preaching at the house of Cornelius. The sermon comes to its climax with these words about Jesus: "Everyone who believes in him receives forgiveness of sins *through his name*" (Acts 10:43).

The implicit necessity of hearing and embracing the name of Jesus, which we see in the story of Cornelius, is made explicit in Acts 4:12 in the climax of another sermon by Peter, this time before the Jewish rulers in Jerusalem: "And there is salvation in no one else, for there is no other name under heaven given among men by which we must be saved."

The situation behind this famous sentence is that the risen Jesus healed a man through Peter and John. The man had been lame from birth, but he got up and ran through the temple praising God. A crowd gathered and Peter preached. His message makes it obvious that what is at stake here is not merely a local religious phenomenon. It has to do with everybody in the world.

Then according to Acts 4:1, the priests and the captain of the temple and the Sadducees came and arrested Peter and John and put them in custody overnight. The next morning the rulers and elders and scribes gather and interrogate Peter and John. In the course of the interrogation, Peter draws out the implication of the universal lordship of Jesus: "There is salvation in no one else, for there is no other name under heaven given among men by which we must be saved" (4:12).

We need to feel the force of this universal claim by taking several phrases very seriously. The reason there is salvation in no one else is that "there is no other name *under heaven* [not just no other name in Israel but no other name under heaven, including the heaven over Greece and Rome and Spain, etc.] given *among men* [not just among Jews but among all humans everywhere] by which we must be saved." These two phrases, "under heaven" and "among men," press the claim of universality to its fullest extent.

But there is even more here that we need to see. Commentators usually interpret Acts 4:12 to mean that without believing in Jesus a person cannot be saved. In other words, Acts 4:12 is seen as a crucial text in answering the question whether those who have never heard the gospel of Jesus can be saved. But Clark Pinnock represents others who say that "Acts 4:12 does not say anything about [this question]. . . . It does not comment on the fate of the heathen. Although it is a question of great importance to us, it is not one on which Acts 4:12 renders a judgment, either positive or negative."[31] Rather, what Acts 4:12 says is that "salvation in its fullness is available to humankind only because God in the person of his Son Jesus provided it."[32] In other words, the verse says that salvation comes only through the *work* of Jesus but not only through faith in Jesus. His work can benefit those who relate to God properly without him, for example, on the basis of general revelation in nature.

The problem with Pinnock's interpretation is that it does not reckon with the true significance of Peter's focus on the *name* of Jesus. "There is

---

31. Pinnock, "Acts 4:12—No Other Name Under Heaven," 110. Pinnock acknowledges that the commentators (e.g., Bruce, Haenchen, Longenecker, Conzelmann) take Acts 4:12 to support the "exclusivist paradigm."

32. Ibid., 109.

no other *name* under heaven *by which* we must be saved." Peter is saying
something more than that there is no other *source* of saving power that
you can be saved by under some *other* name. The point of saying "There
is no other *name*" is that we are saved by calling on the name of the Lord
Jesus. Calling on his name is our entrance into fellowship with God. If
one is saved by Jesus incognito, one does not speak of being saved *by his
name*.

We noticed above that Peter said in Acts 10:43, "Everyone *who believes in
him* receives forgiveness of sins *through his name*." The name of Jesus is the
focus of faith and repentance. In order to believe on Jesus for the forgiveness
of sins, you must believe on his name, which means that you have to have
heard of him and know who he is as a particular man who did a particular
saving work and rose from the dead.

The point of Acts 4:12 for missions is made explicit in the way Paul picks
up on this very issue of the name of the Lord Jesus in Romans 10:13–15.
This passage shows that missions is essential precisely because "'Everyone
who calls on *the name of the Lord* will be saved.' But how are they to call
on him in whom they have not believed? And how are they to believe in
him of whom they have never heard? And how are they to hear without
someone preaching?"

"How Are They to Believe in Him of Whom They Have Never Heard?"

In Romans 10:13, Paul makes the great gospel declaration, quoting Joel 2:32,
"Everyone who calls on the name of the Lord will be saved." He follows
this with rhetorical questions: "But how are they to call on him in whom
they have not believed? And how are they to believe in him of whom they
have never heard?" These are extremely important words relating to the
necessity of the missionary enterprise.

Consider the context of these words in Romans 9:30–10:21. Paul begins
and ends this unit by saying that Gentiles, who never had the advantages of
God's revealed law, have nevertheless attained a right standing with God
through Christ, while Israel, with all her advantages, has not attained a right
standing with God. Here is how he says it in Romans 9:30–31: "Gentiles
who did not pursue righteousness have attained it, that is, a righteousness
that is by faith; but . . . Israel who pursued a law that would lead to righteousness did not succeed in reaching that law." Here is how he says it in
Romans 10:20–21: "Then Isaiah is so bold as to say, 'I have been found by
those who did not seek me; I have shown myself to those who did not ask

for me.' But of Israel he says, 'All day long I have held out my hands to a disobedient and contrary people.'"

Paul is burdened to show that the great reason for this strange reversal—Gentiles getting right with God and actually fulfilling the demands of the law of God, but Israel failing with their own law to get right with God—is that "the goal (or culmination) of the law is Christ for righteousness for everyone who believes" (Rom. 10:4, author's translation). Israel missed the point of her own law, namely, to point her to Christ and the way of justification by faith as the only hope of fulfilling the law (9:32). And then, when Christ appeared, she "stumbled over the stumbling stone" (9:32). The Israelites would not "submit to God's righteousness" (10:3). But Gentiles embraced the promise that "whoever believes in him will not be put to shame" (9:33).

Paul makes the transition to his own gospel and the missionary setting of his life in 10:8, where he says that the message of the Old Testament law, pointing to Christ the Redeemer, is "the word of faith that we proclaim." Then he says explicitly that this Redeemer is Jesus and that all salvation is now had by confessing him—just as salvation in the Old Testament was had by embracing the pointers to his coming, banking on God's grace that he would provide. Thus, verse 9 says, "If you confess with your mouth that *Jesus is Lord* and believe in your heart that God raised him from the dead, you will be saved."

Paul underlines that salvation through believing and confessing Jesus as Lord was the Old Testament hope. He does this by quoting Isaiah 28:16 in Romans 10:11, "For the Scripture says, 'Everyone who believes in him will not be put to shame,'" and by quoting Joel 2:32 in Romans 10:13, "Everyone who calls on the name of the Lord will be saved." So when Romans 10:11 quotes Isaiah 28:16, "Everyone who believes in him will not be put to shame," the reference is clearly to Jesus, the predicted cornerstone. And when 10:13 quotes Joel 2:32, "Everyone who calls on the name of the Lord will be saved," Jesus is the "Lord" referred to, even though in Joel 2:32 "Yahweh" is in view. The reason we know this is that 10:9 said, "If you confess with your mouth that Jesus is Lord . . . you will be saved."

Paul is making clear that in this new era of redemptive history, Jesus is the goal and climax of Old Testament teaching, and therefore, Jesus now stands as Mediator between man and Yahweh as the object of saving faith.

The flow of thought from Romans 10:14–21 is not easy to grasp. The sequence of questions in verses 14–15 are familiar and are often cited in relation to missionary work:

[Therefore,] how are they to call on him in whom they have not believed? And how are they to believe in him of whom they have never heard?[33] And how are they to hear without someone preaching? And how are they to preach unless they are sent? As it is written, "How beautiful are the feet of those who preach the good news!"

But how do these verses fit into the flow of Paul's thought? Why do they begin with the word "therefore" (*oun*)? How does asking a series of questions communicate an inference? Why does the next verse (v. 16) begin with *"But* [or *nevertheless*] they have not all obeyed the gospel"?

The answer seems to be this: The "therefore" at the beginning of verse 14 and the "nevertheless" at the beginning of verse 16 point to the fact that the series of questions in verses 14–15 are really making a statement to the effect that God has already worked to bring about these conditions for calling on the Lord Jesus for salvation. We could paraphrase as follows:

(10–13) Salvation is richly available to both Jews and Gentiles—to everyone who calls upon the name of the Lord Jesus. (14–15) *Therefore*, God has taken steps to provide the prerequisites for calling on the Lord. He is sending those who preach so that Christ can be heard and people can believe and call on the Lord Jesus. (16) Nevertheless, this has not led to obedience, as Isaiah predicted: "Lord, who has believed our report?"

So far then, the main point of verses 14–16 would be that *even though* God has taken steps to provide the prerequisites for calling on the Lord, *nevertheless* most have not obeyed.

But who is in view here when Paul says they have not believed? Differing answers to this question lead to two different ways of construing Paul's line of reasoning in the entire passage. John Murray and Charles Hodge represent these two lines.

Murray says, "At verse 16 the apostle returns to that subject which permeates this section of the epistle, the unbelief of Israel."[34] Similarly, Murray says the focus on Israel's unbelief continues to the end of the paragraph. So, for example, verse 18 also refers to Israel. "But I ask, have they not heard? Indeed they have, for 'Their voice has gone out to all the earth, and their words to the ends of the world.'" He says the quote from Psalm 19:4 (which originally referred to works of nature declaring God's glory)

33. The Greek verb for "hear" (*akouō*) followed by a person in the genitive case means "hear the person," not merely hear about him. Most commentators are agreed on this (e.g., Murray, Cranfield, Moo).

34. John Murray, *The Epistle to the Romans*, vol. 2 (Grand Rapids: Eerdmans, 1965), 60.

is used by Paul to describe the worldwide spread of the gospel of Jesus, and the point is that if the gospel is going out to all the world, "it cannot then be objected that Israel did not hear."[35] So the focus stays on Israel. The point of Paul's thought throughout Romans 10 is that Israel knows the gospel and is nevertheless rejecting it and is thus accountable.

Charles Hodge, on the other hand, sees the focus differently in verses 11–21. "Paul's object in the whole context is to vindicate the propriety of extending the gospel call to all nations." He sees both verses 16 and 18 as references not to Israel but to the nations. "The 16th verse refers to the Gentiles, 'They have not all obeyed the gospel,' and therefore this verse [18], 'Have they not heard?' cannot, without any intimation of change, be naturally referred to a different subject. . . . In the following verse [19], where the Jews are really intended, they are distinctly mentioned, 'Did not Israel know?'"[36]

In spite of this difference between Murray and Hodge, the important thing for our purpose remains fairly clear, and both agree. Whether Paul is focusing in a narrower way on the accountability of Israel or more broadly on the availability of the gospel to the nations (and therefore also to Israel), both agree that calling on the name of the Lord Jesus is necessary for salvation (v. 13).

So necessary is it that Paul feels compelled to show that all the necessary prerequisites for calling on the Lord are being put in place by God (vv. 14–15). Even more relevant for our immediate question is the implication that "calling on the Lord" in a saving way is not something that a person can do from a position of ignorance. One cannot do it from another religion. This is made plain in the questions of verses 14–15.

Each succeeding question rules out an argument from those who say that someone can be saved without hearing the gospel of Jesus. First, "How are they to call on him in whom they have not believed?" shows that effective calling presupposes faith in the one called. This rules out the argument that one might call on God savingly without faith in Christ.

Second, "And how are they to believe in him of whom they have never heard?" shows that faith presupposes hearing Christ in the message of the gospel. This rules out the argument that a person might have saving faith without really knowing or meeting Christ in the gospel.

Third, "And how are they to hear without someone preaching?" shows that hearing Christ in the gospel presupposes a proclaimer of the gospel.

35. Ibid., 62.

36. Charles Hodge, *Commentary on the Epistle to the Romans* (New York: A. C. Armstrong and Son, 1893), 548.

This rules out the argument that one might somehow meet Christ or hear Christ without a messenger to tell the gospel.

Millard Erickson does not seem to take the force of this sequence seriously enough when he suggests that the quotation from Psalm 19:4 in Romans 10:18 teaches that general revelation in nature is all that some need to receive salvation, apart from missionary proclamation.[37]

At first this suggestion may seem compelling. Paul says that people must hear in order to call on the Lord. Then he asks in verse 18, "Have they not heard?" And he answers with the words of Psalm 19:4 (18:4 LXX[38]): "Indeed they have, for 'Their voice has gone out to all the earth, and their words to the ends of the world.'"

In the original context of Psalm 19, "their voice" and "their words" refer to what is communicated through "night" and "day" and "heavens" and "firmament." So one might conclude that the "hearing" that is necessary for saving faith (v. 17) is effectively provided through natural revelation. This is what Erickson concludes.[39]

The problem with this view is that it creates an insurmountable tension with the point of verse 14. There Paul says, "How are they to hear without someone preaching?" If Erickson were correct that a hearing that is effective to save comes through nature, then Paul's question is misleading: "How are they to hear without someone preaching?" He clearly means that one cannot hear what one needs to hear for salvation unless a preacher is sent. He would contradict this if he meant in verse 18 that preachers are not essential for salvation, because an effective message of salvation comes through nature.

Therefore, as most commentators agree, it is unlikely that Paul intends for verse 18 to teach that natural revelation fulfills the saving role of the "word of Christ," which gives rise to faith (v. 17). Murray and Hodge agree that Paul uses the words of the psalm to draw a parallel between the universality of general revelation and the universal spread

37. See note 7.

38. LXX is an abbreviation for the Greek translation of the Old Testament called the Septuagint. It comes from the tradition that the translation was made by seventy (LXX) scholars.

39. He finds support for this conclusion also in Romans 1:18–21. But the problem with this is that though these verses teach the reality of general revelation that is sufficient to hold humanity accountable to glorify God (v. 21), nevertheless, they also teach that men suppress this truth in unrighteousness (v. 18) and do *not* thank God or honor him the way they should (v. 21) and are therefore without excuse (v. 20). General revelation is sufficient to hold all men accountable to worship God but not efficient to bring about the faith that saves. That is why the gospel must be preached to all peoples. God wills to honor his Son by accompanying the preaching of his name with heart-awakening power.

of the gospel.[40] The point is that God has set in motion a missionary movement (the "sending" of v. 15) that will reach to all the peoples of the earth on the analogy of the universal spread of God's glory through natural revelation.[41]

To sum up these thoughts on Romans 10, the theological assumption behind Paul's missionary conviction is that Christ is the fulfillment of all that the Old Testament pointed toward. Before Christ, faith was focused on the mercy of God to forgive sins and to care for his people. As revelation progressed, faith could move more easily from the animal sacrifices to the promised sin-bearer of Isaiah 53. But when Christ came, all faith narrowed in its focus to him alone as the One who purchased and guaranteed all the hopes of the people of God. From the time of Christ onward, God wills to honor Christ by making him the sole focus of saving faith. Therefore, people must call on him and believe in him and hear him and be sent as messengers with the Word of Christ.

Paul's Conception of His Own Missionary Vocation

The indispensability of hearing the gospel for salvation is seen in the biblical texts that show how Paul conceived of his own missionary vocation.

40. Murray, *Epistle to the Romans*, 61: "Since the gospel proclamation is not to all without distinction, it is proper to see the parallel between the universality of general revelation and the universalism of the gospel. The former is the pattern now followed in the sounding forth of the gospel to the uttermost parts of the earth. The application which Paul makes of Psalm 19:4 can thus be seen to be eloquent not only of this parallel but also of that which is implicit in the parallel, namely, the widespread diffusion of the gospel of grace." Hodge, *Commentary on the Epistle to the Romans*, 549: "This verse, therefore is to be considered as a strong declaration that what Paul had proved ought to be done, had in fact been accomplished. The middle wall of partition had been broken down, the gospel of salvation, the religion of God, was free from its trammels, the offers of mercy were as wide and general as the proclamation of the heavens. . . . His object in using the words of the Psalmist was, no doubt, to convey more clearly and affectingly to the minds of his hearers the idea that the proclamation of the gospel was now as free from all nations or ecclesiastical restrictions, as the instructions shed down upon all people by the heavens under which they dwell. Paul, of course, is not to be understood as quoting the Psalmist as though the ancient prophet was speaking of the preaching of the gospel. He simply uses scriptural language to express his own ideas, as is done involuntarily almost by every preacher in every sermon."

41. The words "Their voice has gone out" does not have to mean that the spread of the message is finished. In Paul's context, the natural meaning is that the gospel has been propelled into the world to reach all peoples. Olshausen suggests that "'their voice has gone out' is to be understood as prophetically spoken; that which is begun is viewed as if already completed, and therefore we need not seek for any further explanation how it is that St. Paul can represent Christ's messengers as spread all over the earth, whereas, when he wrote these words, they had not so much as carried the preaching of Christ through the whole of the Roman empire." Hermann Olshausen, *Studies in the Epistle to the Romans* (1849; reprint, Minneapolis: Klock and Klock Christian Publishers: 1983), 354.

At his conversion, Paul received a commission from the Lord that clarifies the condition of those without Christ. He refers to this in Acts 26:15–18.

> And I said, "Who are you, Lord?" And the Lord said, "I am Jesus whom you are persecuting. But rise and stand upon your feet, for I have appeared to you for this purpose, to appoint you as a servant and witness to the things in which you have seen me and to those in which I will appear to you, delivering you from your people and from the Gentiles—to whom *I am sending you to open their eyes, so that they may turn from darkness to light and from the power of Satan to God, that they may receive forgiveness of sins* and a place among those who are sanctified by faith in me."

Here we see what was at stake in Paul's ministry. Without making any distinctions, the Lord says that those who do not yet have the gospel are in darkness and in the power of Satan and without the forgiveness of sins. Christ commissioned Paul with a word of power that actually opens the eyes of the spiritually blind, not so that they can see they are forgiven but so that they can be forgiven. His message delivers from the power of Satan. The picture of nations without the gospel is that they are blind and in the darkness and in bondage to Satan and without forgiveness of sins and unacceptable to God because they are unsanctified.

This accords with what Paul says elsewhere about the condition of man without the power of the gospel: All are under sin with their mouths stopped before God (Rom. 3:9–19); they are in the flesh and unable to submit to God or please God (Rom. 8:7–8); they are natural and not spiritual and therefore unable to receive the things of the Spirit (1 Cor. 2:14–16); they are dead in trespasses and children of wrath (Eph. 2:3–5); and they are darkened and alienated from God and hard in heart (Eph. 4:17–18).

With the coming of Christ came a message that has power to save (Rom. 1:16; 1 Cor. 15:2; 1 Thess. 2:16) and bear fruit (Col. 1:6) and triumph (2 Thess. 3:1), and it is the mission of Paul and all his heirs to preach that message to the nations. "Since, in the wisdom of God, the world did not know God through wisdom [or false religion], it pleased God through the folly of what we preach to save those who believe" (1 Cor. 1:21).

Salvation is at stake when Paul speaks to Jews in the synagogue as well. Paul does not assume that God-fearing Gentiles or Jews are saved by virtue of knowing the Old Testament Scriptures. What does he say in the synagogue at Antioch of Pisidia?

Let it be known to you therefore, brothers, that through this man forgiveness of sins is proclaimed to you, and by him everyone who believes is freed from everything from which you could not be freed by the law of Moses.

Acts 13:38–39

Paul does not tell them that even the best of them are already forgiven by virtue of their obedience to the law. He offers them forgiveness through Christ. And he makes "freeing" ("justification") from sin conditional on believing on Christ. When the synagogue later opposes this message, Paul says in Acts 13:46–48:

It was necessary that the word of God be spoken first to you. Since you thrust it aside and judge yourselves unworthy of eternal life, behold, we are turning to the Gentiles. For so the Lord has commanded us, saying, "I have made you a light for the Gentiles, that you may bring salvation to the ends of the earth." And when the Gentiles heard this, they began rejoicing and glorifying the word of the Lord, and as many as were appointed to eternal life believed.

Paul's vocation is to bring salvation to the ends of the earth. The assumption is that salvation is not already at the ends of the earth. Paul is to take it there. Paul's message is the means of salvation. There is no salvation without it: "As many as were appointed to eternal life believed" Paul's message and were saved. God has ordained that salvation come to the nations through sent messengers whose obedient preaching of the gospel brings salvation to the nations.

Through Paul's preaching, God is now doing the sovereign work that he had overlooked for so long during the times of ignorance. He is bringing Gentiles to faith according to his preordained plan. He is opening their hearts to the gospel (Acts 16:14), granting them repentance (Acts 11:18), and cleansing their hearts by faith (Acts 15:9).

Before this time of gospel privilege, these things were not possible, for God was allowing the nations to go their own way (Acts 14:16). But now a great movement is under way to gather a people for his name from all the nations, and God himself is active in the ministry of his messengers to sanctify a people for himself. This becomes wonderfully clear in Romans 15, where Paul describes his own vocation in its relation to the work of Christ in and through him.

But on some points I have written to you very boldly by way of reminder, because of the grace given me by God to be a minister of Christ Jesus to the Gentiles in the priestly service of the gospel of God, so that the offering of the Gentiles may be acceptable, sanctified by the Holy Spirit. In Christ Jesus, then, I have reason to be proud of my work for God. For I will not venture to speak of anything except what Christ has accomplished through me to bring the Gentiles to obedience—by word and deed.

verses 15–18

Notice the initiative of God in these verses. First, God gave Paul the grace of apostleship and called him to the ministry of the gospel (vv. 15–16). Second, the Gentiles who believe Paul's message are acceptable to God because they are sanctified by the Holy Spirit (v. 16). Third, it is not Paul who has won obedience from the Gentiles; it is what Christ has accomplished through him (v. 18).

Therefore, the Gentile mission is the new work of God. It is the fulfillment of divine prophecy that once God allowed the nations to go their own way, but *now*

God . . . visited the Gentiles, to take from them a people for his name. And with this the words of the prophets agree, just as it is written, "After this I will return, and I will rebuild the tent of David that has fallen; I will rebuild its ruins, and I will restore it, *that the remnant of mankind may seek the Lord*, and all the Gentiles who are called by my name, says the Lord, who makes these things known from of old."

Acts 15:14–18

A new day has come with Jesus Christ. The people of God are being rebuilt in such a way that they will no longer fail in their task of reaching the nations. In this new day, God will not suffer his people to neglect their mission; he will no longer allow the nations to go their own way. He is establishing a church "that the remnant of mankind may seek the Lord."

And he will now gather in all those among the nations who are called by his name! It is *his* new work! All those who are predestined *will* be called (Rom. 8:30). All those who are foreordained to eternal life *will* believe (Acts 13:48). All those who are ransomed *will* be gathered from every people under heaven (Rev. 5:9). God himself is the chief agent in this new movement, and he *will* take out a people for his name among the nations (Acts 15:14).

The Writings of John

John's conception of the new missionary task parallels Paul's. Just as Paul said that no one could believe in a Christ of whom they had not heard (Rom.

10:14), so Jesus says in John 10:27, "My sheep hear my voice, and I know them, and they follow me" (cf. 10:4, 14). In other words, Jesus gathers his redeemed flock by calling them with his own voice. The true sheep hear his voice and follow, and he gives them eternal life (10:28).

Whom does Jesus have in mind when he speaks of those who will hear his voice and follow him? He is referring to more than the Jews who actually heard him on earth. He says, "I have *other sheep that are not of this fold. I must bring them also, and they will listen to my voice.* So there will be one flock, one shepherd" (10:16). "Other sheep that are not of this fold" refers to the Gentiles, who are not part of the Jewish fold.

But how will these Gentiles hear his voice? The answer is the same as with Paul: They hear the voice of Jesus, not in nature or in an alien religion but in the voice of Christ's messengers. We see this in the way Jesus prays for his future disciples in John 17:20–21: "I do not ask for these only, but also for those *who will believe in me through their word,* that they may all be one." We infer from this then that the "sheep that are not of this fold" will hear the voice of the Shepherd through the voice of his messengers.

Eternal life, therefore, comes only to those who hear the voice of the Shepherd and follow him. "My sheep hear my voice, and I know them, and they follow me. I give them eternal life" (10:27–28). This hearing is through the messengers of the Shepherd. This is what Jesus means in John 14:6 when he says, "I am the way, and the truth, and the life. No one comes to the Father except through me." "Through me" does not mean that people in other religions can get to God because Jesus died for them, though they don't know about it. The "through me" must be defined in the context of John's Gospel as believing in Jesus through the word of his disciples (John 6:35; 7:38; 11:25; 12:46; 17:20).

Eternal life is owing to the death of Jesus for his sheep (10:15)—a death that atoned not for a few Jewish sheep only but for sheep from every nation. We see this in John 11:51–53, where John interprets the words of Caiaphas: "Being high priest that year he prophesied that Jesus would die for the nation, *and not for the nation only, but also to gather into one the children of God who are scattered abroad.*"

The "children of God scattered abroad" (11:52) are the "other sheep that are not of this fold" (10:16). And when we look at John's picture of the consummation of the missionary cause in Revelation, we see that these "sheep" and "children" are truly from all the nations.

> And they sang a new song, saying, Worthy are you to take the scroll and to open its seals, for you were slain, and by your blood you ransomed people

for God *from every tribe and language and people and nation*, and you
have made them a kingdom and priests to our God, and they shall reign
on the earth."

Revelation 5:9–10

Here we see the true extent of the word "scattered" in John 11:52. Jesus
died to gather the "children of God" who are scattered among "every tribe
and language and people and nation." The implication is that the messengers of the Shepherd must (Mark 13:10) and *will* (Matt. 24:14) reach every
people under heaven with the message of the gospel and the voice of the
Shepherd. The redeemed in heaven from all the peoples are not redeemed
without knowing it. Rather, as Revelation 7:14 makes clear, those "from
every nation, from all tribes and peoples and languages" (Rev. 7:9) are those
who "have washed their robes and made them white in the blood of the
Lamb" (Rev. 7:14; cf. 22:14). They are those who "keep the commandments
of God and hold to the testimony of Jesus" (Rev. 12:17). The gospel of the
blood of Christ crucified for sinners and risen in victory must be preached
to all the nations so that they can believe and be saved.

Conclusion

The question we have been trying to answer in this section is whether some
people are quickened by the Holy Spirit and saved by grace through faith
in a merciful Creator even though they never hear of Jesus in this life.
Are there devout people in religions other than Christianity who humbly
rely on the grace of a God whom they know only through nature or non-
Christian religious experience?

The answer of the New Testament is a clear and earnest no. Rather,
the message throughout is that with the coming of Christ a major change
occurred in redemptive history. Saving faith was once focused on the mercy
of God known in his redemptive acts among the people of Israel and in
the system of animal sacrifices and in the prophecies of coming redemption. Outside Israel we hear of Melchizedek (Genesis 14), who seems to
know the true God apart from connection with special revelation in the
line of Abraham.

But now the focus of faith has been narrowed down to one man, Jesus
Christ, the fulfillment and guarantee of all redemption and all sacrifices
and all prophecies. It is to his honor that henceforth all saving faith shall
be directed to him.

Therefore, this great turn in redemptive history is accompanied by a new mission thrust ordained by God. God no longer allows the nations to walk their own way (Acts 14:16) but sends his messengers everywhere to call all to repent and believe the gospel (Acts 17:30).

God in Christ is himself the power behind this mission. He has ordained his people to life (Acts 13:48) and ransomed them by laying down his life for them (John 10:15; Rev. 5:9). Now he is commissioning Spirit-filled messengers to preach to them (Rom. 1:5; 10:15), and he is speaking through these messengers with power (Luke 12:12; 21:15; 1 Thess. 2:13) and calling the lost effectually to faith (Rom. 8:30; 1 Cor. 1:24) and keeping them by his almighty power (Jude 24).

Those who affirm that people who have no access to the gospel may nevertheless be saved without knowing Christ try to argue that this idea enhances the motivation to evangelize the lost. As we saw above, this is a futile effort. The arguments fall apart as you pick them up. For example, John Ellenberger cites four ways our motivation will be "enhanced."

1. Citing Acts 18:10 ("I have many in this city who are my people"), he says that "the knowledge that the Holy Spirit has been working in the hearts of people prior to hearing the good news should encourage us."[42] I agree. But that is not the issue. Working in people's hearts to prepare them to respond to the gospel is very different from working in their hearts so that they are saved apart from the gospel. The first motivates missions; the second does not.

2. He argues unintelligibly that "because the great majority have not responded to general revelation, they need to be confronted by the claims of Jesus."[43] This amounts to saying that if you believe some are saved without hearing the claims of Christ, you will be more motivated to share those claims because most are not saved that way. But that is *not* an argument that the view that some can be saved without the gospel "enhances" our motivation to evangelize the lost. On the contrary, it's an argument that the more needed the claims of Christ are, the greater the motivation to share them.

3. Third, he argues that believing that some are saved apart from the preaching of the gospel "broadens our understanding of the whole gospel."[44] In other words, if we are going to pursue missions with

42. John Ellenberger, "Is Hell a Proper Motivation for Missions?" in *Through No Fault of Their Own*, 225.
43. Ibid., 226.
44. Ibid.

zeal, we need to do so for reasons other than merely providing escape from hell (which some already have before we get there). We need to desire to bring the blessings of salvation in this life. I suppose this is true. But why should we assume that the church will be more motivated to bring *these* blessings to people than it is to bring the blessing of eternal life? The risk I am willing to take to save a person from execution is not increased by telling me, "He is no longer on death row, but surely you will want to feel all the same urgency to help him find a good life."

4. Finally, Ellenberger argues that believing some are saved apart from the preaching of the gospel "reaffirms love as the primary motivation."[45] Again this is unintelligible to me, because it seems to assume that the urgency of missions driven by the desire to rescue people from eternal torment is not love. How does saying some are saved without the gospel make a greater appeal to love?

So I affirm again that the contemporary abandonment of the universal necessity of hearing the gospel for salvation does indeed cut a nerve in missionary motivation. I say *a* nerve rather than *the* nerve because I agree that the universal lostness of man is not the only focus for missionary motivation. Arching over it is the great goal of bringing glory to Christ.[46]

Therefore, the church is bound to engage with the Lord of glory in his cause. Charles Hodge is right that "the solemn question, implied in the language of the apostle, how can they believe without a preacher? should sound day and night in the ears of the churches."[47]

It is our unspeakable privilege to be caught up with him in the greatest movement in history—the ingathering of the elect "from all tribes and languages and peoples and nations" until the full number of the Gentiles comes in, all Israel is saved, the Son of Man descends with power and great glory as King of kings and Lord of lords, and the earth is full of the knowledge of his glory as the waters cover the sea forever and ever. Then the supremacy of Christ will be manifest to all, he will deliver the kingdom to God the Father, and God will be all in all.

45. Ibid.
46. For my understanding, following Jonathan Edwards, on the relationship between passion for the supremacy and compassion for the souls of men, see chapter 6.
47. Hodge, *Commentary on the Epistle to the Romans*, 553.

5

The Supremacy of God among "All the Nations"

Can Love Decide?

How do we decide what the task of missions is, or even if there should be such a thing as missions? One answer would be that love demands it and love defines it. If people all over the world are under condemnation for sin and cut off from eternal life (Eph. 2:2–3, 12; 4:17; 5:6), and if calling on Jesus is their only hope for eternal, joyful fellowship with God (as chap. 4 shows), then love demands missions.

But can love define missions? Not without consulting the strange ways of God. Sometimes the ways of God are not the way we would have done things with our limited views. But God is love, even when his ways are puzzling. It may not look like love for your life if you sold all that you had and bought a barren field. But it might in fact be love from another perspective, namely, that there is a treasure buried in the field. So, of course, love will consult God's perspective on missions. Love will refuse to define missions with a limited human perspective. Love will test its logic by the larger picture of God's ways.

Two Sinking Ocean Liners

The limits of love's wisdom become plain when we imagine missions as a rescue operation during a tragedy at sea.

177

Suppose there are two ocean liners on the sea, and both begin to sink at the same time with large numbers of people on board who do not know how to swim. There are some lifeboats but not enough. And suppose you are in charge of a team of ten rescuers in two large boats.

You arrive on the scene of the first sinking ship and find yourself surrounded by hundreds of screaming people, some going down before your eyes, some fighting over scraps of debris, others ready to jump into the water from the sinking ship. Several hundred yards away the very same thing is happening to the people on the other ship.

Your heart breaks for the dying people. You long to save as many as you can, so you cry out to your two crews to give every ounce of energy they have. There are five rescuers in each boat, and they are working with all their might. They are saving many. There is lots of room in the rescue boats.

Then someone cries out from the other ship, "Come over and help *us*!" What would love do? Would love go or stay?

I cannot think of any reason that love would leave its life-saving labor and go to the other ship. Love puts no higher value on distant souls than on nearer souls. In fact, love might well reason that in the time it would take to row across the several hundred yards to the other ship, an overall loss of total lives would result.

Love might also reason that the energy of the rescuers would be depleted by rowing between ships, which would possibly result in a smaller number of individuals being saved. Not only that, but from past experience you may know that the people on the other boat were probably all drunk at this time in the evening and would be less cooperative with your saving efforts. This too might mean fewer lives saved.

So love, by itself, may very well refuse to leave its present rescue operation. It may stay at its present work in order to save as many individuals as possible.

This imaginary scene on the sea is not, of course, a perfect picture of the church in the world, if for no other reason than that the rescue potential of the church is *not* fully engaged even where it is. But the point of the illustration still stands: Love alone (from our limited human perspective) may not see the missionary task the way God does.

God May Have Another View

God may have in mind that the aim of the rescue operation should be to gather saved sinners from every people in the world (from *both* ocean liners), even if some of the rescuers must leave a fruitful *reached* people (the first ocean liner) in order to labor among an (possibly less fruitful) *unreached* people (the second ocean liner).

In other words, the task of missions may not be merely to win[1] as many individuals as possible from the most responsive people groups of the world but rather to win individuals from *all* the people groups of the world. It may not be enough to define missions as leaving the safe shore of our own culture to conduct rescue operations on the strange seas of other languages and cultures. Something may need to be added to that definition that impels us to leave one rescue operation to take up another.

This chapter shows that God's call for missions in Scripture *cannot* be defined in terms of crossing cultures to maximize the total number of individuals saved. Rather, God's will for missions is that every people group be reached with the testimony of Christ and that a people be called out for his name from all the nations.[2]

I believe that this definition of missions will in fact result in the greatest possible number of white-hot worshipers for God's Son. But that remains for God to decide. Our responsibility is to define missions his way and then obey. That means we must conduct a careful investigation of how the New Testament portrays the special missionary task of the church. More specifically, we must assess biblically the widespread concept of "unreached peoples" as the focus of missionary activity.

The Indictment of 1974: People Blindness

Since 1974, the task of missions has increasingly focused on evangelizing[3] unreached peoples as opposed to evangelizing unreached territories. That

---

1. I use the word "win" in the sense that Paul does in 1 Corinthians 9:19–22. The use of "save" in verse 22 shows that this is what he has in mind: to be used by God in love and witness to win people over to faith in Christ and so to save them from sin and condemnation. "For though I am free from all, I have made myself a servant to all, that I might *win* more of them. To the Jews I became as a Jew, in order to *win* Jews. To those under the law I became as one under the law (though not being myself under the law) that I might *win* those under the law. To those outside the law I became as one outside the law (not being outside the law of God but under the law of Christ) that I might *win* those outside the law. To the weak I became weak, that I might *win* the weak. I have become all things to all people, that by all means I might save some."

2. The word "nations" in this chapter does not refer to the modern political state as in the "United Nations" or the "nation" of England. We will see that its biblical meaning has to do with an ethnic group that may or may not have political dimensions.

3. I use the word "evangelize" in the broad New Testament sense of speaking the Good News of Christ and his saving work. The speaking is with a view of bringing about faith and establishing the church of Christ (Rom. 10:14–15; 15:20), but true evangelizing does not depend

year at the Lausanne Congress on World Evangelization, Ralph Winter shocked and indicted the Western missionary enterprise with what he called "people blindness." Since that time he and others have relentlessly pressed the "people-group" focus onto the agenda of most mission-minded churches and agencies. The "shattering truth" that he revealed at Lausanne was this: In spite of the fact that every country of the world has been penetrated with the gospel, four out of five non-Christians are still cut off from the gospel because the barriers are cultural and linguistic, not geographic.

> Why is this fact not more widely known? I'm afraid that all our exultation about the fact that every *country* of the world has been penetrated has allowed many to suppose that every *culture* has by now been penetrated. This misunderstanding is a malady so widespread that it deserves a special name. Let us call it "people blindness," that is, blindness to the existence of separate *peoples* within *countries*—a blindness, I might add, which seems more prevalent in the U.S. and among U.S. missionaries than anywhere else.[4]

Winter's message was a powerful call for the church of Christ to reorient its thinking so that missions would be seen as the task of evangelizing unreached *peoples*, not the task of merely evangelizing more territories. In a most remarkable way, in the next fifteen years the missionary enterprise responded to this call. In 1989, Winter was able to write, "Now that the concept of Unreached Peoples has taken hold very widely, it is immediately possible to make plans . . . with far greater confidence and precision."[5]

A Milestone Definition, 1982

Probably the most significant unified effort to define "people group" came in March 1982 as a result of the work of the Lausanne Strategy Working Group. This meeting defined a "people group" as:

> a significantly large grouping of individuals who perceive themselves to have a common affinity for one another because of their shared language,

---

on a believing response (Heb. 4:6). For a remarkably thorough historical survey of the concept, see David B. Barrett, *Evangelize! A Historical Survey of the Concept* (Birmingham, Ala.: New Hope, 1987).

4. Ralph D. Winter, "The New Macedonia: A Revolutionary New Era in Mission Begins," in *Perspectives on the World Christian Movement: A Reader*, 3d ed., ed. Ralph D. Winter and Steven C. Hawthorne (Pasadena, Calif.: William Carey Library, 1999), 346.

5. Ralph Winter, "Unreached Peoples: Recent Developments in the Concept," *Mission Frontiers* (August/September 1989): 18.

religion, ethnicity, residence, occupation, class or caste, situation, etc. or combinations of these. . . . [It is] the largest group within which the Gospel can spread as a church planting movement without encountering barriers of understanding or acceptance.[6]

We should be aware that this definition was developed not merely on the basis of biblical teaching about the specific nature of people groups but also on the basis of what would help missionaries identify and reach various groups. This is a legitimate method for advancing evangelistic strategy. But we need to distinguish it from the method I will use in this chapter.[7]

We also need to make clear at the outset that I am not going to use the term "people group" in a precise sociological way as distinct from "people." I agree with those who say that the biblical concept of "peoples" or "nations" cannot be stretched to include individuals grouped on the basis of things such as occupation, residence, or handicaps. These are sociological groupings that are very relevant for evangelistic strategy but do not figure into defining the *biblical* meaning of "peoples" or "nations." Harley Schreck and David Barrett have proposed distinguishing the sociological category "people group" from the ethnological category "peoples."[8] I agree with the category distinction but have found the terminology to be a linguistic straitjacket that I can't wear. The singular "people" in the English language does not clearly signify a distinctive grouping. Therefore, when I use "people group," I am only calling attention to the group concept over against individuals. The context will make clear the nature of the grouping.

"Test All Things"—Including People-Group Thinking

My aim is to test the people-group focus by the Scriptures. Is the missionary mandate of the Bible (1) a command to reach as many individuals as possible, or (2) a command to reach all the "fields," or (3) a command to reach all the "people groups" of the world, as the Bible defines people groups? Is the emphasis that has dominated discussion since 1974 a biblical teaching, or is it simply a strategic development that gives missions effort a sharper focus?

6. Ibid., 12.
7. See note 38 on this difference of perspective and its effects.
8. Harley Schreck and David Barrett, eds., *Unreached Peoples: Clarifying the Task* (Monrovia, Calif.: New Hope, 1987), 6–7.

So we turn now to the basic question of this chapter: Is it biblical to define the missionary task of the church as reaching all the unreached[9] *peoples* of the world? Or is it sufficient to say that missions is simply the effort to reach as many individuals as possible in places different from our own?

The Most Famous Commission

And Jesus came and said to them, "All authority in heaven and on earth has been given to me. Go therefore and make disciples of all nations, baptizing them in the name of the Father and of the Son and of the Holy Spirit, teaching them to observe all that I have commanded you. And behold, I am with you always, to the end of the age."

Matthew 28:18–20

This passage is often called the Great Commission. The first thing to make clear about it is that it is still binding on the modern church. It was given not only to the apostles for their ministry but also to the church for its ministry as long as this age lasts.

The basis for saying this comes from the text itself. The undergirding promise of verse 20 says, "And behold, I am with you always, to the end of the age." The people referred to in the word "you" cannot be limited to the apostles, because they died within one generation. The promise extends to "the end of the age," that is, to the day of judgment at Christ's second coming (cf. Matt. 13:39–40, 49). Jesus is speaking to the apostles as representatives of the church, which would endure to the end of the age. He is assuring the church of his abiding presence and help as long as this age lasts. This is significant because the promise of verse 20 is given to sustain and encourage the command to make disciples of all nations. Therefore, if the sustaining promise is expressed in terms that endure to the end of the age, we may rightly assume that the command to make disciples also endures to the end of the age.

I conclude then that the Great Commission was given not just to the apostles but also to the church, which would endure to the end of the age. This is further buttressed by the authority Jesus claims in verse 18. He lays claim to "all authority in heaven and on earth." This enables him to do what he had earlier promised in Matthew 16:18, when he said, "I will build my church." So the abiding validity of the Great Commission rests

9. See below in this chapter for a discussion of what reached and unreached means.

on the ongoing authority of Christ over all things (Matt. 28:18) and on the purpose of Christ to build his church (Matt. 16:18) and on his promise to be present and help in the mission of the church to the end of the age (Matt. 28:20).

Therefore, these words of the Lord are crucial for deciding what the missionary task of the church should be today. Specifically, the words "make disciples of all nations" must be closely examined. They contain the very important phrase "all nations," which is often referred to in the Greek form *panta ta ethnē* (*panta* = all; *ta* = the; *ethnē* = nations). The reason this is such an important phrase is that *ethnē*, when translated as "nations," sounds like a political or geographic grouping. That is its most common English usage. But this is not what the Greek means, nor does the English always mean this. For example, we say the Cherokee nation or the Sioux nation, which means something like "people with a unifying ethnic identity." In fact, the word "ethnic" comes from the Greek word *ethnos* (singular of *ethnē*). Our inclination then might be to take *panta ta ethnē* as a reference to "all the ethnic groups." "Go and disciple all the ethnic groups."

But this is precisely what needs to be tested by a careful investigation of the wider biblical context and especially the use of *ethnos* in the New Testament and its Old Testament background.

The Singular Use of *Ethnos* in the New Testament

In the New Testament, the singular *ethnos* never refers to an individual.[10] This is a striking fact. Every time the singular *ethnos* does occur it refers to a people group or nation—often the Jewish nation, even though in the plural it is usually translated "Gentiles" in distinction from the Jewish people.[11]

Here are some examples to illustrate the corporate meaning of the singular use of *ethnos*.

10. Galatians 2:14 appears to be an exception in the English text ("If you, though a Jew, live like a Gentile and not like a Jew, how can you force the Gentiles to live like Jews?"). But the Greek word here is not *ethnos* but the adverb *ethnikōs*, which means to have the life patterns of Gentiles.

11. Following are all the singular uses in the New Testament: Matt. 21:43; 24:7 (= Mark 13:8 = Luke 21:10); Luke 7:5; 23:2 (both references to the Jewish nation); Acts 2:5 ("Jews from every nation"); 7:7; 8:9; 10:22 ("whole nation of the Jews"), 35; 17:26; 24:2, 10, 17; 26:4; 28:19 (the last five references are to the Jewish nation); John 11:48, 50, 51, 52; 18:35 (all in reference to the Jewish nation); Rev. 5:9; 13:7; 14:6; 1 Peter 2:9. Paul never uses the singular.

Nation [*ethnos*] will rise against nation [*ethnos*], and kingdom against kingdom, and there will be famines and earthquakes in various places.

Matthew 24:7

Now there were dwelling in Jerusalem Jews, devout men from every nation [*ethnous*] under heaven.

Acts 2:5

There was a man named Simon, who . . . amazed the people [*ethnos*] of Samaria.

Acts 8:9

You are a chosen race, a royal priesthood, a holy nation [*ethnos*], a people for his own possession.

1 Peter 2:9

By your blood you ransomed people for God from every tribe and language and people and nation [*ethnous*].

Revelation 5:9

What this survey of the singular establishes is that the word *ethnos* very naturally and normally carried a corporate meaning in reference to people groups with a certain ethnic identity. In fact, the reference in Acts 2:5 to "every nation" is very close in form to "all the nations" in Matthew 28:19. And in Acts 2:5 it must refer to people groups of some kind. At this stage, therefore, we find ourselves leaning toward a corporate "people group" understanding of "all the nations" in the Great Commission of Matthew 28:19.

The Plural Use of *Ethnos* in the New Testament

Unlike the singular, the plural of *ethnos* does not always refer to people groups. It sometimes simply refers to Gentile individuals.[12] Many instances are ambiguous. What is important to see is that in the plural the word can refer either to an ethnic group or simply to Gentile individuals who may

12. For example, Matt. 6:32; 10:5; 12:21; 20:25; Luke 2:32; 21:24; Acts 9:15; 13:46, 47; 15:7, 14, 23; 18:6; 21:11; 22:21; Rom. 3:29; 9:24; 15:9, 10, 11, 12, 16; 16:26; Gal. 2:9; 3:14; 2 Tim. 4:17; Rev. 14:18; 16:19; 19:15; 20:8; 21:24. When I use the term "Gentile individuals" in this chapter, I do not mean to focus undue attention on specific persons. Rather, I mean to speak of non-Jews in a comprehensive way without reference to their ethnic groupings.

not make up an ethnic group. For example, consider the following texts, which illustrate the meaning of Gentile individuals.

> Acts 13:48—When Paul turns to the Gentiles in Antioch after being rejected by the Jews, Luke says, "And when *the Gentiles* heard this, they began rejoicing and glorifying the word of the Lord." This is a reference not to nations but to the group of Gentile individuals at the synagogue who heard Paul.
>
> 1 Corinthians 12:2—"You know that when you were *pagans*, you were led astray to mute idols." In this verse, "you" refers to the individual Gentile converts at Corinth. It would not make sense to say, "When you were nations . . ."
>
> Ephesians 3:6—Paul says that the mystery of Christ is "that *the Gentiles* are fellow heirs, members of the same body." It would not make sense to say that nations are fellow heirs and *members* (a definite reference to individuals) of the same body. Paul's conception is that the local body of Christ has many *individual* members who are *Gentiles*.

These are perhaps sufficient to show that the plural of *ethnos* does not have to mean nation or people group. On the other hand, the plural, like the singular, certainly can, and often does, refer to people groups. For example:

> Acts 13:19—Referring to the taking of the Promised Land by Israel, Paul says, "After destroying seven nations [*ethnē*] in the land of Canaan, he gave them their land as an inheritance."
>
> Romans 4:17—"As it is written, 'I have made you the father of many nations.'" Here Paul is quoting Genesis 17:4, where "father of a multitude of nations" does not refer to individuals but to people groups. *Ethnōn* is a Greek translation of the Hebrew *goyim*, which virtually always means nations or people groups. For example, in Deuteronomy 7:1, Moses says that God will clear "away many nations before you, the Hittites, the Girgashites, the Amorites, the Canaanites, the Perizzites, the Hivites, and the Jebusites." The word "nations" here is *goyim* in Hebrew and *ethnē* in Greek.
>
> Revelation 11:9—"For three and a half days some from the peoples and tribes and languages and nations [*ethnōn*] will gaze at their dead

bodies." In this sequence, it is clear that "nations" refers to some kind of ethnic grouping, not just to Gentile individuals.

What we have seen then is that in the plural *ethnē* can mean Gentile individuals who may not be part of a single people group, or it can mean (as it always does in the singular) a people group with ethnic identity. This means that we cannot yet be certain which meaning is intended in Matthew 28:19. We cannot yet answer whether the task of missions is merely reaching as many individuals as possible or reaching all the people groups of the world.

Nevertheless, the fact that in the New Testament the singular *ethnos* never refers to an individual but always to a people group should perhaps incline us toward the people-group meaning unless the context leads us to think otherwise. This will be all the more true when we consider the Old Testament context and the impact it had on the writings of John and Paul. But first we should examine the New Testament use of the crucial phrase *panta ta ethnē* ("all the nations").

The Use of *Panta ta Ethnē* in the New Testament

Our immediate concern is with the meaning of *panta ta ethnē* in Matthew 28:19: "Go and make disciples of all nations." Since this is such a crucial phrase in the understanding of missions, and since it is tossed about as a Greek phrase today even in nontechnical writings, it is important to make all the uses of it readily accessible for the non-Greek reader to consider. Therefore, the following discussion provides all the texts in which the combination of *pas* ("all") and *ethnos* ("nation/Gentile") occur in the New Testament, either in the singular ("every nation") or plural ("all nations/Gentiles"). The different forms of *pan, panta, pasin,* and *pantōn* are simply changes in the grammatical case of the same word to agree with the various forms of the noun *ethnos* (*ethnē, ethnesin*).

> Matthew 24:9—"You will be hated by *pantōn tōn ethnōn* for my name's sake."
> Matthew 24:14 (= Mark 13:10)—"This gospel of the kingdom will be proclaimed throughout the whole world as a testimony to *pasin tois ethnesin,* and then the end will come."
> Matthew 25:32—"Before him will be gathered *panta ta ethnē,* and he will separate people one from another as a shepherd separates the sheep from the goats." (This context seems to demand the meaning

"Gentile individuals," not people groups, because it says that Jesus will "separate people from one another as a shepherd separates the sheep from the goats." This is a reference to individuals who are being judged as the "cursed" and the "righteous" who enter hell or eternal life. Cf. verses 41, 46.)

Matthew 28:19—"Make disciples of *panta ta ethnē*."

Mark 11:17—"My house shall be called a house of prayer for *pasin tois ethnesin*." (This is a quote from Isaiah 56:7. The Hebrew phrase behind *pasin tois ethnesin* is *lekol ha'ammim*, which has to mean "all peoples" rather than "all people.")

Luke 12:29–30—"Do not seek what you are to eat and what you are to drink, nor be worried. For *panta ta ethnē* of the world seek after these things."

Luke 21:24—"They will fall by the edge of the sword and be led captive among *ta ethnē panta*." (This warning echoes the words of Ezekiel 32:9, where the corresponding Hebrew word is goyim, which means "nations" or "people groups." See also Deuteronomy 28:64.)

Luke 24:47—"Repentance and forgiveness of sins should be proclaimed in his name to *panta ta ethnē*, beginning from Jerusalem."

Acts 2:5—"Now there were dwelling in Jerusalem Jews, devout men from *pantos ethnous* under heaven." (This must clearly refer to people groups rather than individuals. The reference is to various ethnic or national groups from which the diaspora Jews had come to Jerusalem.)

Acts 10:35—"In *panti ethnei* anyone who fears him and does what is right is acceptable to him." (Again, this must be a reference to people groups or nations, not to individual Gentiles, because the individuals who fear God are "in every nation.")

Acts 14:16—"In past generations he allowed *panta ta ethnē* to walk in their own ways."

Acts 15:16–17—"I will rebuild the tent of David that has fallen . . . that the remnant of mankind may seek the Lord, and *panta ta ethnē* upon whom is called my name upon them." (I render this verse with this awkwardly literal translation simply to highlight the fact that this is a quotation from Amos 9:12, which in Greek follows the Hebrew with similar literalness. Again, the Hebrew word behind *ethnē* is goyim, which means "nations" or "people groups.")

Acts 17:26—"And he made from one man *pan ethnos* of mankind to live on all the face of the earth." (As with Acts 2:5 and 10:35, this is a reference to every people group rather than to individuals because it says that every nation is made up "of mankind." It would not make sense to say that every individual Gentile was made up "of mankind." Nor does the suggestion of some that it means "the whole human race" fit the meaning of *ethnos* or the context.)[13]

Romans 1:5—"We have received grace and apostleship to bring about the obedience of faith for the sake of his name among *pasin tois ethnesin.*"

Galatians 3:8—"And the Scripture, foreseeing that God would justify the Gentiles by faith, preached the gospel beforehand to Abraham, saying, 'In you shall *panta ta ethnē* be blessed.'" (This is a quote from Genesis 12:3 that clearly refers to people groups. The corresponding Hebrew phrase, *kol mishpehot*, means "all families." See discussion below on Genesis 12:3 for more concerning Paul's translation.)

2 Timothy 4:17—"But the Lord stood by me and strengthened me, so that through me the message might be fully proclaimed and *panta ta ethnē* might hear it."

Revelation 12:5—"She gave birth to a male child, one who is to rule *panta ta ethnē* with a rod of iron." (Cf. Psalm 2:9. The Old Testament allusion makes it likely that the Old Testament reference to nations in Psalm 2:8 is intended here as well.)

Revelation 15:4—"Who shall not fear, O Lord, and glorify your name? For you alone are holy. *Panta ta ethnē* will come and worship you, for your righteous acts have been revealed." (Cf. Psalm 86:9; 85:9 LXX.[14] Again, the Old Testament allusion suggests a corporate understanding of nations coming to worship the Lord.)

Out of these eighteen uses of *panta ta ethnē* (or its variant), only the one in Matthew 25:32 seems to demand the meaning "Gentile individu-

---

13. Following Dibelius this is suggested by F. F. Bruce, *Commentary on the Book of Acts* (Grand Rapids: Eerdmans, 1954), 358. But Lenski is surely right that the very next clause in Acts 17:26 militates against such a translation: ". . . having determined allotted periods and boundaries of their dwelling place." This naturally refers, as John Stott also says, to various ethnic groups with "the epochs of their history and the limits of their territory." R. C. H. Lenski, *The Interpretation of the Acts of the Apostles* (Minneapolis: Augsburg, 1934), 729; John Stott, *The Spirit, The Church, and the World* (Downers Grove, Ill.: InterVarsity, 1990), 286. The point of the verse is to take the air out of the sails of ethnic pride in Athens. All the other *ethnē* have descended from the same "one" as the Greeks, and not only that, but whatever time and territory a people has, it is God's sovereign doing and nothing to boast in. "Both the history and the geography of each nation are ultimately under [God's] control" (Stott).

14. See note 38 in chapter 4.

als." (See the comments above on that verse.) Three others demand the people-group meaning on the basis of the context (Acts 2:5; 10:35; 17:26). Six others require the people-group meaning on the basis of the Old Testament connection (Mark 11:17; Luke 21:24; Acts 15:17; Gal. 3:8; Rev. 12:5; 15:4). The remaining eight uses (Matt. 24:9; 24:14; 28:19; Luke 12:30; 24:47; Acts 14:16; Rom. 1:5; 2 Tim. 4:17) could go either way.

What can we conclude so far concerning the meaning of *panta ta ethnē* in Matthew 28:19 and its wider missionary significance?

The singular use of *ethnos* in the New Testament always refers to a people group. The plural use of *ethnos* sometimes must be a people group and sometimes must refer to Gentile individuals but usually can go either way. The phrase *panta ta ethnē* must refer to Gentile individuals only once but must refer to people groups nine times. The remaining eight uses may refer to people groups. The combination of these results suggests that the meaning of *panta ta ethnē* leans heavily in the direction of "all the nations (people groups)." It cannot be said with certainty that this phrase always carries this meaning wherever it is used, but it is far more likely that it does in view of what we have seen so far.

This likelihood increases even more when we realize that the phrase *panta ta ethnē* occurs in the Greek Old Testament nearly one hundred times and virtually never carries the meaning "Gentile individuals" but always carries the meaning "all the nations" in the sense of people groups outside Israel.[15] That the New Testament vision for missions has this focus will appear even more probable when we examine the Old Testament background.

The Old Testament Hope

The Old Testament is replete with promises and expectations that God would one day be worshiped by people from all the nations of the world.

15. My survey was done searching for all case variants of *panta ta ethnē* in the plural. The following texts are references to Greek Old Testament (LXX) verse and chapter divisions, which occasionally do not correspond to the Hebrew and English versions: Gen. 18:18; 22:18; 26:4; Exod. 19:5; 23:22, 27; 33:16; Lev. 20:24, 26; Deut. 2:25; 4:6, 19, 27; 7:6, 7, 14; 10:15; 11:23; 14:2; 26:19; 28:1, 10, 37, 64; 29:23; 30:1, 3; Josh. 4:24; 23:3, 4, 17, 18; 1 Sam. 8:20; 1 Chron. 14:17; 18:11; 2 Chron. 7:20; 32:23; 33:9; Neh. 6:16; Esth. 3:8; Pss. 9:8; 46:2; 48:2; 58:6, 9; 71:11, 17; 81:8; 85:9; 112:4; 116:1; 117:10; Isa. 2:2; 14:12, 26; 25:7; 29:8; 34:2; 36:20; 40:15, 17; 43:9; 52:10; 56:7; 61:11; 66:18, 20; Jer. 3:17; 9:25; 25:9; 32:13, 15; 33:6; 35:11, 14; 43:2; 51:8; Ezek. 25:8; 38:16; 39:21, 23; Dan. 3:2, 7; 7:14; Joel 4:2, 11, 12; Amos 9:12; Obad. 15, 16; Hab. 2:5; Hag. 2:7; Zech. 7:14; 12:3, 9; 14:2, 16, 18, 19; Mal. 2:9; 3:12.

These promises form the explicit foundation of New Testament missionary vision.

All the Families of the Earth Will Be Blessed

Foundational for the missionary vision of the New Testament was the promise that God made to Abram in Genesis 12:1–3:

> Now the LORD said to Abram, "Go from your country and your kindred and your father's house to the land that I will show you. And I will make of you a great nation and I will bless you and make your name great, so that you will be a blessing. I will bless those who bless you, and him who dishonors you I will curse, and in you all the families of the earth shall be blessed."

This promise for universal blessing to the "families" of the earth is essentially repeated in Genesis 18:18; 22:18; 26:4; 28:14.

In 12:3 and 28:14, the Hebrew phrase for "all the families" (*kol mishpehot*) is rendered in the Greek Old Testament by *pasai hai phylai*. The word *phylai* means "tribes" in most contexts. But *mishpahah* can be and usually is smaller than a tribe.[16] For example, when Achan sinned, Israel is examined in decreasing order of size: first by tribe, then by *mishpahah* ("family"), then by household (Josh. 7:14).

So the blessing of Abraham is intended by God to reach to fairly small groupings of people. We need not define these groups with precision in order to feel the impact of this promise. The other three repetitions of this Abrahamic promise in Genesis use the phrase "all the nations" (Hebrew: *kol goye*), which the Septuagint translates with the familiar *panta ta ethnē* in each case (18:18; 22:18; 26:4). This again strongly suggests that the term *panta ta ethnē* in missionary contexts refers to people groups rather than to Gentile individuals.

The New Testament explicitly cites this particular Abrahamic promise twice. In Acts 3:25, Peter says to the Jewish crowd, "You are the sons of the prophets and of the covenant that God made with your fathers, saying to Abraham, 'And in your offspring shall all the families of the earth be blessed.'" The Greek phrase in Acts 3:25 for "all the families" is *pasai hai patriai*. This is an independent translation of Genesis 12:3, differing from both the Greek Old Testament (*pasai hai phylai*) and the way Paul

---

16. Karl Ludwig Schmidt argues that the *mishpehot* are "smaller clan-like societies within the main group or nation." Gerhard Kittel, ed., Geoffrey Bromiley, trans. *Theological Dictionary of the New Testament*, vol. 2 (Grand Rapids: Eerdmans, 1964), 365.

translates it in Galatians 3:8 (*panta ta ethnē*).[17] But by choosing another word that refers to people groups (*patriai*), the writer confirms that the promise was understood in the early church in terms of people groups, not in terms of Gentile individuals. *Patria* can be a subgroup of a tribe or more generally a clan or tribe.

The other New Testament quotation of the Abrahamic promise is in Galatians 3:6–8:

> Just as Abraham "believed God, and it was counted to him as righteousness?"
> . . . Know then that it is those of faith who are the sons of Abraham. And the Scripture, foreseeing that God would justify the Gentiles [*ta ethnē*] by faith, preached the gospel beforehand to Abraham, saying, "In you shall all the nations [*panta ta ethnē*] be blessed."

Interestingly, all English versions translate the word *ethnē* differently in its two uses in verse 8: in the first case, "Gentiles," and in the next, "nations."

One could try to argue that Paul's use of the promise to support the justification of individual Gentiles means that he did not see people groups in the Abrahamic promise, since it is individuals who are justified. But that is not a necessary conclusion. More likely is the possibility that Paul recognized the Old Testament meaning of *panta ta ethnē* in Genesis 18:18 (the closest Old Testament parallel) and drew the inference that individual Gentiles are necessarily implied. So the English versions are correct to preserve the two meanings in the two uses of *ethnē* in Galatians 3:8.

Paul's use of the promise warns us not to get so swept up into people-group thinking that we forget that the "blessing of Abraham" is indeed experienced by *individuals*, or not at all.

What we may conclude from the wording of Genesis 12:3 and its use in the New Testament is that God's purpose for the world is that the blessing of Abraham, namely, the salvation achieved through Jesus Christ, the seed of Abraham, would reach to all the ethnic people groups of the world. This would happen as people in each group put their faith in Christ and thus become "sons of Abraham" (Gal. 3:7) and heirs of the promise (Gal. 3:29). This event of individual salvation as persons trust Christ will happen

---

17. Paul may have chosen to use *panta ta ethnē* because this is how the Greek Old Testament translates the promise of God to Abraham in three of its five occurrences (Gen. 18:18; 22:18; 26:4; but not 12:3 and 28:14, which translate it *pasai hai phylai*). But Paul's words do not correspond exactly with any of these five texts, so he may well have been giving his own composite translation from the Hebrew.

among "all the nations." The size and makeup of the nations or people groups referred to in this promise and its New Testament usage are not precise. But the words point to fairly small groupings, since the reference to "all the nations" in Genesis 18:18 (= Gal. 3:8) is an echo of "all the families" in Genesis 12:3.

The smallness of the people groups envisioned in the Old Testament hope is brought out again by the phrase "families of the nations" in Psalms 22:27 (21:28 LXX) and 96:7 (95:7 LXX).

> All the ends of the earth shall remember and turn to the LORD, and *all the families of the nations* shall worship before you. For kingship belongs to the LORD, and he rules over the nations.
>
> Psalm 22:27–28

The phrase "all the families of the nations" is *pasai hai patriai tōn ethnōn*. So the hope in view is not just that "all the nations" (*panta ta ethnē*) would respond to the truth and worship God but that even smaller groupings, "all the families of the nations," would. "Family" does not carry our modern meaning of nuclear family but something more like clan.[18] This will be confirmed when we look at the hope expressed in Revelation 5:9, where worshipers have been redeemed not only from every "nation" (*ethnous*) but also from every "tribe" (*phylēs*).

The Hope of the Nations

One of the best ways to discern the scope of the Great Commission as Jesus gave it and the apostles pursued it is to immerse ourselves in the atmosphere of hope that they felt in reading their Bible, the Old Testament. One overwhelming aspect of this hope is its expectation that the truth of God would reach to all the people groups of the world and that these groups would come and worship the true God. This hope was expressed in people-group terminology again and again (peoples, nations, tribes, families, etc.). Here is a sampling from the Psalms and Isaiah of the kind of hope that set the stage for Jesus' Great Commis-

---

18. The evidence for this would be, for example, the repeated use in the Greek Old Testament of the phrase "houses (or households) of the families," which shows that the "family" (*patria*) is a larger grouping than a household. Cf. Exod. 6:17; Num. 1:44; 3:24; 18:1; 25:14–15; Josh. 22:14; 1 Chron. 23:11; 24:6; 2 Chron. 35:5; Ezra 2:59. See below on "How Small Is a Family?"

sion. The texts fall into four categories of exhortation, promise, prayers, and plans.

"DECLARE HIS GLORY AMONG THE NATIONS!"

The first category of texts expressing the hope of the nations is a collection of *exhortations* that God's glory be declared and praised among the nations and by the nations.

> Sing praises to the LORD, who sits enthroned in Zion! Tell among the *peoples* his deeds!
>
> Psalm 9:11

> Clap your hands, *all peoples*! Shout to God with loud songs of joy!
>
> Psalm 47:1

> Bless our God, O *peoples*; let the sound of his praise be heard.
>
> Psalm 66:8

> Declare his glory among the nations, his marvelous works among *all the peoples*!
>
> Psalm 96:3

> Ascribe to the LORD, O *families of the peoples*, ascribe to the LORD glory and strength! . . . Say among the nations, "The LORD reigns! Yes, the world is established; it shall never be moved; he will judge the *peoples* with equity."
>
> Psalm 96:7, 10

> Oh give thanks to the LORD; call upon his name; make known his deeds among the *peoples*!
>
> Psalm 105:1

> Praise the LORD, *all nations*! Extol him, *all peoples*!
>
> Psalm 117:1

> And you will say in that day: "Give thanks to the LORD, call upon his name, make known his deeds among the *peoples*, proclaim that his name is exalted.
>
> Isaiah 12:4

Draw near, O *nations*, to hear, and give attention, O *peoples*! Let the earth hear, and all that fills it; the world, and all that comes from it.

Isaiah 34:1

"Nations Shall Come to Your Light!"

The second category of texts expressing the hope of the nations is a collection of *promises* that the nations will one day worship the true God.

I will make the *nations* your heritage.

Psalm 2:8; cf. 111:6

I will cause your name to be remembered in all generations; therefore *nations* will praise you[19] forever and ever.

Psalm 45:17

The *princes of the peoples* gather as the people of the God of Abraham. For the shields of the earth belong to God; he is highly exalted!

Psalm 47:9

All the nations you have made shall come and worship before you, O Lord, and shall glorify your name.

Psalm 86:9

The Lord records as he registers the *peoples*, "This one was born there."

Psalm 87:6

Nations will fear the name of the Lord, and all the kings of the earth will fear your glory.

Psalm 102:15

Peoples gather together, and kingdoms, to worship the Lord.

Psalm 102:22

He has shown his people the power of his works, in giving them the inheritance of the *nations*.

Psalm 111:6

---

19. This is a psalm to the king and refers in its final application to Christ the Messiah, as is shown by the use made of verse 7 in Hebrews 1:9.

In that day the root of Jesse, who shall stand as a signal for the peoples—of him shall the *nations* inquire, and his resting place shall be glorious.

Isaiah 11:10

On this mountain the LORD of hosts will make for *all peoples* a feast of rich foods, a feast of well-aged wine, of rich food full of marrow, of aged wine well refined. And he will swallow up on this mountain the covering that is cast over all peoples, the veil that is spread over all nations.

Isaiah 25:6–7

[The LORD] says: "It is too light a thing that you should be my servant to raise up the tribes of Jacob and to bring back the preserved of Israel; I will make you as a light for the *nations*, that my salvation may reach to the end of the earth."

Isaiah 49:6

My righteousness draws near, my salvation has gone out, and my arms will judge the *peoples*; the coastlands hope for me, and for my arm they wait.

Isaiah 51:5

The LORD has bared his holy arm before the eyes of all the *nations*, and all the ends of the earth shall see the salvation of our God.

Isaiah 52:10

So shall [my Servant] sprinkle many *nations*; kings shall shut their mouths because of him; for that which has not been told them they see, and that which they have not heard they understand.

Isaiah 52:15

Behold, you shall call a *nation* that you do not know, and a *nation* that did not know you shall run to you, because of the LORD your God, and of the Holy One of Israel, for he has glorified you.

Isaiah 55:5

These I will bring to my holy mountain, and make them joyful in my house of prayer; their burnt offerings and their sacrifices will be accepted on my altar; for my house shall be called a house of prayer for all *peoples*.

Isaiah 56:7

And *nations* shall come to your light, and kings to the brightness of your rising.

Isaiah 60:3

For I know their works and their thoughts, and the time is coming to gather *all nations and tongues*. And they shall come and shall see my glory.

Isaiah 66:18

The time is coming to gather *all nations and tongues*. And they shall come and shall see my glory, and I will set a sign among them. And from them I will send survivors to the nations, to Tarshish, Pul, and Lud, who draw the bow, to Tubal and Javan, to the coastlands afar off, that have not heard my fame or seen my glory. And they shall declare my glory among the nations.

Isaiah 66:18–19

"LET ALL THE PEOPLES PRAISE YOU, O GOD!"

The third category of texts that express the hope of the nations does so with confident *prayers* that God be praised among the nations.

May God be gracious to us and bless us and make his face to shine upon us, that your way may be known on earth, your saving power among *all nations*. Let *the peoples* praise you, O God; let all the peoples praise you! Let the nations be glad and sing for joy, for you judge the peoples with equity and guide the nations upon earth. Let the peoples praise you, O God; let *all the peoples* praise you!

Psalm 67:1–5

May all kings fall down before him, *all nations* serve him!

Psalm 72:11

May his name endure forever, his fame continue as long as the sun! May people be blessed in him, *all nations* call him blessed!

Psalm 72:17

"I WILL SING PRAISES TO YOU AMONG THE NATIONS"

The fourth category of texts that express the hope of the nations announces the *plans* of the psalmist to do his part in making God's greatness known among the nations.

For this I will praise you, O LORD, among the *nations*, and sing to your name.

Psalm 18:49

I will give thanks to you, O Lord, among the *peoples*; I will sing praises to you among the *nations*.

Psalm 57:9

I will give thanks to you, O LORD, among the *peoples*; I will sing praises to you among the *nations*.

Psalm 108:3

Blessed to Be a Blessing

What these texts demonstrate is that the blessing of forgiveness and salvation that God had granted to Israel was meant eventually to reach all the people groups of the world. Israel was blessed in order to be a blessing among the nations. This is expressed best in Psalm 67:1–2: "May God be gracious to us and bless us and make his face to shine upon us, [Why?] that your way may be known on earth, your saving power among *all nations*." Blessing came to Israel as a means of reaching the nations. This is the hope of the Old Testament: The blessings of salvation are for the nations.

The Missionary God versus the Reluctant Prophet

One of the most vivid Old Testament confirmations and illustrations of God's saving purpose for the nations is found in the Book of Jonah. The prophet was commissioned to preach to the pagan city of Nineveh. He tried to run away because he knew God would be gracious to the people and forgive them. The point of the book is not the fish. It's about missions and racism and ethnocentrism. The point is: Be merciful like God, not miserly like Jonah.

Nineveh did in fact repent at the begrudging preaching of Jonah. When God saw the repentance of Nineveh, "God relented of the disaster that he had said he would do to them, and he did not do it" (Jonah 3:10). This is what Jonah was afraid of.

> It displeased Jonah exceedingly, and he was angry. And he prayed to the LORD and said, "O LORD, is not this what I said when I was yet in my country? That is why I made haste to flee to Tarshish; for I knew that you are a gracious God and merciful, slow to anger and abounding in steadfast love, and relenting from disaster. Therefore now, O LORD, please take my life from me, for it is better for me to die than to live."
>
> Jonah 4:1–3

Jonah is not the model missionary. His life is an example of how not to be. As he sulks on the outskirts of town, God appoints a plant to grow up over Jonah to give him shade. When the plant withers, Jonah pities the plant! So God comes to him with these words: "You pity the plant, for which you did not labor, nor did you make it grow, which came into being in a night and perished in a night. And should not I pity Nineveh, that great city, in which there are more than 120,000 persons who do not know their right hand from their left, and also much cattle?" (Jonah 4:10–11).

The missionary implications of Jonah are not merely that God is more ready to be merciful to the nations than his people are but also that Jesus identifies himself as "something greater than Jonah" (Matt. 12:39–41). He is greater not only because his resurrection is greater than surviving a fish's belly but also because he stands in harmony with the mercy of God and extends it now to *all the nations*. Thomas Carlisle's poem "You Jonah" closes with these lines:

> And Jonah stalked
> to his shaded seat
> and waited for God
> to come around
> to his way of thinking.
> And God is still waiting for a host of Jonahs
> in their comfortable houses
> to come around
> to his way of loving.[20]

To see what power this Old Testament hope had on the missionary vision of the New Testament, we turn now to the apostle Paul and his idea of the missionary task. The Old Testament hope is the explicit foundation of his life's work as a missionary.

Paul's Idea of the Missionary Task

We examined Paul's use of Genesis 12:3 (Gal. 3:8) earlier in this chapter. He saw the promise that in Abraham all the nations would be blessed, and he reasoned that Christ was the true offspring of Abraham and thus the heir of the promises (Gal. 3:16). Further, he reasoned that all who are united to Christ by faith also become sons of Abraham and heirs of the promise. "It is those of faith who are the sons of Abraham. . . . If you are Christ's, then you are Abraham's offspring, heirs according to promise" (Gal. 3:7, 29). This is how Paul saw Abraham's blessing coming to the

---

20. Quoted in Johannes Verkuyl, "The Biblical Foundation of the Worldwide Mission Mandate," in *Perspectives on the World Christian Movement*, 33.

nations. It came through Christ, who was the seed of Abraham. By faith people are united to Christ and inherit the blessing of Abraham. "Christ redeemed us from the curse of the law . . . that in Christ Jesus the blessing of Abraham might come to the Gentiles" (Gal. 3:13–14). So the promise of Genesis 12:3 comes true as the missionaries of the Christian church extend the message of the gospel to all the families of the earth.

How Would Abraham Be the Father of Many Nations?

But Paul saw another connection between the promise to Abraham and Paul's own calling to reach the nations. He read in Genesis 17:4–5 that God promised to make Abraham the father of a multitude of nations. "Behold, my covenant is with you, and you shall be *the father of a multitude of nations*. No longer shall your name be called Abram, but your name shall be Abraham, for I have made you *the father of a multitude of nations*."

We saw earlier that "nations" here refers to people groups, not Gentile individuals. But how was this promise supposed to come true? How could a Jew become the father of a multitude of nations? It would not be enough to say that Abraham became the great-grandfather of the twelve tribes of Israel plus the father of Ishmael and his descendants plus the grandfather of Esau and the Edomites. Fourteen does not make a multitude.

Paul's answer to this was that all who believe in Christ become the children of Abraham. In this way, Abraham becomes the father of a multitude of nations, because believers will be found in every nation as missionaries reach all the unreached people groups. Paul argues like this: In Romans 4:11, he points out that Abraham received circumcision as the sign of righteousness which he had by faith before he was circumcised. "The purpose was to make *him the father of all who believe* without being circumcised, so that righteousness would be counted to them as well." In other words, the decisive thing that happened to Abraham in his relation to God happened before he received the distinguishing mark of the Jewish people, circumcision. So true spiritual sonship to Abraham is to share his faith, not his Jewish distinctives.

The way Abraham becomes the father of many nations is by those nations coming to share his faith and being united to the same source of blessing that flows through the covenant God made with him. So Paul says in Romans 4:16–17, "That is why it depends on faith, in order that the promise may rest on grace and be guaranteed to all his offspring—not only to the adherent of the law [that is, Jews] but also to the one who shares the faith of Abraham [that is, the non-Jewish nations], who is the father of us all, as it is written, 'I have made you the father of many nations.'"

When Paul read that Abraham would be made "the father of many nations," he heard the Great Commission. These nations would come into their sonship and enjoy the blessing of Abraham only if missionaries reached them with the gospel of salvation by faith in Jesus Christ. It is not surprising then that Paul supports his own missionary calling with other Old Testament promises that predicted the reaching of the nations with God's light and salvation.

"I Have Set You to Be a Light to the Nations"

For example, in Acts 13:47, Paul's explanation of his ministry to the Gentile nations is rooted in the promise of Isaiah 49:6 that God would make his servant a light to the nations. As Paul preached in the synagogue of Antioch of Pisidia on his first missionary journey, the Jews "were filled with jealousy and began to contradict what was spoken by Paul, reviling him" (Acts 13:45). So Paul and Barnabas turned away from the synagogue and focused their ministry on the people from other people groups. To give an account of this decision, Paul cites Isaiah 49:6: "Since you thrust [the Word of God] aside and judge yourselves unworthy of eternal life, behold, we are turning to the Gentiles. For so the Lord has commanded us, saying, 'I have made you a light for the Gentiles [*ethnōn*, "nations"], that you may bring salvation to the ends of the earth'" (Acts 13:46–47).

It is difficult to know why the English versions do not preserve the Old Testament sense of Isaiah 49:6 and translate, "I have made you a light for the *nations*." The Hebrew word in Isaiah 49:6 is *goyim*, which means people groups, not Gentile individuals. Then Paul would be doing just what he apparently did in Galatians 3:8. He would be drawing a necessary inference about individual Gentiles from an Old Testament reference to nations. Thus, Paul's own missionary vision was guided by meditating not only on the promises to Abraham but also on the wider Old Testament hope that salvation would come to all the nations.

Paul's Passion for Unreached Peoples

This is remarkably confirmed in Romans 15. Here it becomes crystal clear that Paul saw his missionary calling as reaching more and more people groups, not just more and more Gentile individuals.

In Romans 15:8–9, Paul states the twofold purpose for Christ's coming. "For I tell you that Christ became a servant to the circumcised [that is, became incarnate as a Jew] to show God's truthfulness, in order [1] *to confirm the promises given to the patriarchs*, and in order [2] that *the Gentiles* [ta ethnē] *might glorify God for his mercy.*" The first purpose for Christ's coming was to prove that God is truthful and faithful in keeping, for example, the promises made to Abraham. The second purpose for Christ's coming is that the nations might glorify God for his mercy.

These two purposes overlap since clearly one of the promises made to the patriarchs was that the blessing of Abraham would come to "all the families of the earth." This is in perfect harmony with what we saw of the Old Testament hope. *Israel* is blessed that the *nations* might be blessed (Psalm 67). In the same way, Christ comes to Israel so that the nations might receive mercy and give God glory.

Saturated with the Hope of the Nations

To support this claim of God's purpose for the nations, Paul gathers four Old Testament quotations about the *ethnē*, all of which in their Old Testament context refer to nations, not just to Gentile individuals.

As it is written, "Therefore I will praise you among the *nations* [*ethnesin*] and sing to your name."

Romans 15:9 = Psalm 18:49,
author's translation

Rejoice, O *nations* [*ethnē*], with his people.
Romans 15:10 = Deuteronomy 32:43,
author's translation

Praise the Lord, all you *nations* [*panta ta ethnē*], and let all the peoples praise him.

Romans 15:11 = Psalm 117:1,
author's translation

The root of Jesse will come, even he who arises to rule the *nations* [*ethnōn*]; in him will the *nations* [*ethnē*] hope.

Romans 15:12 = Isaiah 11:10,
author's translation

What is so remarkable about this series of texts that Paul strings together is that Paul either had them memorized or took the trouble to find them in the Old Testament—without a concordance! Either way it shows that he was intent on seeing his missionary calling in the light of the Old Testament hope that all the nations would be reached with the gospel. The people-group focus of these texts is unmistakable from the Old Testament context.

From Jerusalem to Illyricum: The Work Is Finished!

What we see next, therefore, is how the people-group focus governed Paul's missionary practice. Was his aim to win as many Gentile individuals as possible or to reach as many people groups or nations as possible? Romans 15:18–21 gives a startling answer:

> For I will not venture to speak of anything except what Christ has accomplished through me to bring the Gentiles [ethnōn, "nations"], to obedience—by word and deed, by the power of signs and wonders, by the power of the Spirit of God—so that *from Jerusalem and all the way around to Illyricum I have fulfilled the ministry of the gospel of Christ*; and thus I make it my ambition to preach the gospel, *not where Christ has already been named*, lest I build on someone else's foundation, but as it is written, "Those who have never been told of him will see, and those who have never heard will understand."

Literally, Paul says, "From Jerusalem and around to Illyricum I have *fulfilled* [*peplērōkenai*] the gospel." What can that possibly mean? We know that there were thousands of souls yet to be saved in that region because this was Paul's and Peter's assumption when they wrote letters to the churches in those regions. It is a huge area that stretches from southern Palestine to northern Italy. Yet Paul says he has *fulfilled the gospel* in that whole region, even though his work of evangelism is only ten or fifteen years old.

We know that Paul believed work was still needed there because he left Timothy in Ephesus (1 Tim. 1:3) and Titus in Crete (Titus 1:5) to do the work. Nevertheless, he says he *has fulfilled the gospel* in the whole region. In fact, he goes so far as to say in Romans 15:23–24, "But now, since *I no longer have any room for work in these regions* . . . I hope to see you in passing as I go to Spain." This is astonishing! How can he say not only that he has fulfilled the gospel in that region but also that he has no more room for work? He is finished and going to Spain (Rom. 15:24). What does this mean?

It means that Paul's conception of the *missionary task* is not merely the winning of more and more people to Christ (which he could have done very efficiently in these familiar regions) but the reaching of more and more peoples or nations. His focus was not primarily on new geographic areas. Rather, he was gripped by the vision of unreached peoples. Romans 15:9–12 (just quoted) shows that his mind was saturated with Old Testament texts that relate to the hope of the nations.

Driven by a Prophetic Vision of Hope

What was really driving Paul when he said in Romans 15:20 that his aim is to preach not where Christ has been named "*lest I build on someone else's foundation*"? One could uncharitably assume a kind of ego that likes to be able to take all the credit for a church-planting effort. But this is not the Paul we know from Scripture, nor is it what the context suggests.

The next verse (Rom. 15:21) shows what drives Paul. The Old Testament conception of God's worldwide purpose gives Paul his vision as a pioneer missionary. He is driven by a prophetic vision of hope. He quotes Isaiah 52:15: "Those who have never been told of him will see, and those who have never heard will understand."

In the Old Testament, these words are immediately preceded by, "So shall he sprinkle *many nations* [*ethnē polla*]; kings shall shut their mouths because of him" (Isa. 52:15). No doubt Paul reflected on the fact that his commission from the Lord came to him in similar words. In a close parallel to Isaiah 52:15, the risen Lord Jesus had said to Paul that he was "to carry [Christ's] name before the *Gentiles* [*ethnōn*, "nations"] and *kings*" (Acts 9:15).

In other words, Paul was driven by a personal commission from the Lord that was richly buttressed and filled out with a prophetic vision of hope. He was gripped by the Old Testament purpose of God to bless all the nations of the earth (Gal. 3:8), to be praised by all the peoples (Rom. 15:11), to send salvation to the ends of the earth (Acts 13:47), to make Abraham the father of many nations (Rom. 4:17), and to be understood in every group where he is not known (Rom. 15:21).[21]

---

21. To these reflections could be added Paul's crucial words in Romans 10:14–15 concerning the necessity of people being sent so that they can preach so that people can hear so that they can believe so that they can call on the Lord so that they can be saved. See the discussion of these verses in chapter 4.

So Paul's conception of his specifically missionary task was that he must press on beyond the regions and peoples where Christ is now preached to places such as Spain and to peoples "who have never been told of him." God's missionary "grace" for Paul was that he be a foundation-layer in more and more places and peoples. His aim was not to reach as many Gentile individuals as he could but to reach as many unreached peoples as he could. This was Paul's specific missionary vision.

Obedience for the Sake of His Name among All the Nations

Against this backdrop, the missionary statements at the beginning and end of the Book of Romans take on a distinct people-group coloring. Earlier we said that *panta ta ethnē* in these two verses is ambiguous. But from what we have seen now, from the phrase's use in the Old Testament and from Paul's dependence on that Old Testament hope, it is likely that Paul has in view nations or people groups and not just Gentile individuals.

> Through [Christ] we have received grace and apostleship to bring about the obedience of faith for the sake of his name among *all the nations* [*pasin tois ethnesin*].
>
> Romans 1:5

> [The mystery] has now been disclosed and through the prophetic writings has been made known to *all nations* [*panta ta ethnē*], according to the command of the eternal God, to bring about the obedience of faith.
>
> Romans 16:26

Paul saw his special missionary "grace and apostleship" as one of God's appointed means of fulfilling the "command" that the obedience of faith be pursued among all the nations. To this he gave his life.

John's Vision of the Missionary Task

The vision of the missionary task in the writings of the apostle John confirms that Paul's grasp of the Old Testament hope of reaching all the peoples was not unique among the apostles. What emerges from Revelation and the Gospel of John is a vision that assumes the central missionary task of reaching people groups, not just Gentile individuals.

The decisive text is Revelation 5:9–10. John is given a glimpse of the climax of redemption as redeemed people worship at the throne of God. The composition of that assembly is crucial.

> [The four living creatures and the twenty-four elders] sang a new song, saying, "Worthy are you to take the scroll and to open its seals, for you were slain, and by your blood you ransomed people for God *from every tribe and language and people and nation*, and you have made them a kingdom and priests to our God, and they shall reign on the earth."

The missionary vision behind this scene is that the task of the church is to gather the ransomed from all peoples, languages, tribes, and nations.[22] All peoples must be reached because God has appointed people to believe the gospel whom he has ransomed through the death of his Son. The design of the atonement prescribes the design of mission strategy. And the design of the atonement (Christ's ransom, verse 9) is *universal* in the sense that it extends to all peoples and *definite* in that it effectually ransoms some from each of those peoples. Therefore, the missionary task is to gather the ransomed from all the peoples through preaching the gospel.

Gathering the Scattered Children

This understanding of John's vision of missions is powerfully confirmed from his Gospel. In John 11:50–52, Caiaphas, the high priest, admonishes the irate Jewish council to get Jesus out of the way because "it is better for you that one man should die for the people, not that the whole nation should perish." Then John comments on this word from Caiaphas. His words are crucial for understanding John's missionary vision. John says:

> [Caiaphas] did not say this of his own accord, but being high priest that year he prophesied that Jesus would die for the nation, and not for the nation only, but also *to gather into one the children of God who are scattered abroad.*

This ties in remarkably well with John's conception of missions in Revelation 5:9. There it says that Christ's death ransomed men "from every

---

22. One cannot help but sense that John means for us to see a great reversal of the idolatry so prevalent on the earth, expressed, for example, in Daniel 3:7. Nebuchadnezzar had erected an idol and called everyone to worship it. The words used to describe the extent of that worship are almost identical to the words John uses in Revelation 5:9 to describe the extent of the true worship of God: "All the peoples, nations, and languages fell down and worshiped the golden image that King Nebuchadnezzar had set up."

tribe and language and people and nation." Here in John 11:52 it says that Christ's death gathers the children of God who are scattered among all those nations. In other words, both texts picture the missionary task as gathering in those who are ransomed by Christ. John calls them "the children of God."

Therefore, "scattered" (in John 11:52) is to be taken in its fullest sense: The "children of God" will be found as widely scattered as there are *peoples* of the earth. The missionary task is to reach them in every tribe, language, people, and nation. The way they are to be reached is by the preaching of missionaries. This is what Jesus implies when he says in John 17:20, "I do not ask for these only, but also for those who will believe in me through their word." This parallels John 11:52, which says that Jesus did not die for the nation only but to gather into one the children of God who are scattered abroad. The saving power of his death will extend to people in all the nations of the world, but it will do so only through the word of those whom he sends.

I Must Bring the Other Sheep Also!

The same conception also lies behind the missionary text in John 10:16. Jesus says, "I have other sheep that are not of this fold. I must bring them also, and they will listen to my voice." "This fold" refers to the people of Israel. The "other sheep" refers to the "children of God" who are scattered abroad (John 11:52). These are the "ransomed from every tribe" in Revelation 5:9. Therefore, the words "I *must* bring them also" are a very strong affirmation that the Lord *will* see his missionary purpose completed. He will gather his "sheep" or "the children of God" or the "ransomed" from all the peoples of the earth. As he says in Matthew 16:18, he will build his church.

Thus, the Gospel of John lends tremendous force to the missionary purpose and missionary certainty implied in Revelation 5:9. Jesus has *ransomed* persons in all the peoples of the world. He *died* to gather these "children of God" who are scattered among all the peoples. Therefore, he *must* bring all these wandering sheep into his fold! And they will be brought in through the Word preached by his messengers.

Again and Again: Nations, Tribes, Peoples, and Languages

Four other passages from Revelation confirm that John understands the task of missions as reaching all the people groups of the world so that the redeemed can be gathered in.

After this I looked, and behold, a great multitude that no one could number, from every nation, from *all tribes and peoples and languages*, standing before the throne and before the Lamb, clothed in white robes, with palm branches in their hands, and crying out with a loud voice, "Salvation belongs to our God who sits on the throne, and to the Lamb!"

7:9–10

Unless we restrict this multitude to the converts of the great tribulation and say that God's missionary purpose at that time will be different from what it is now, the implication of God's worldwide purpose is clear: He aims to be worshiped by converts from all the nations, tribes, peoples, and languages.

Then I saw another angel flying directly overhead, with an *eternal gospel to proclaim to those who dwell on earth, to every nation* [*pan ethnos*] *and tribe and language and people.* And he said with a loud voice, "Fear God and give him glory, because the hour of his judgment has come, and worship him who made heaven and earth, the sea and the springs of water."

14:6–7

Again the intention is that the gospel be proclaimed not just to more and more individuals but to "every nation, tribe, language, and people."

Who will not fear, O Lord, and glorify your name? For you alone are holy. *All nations* [*panta ta ethnē*] will come and worship you, for your righteous acts have been revealed.

15:4

In view of the Old Testament allusion here to Psalm 86:9,[23] and in view of the context of Revelation with its repeated use of *ethnos* in reference to "nations" (at least ten times) and not persons, *panta ta ethnē* in 15:4 no doubt refers to people groups and not merely to Gentile individuals. Therefore, what John foresees as the goal of missions is a worshiping multitude of saints from all the peoples of the world.

And I heard a loud voice from the throne saying, "Behold, the dwelling of God is with man. He will dwell with them, and they will be his peoples [*laoi*], and God himself will be with them as their God."

21:3

23. Psalm 85:9 LXX. See a discussion of this text earlier in this chapter.

This is a surprising and remarkable glimpse of the new heavens and the new earth. It pictures *peoples*, not just people, in the age to come. It seems that *laoi* ("peoples") and not *laos* ("people") is the genuine, original reading.[24] Therefore, John (recording the angelic voice) seems to make explicit (in distinction from Leviticus 26:12, *laos*) that the final goal of God in redemption is not to obliterate the distinctions of the peoples but to gather them all into one diverse but unified assembly of peoples.

We may conclude from this inquiry into John's writings that his conception of the unique task of missions is to reach more and more people groups until there are converts from "every tribe and language and people and nation." It is a task that he is utterly certain will be accomplished, for he sees it as already complete in the Lord's vision of the age to come.

Did Paul and John Get This Focus on Peoples from Jesus?

Was this focus on peoples the intention of Jesus as he gave his apostles their final commission? Paul's conception of his own missionary task, which he received from the risen Lord, would certainly suggest that this is what the Lord commanded, not only to him but to all the apostles as the special missionary task of the church.

The Great Commission: It Was Written!

But there is also evidence of this intention in the context of Luke's record of the Lord's words in Luke 24:45–47:

> Then he opened their minds to understand the Scriptures, and said to them, "Thus it is written, that the Christ should suffer and on the third day rise from the dead, and that repentance and forgiveness of sins should be proclaimed in his name to all nations [*panta ta ethnē*], beginning from Jerusalem."

The context here is crucial. First, Jesus "opens their minds to understand the Scriptures." Then he says, "Thus it is written" (in the Old Testament), followed (in the original Greek) by three coordinate infinitive clauses that make explicit what is written in the Old Testament: first, that the Christ is to suffer; second, that he is to rise on the third day; and third, that repentance and forgiveness of sins are to be preached in his name to "all nations."

24. The United Bible Societies *Greek New Testament* (4th ed.) and the Nestle-Aland Greek New Testament (27th ed.) chose *laoi* as original. The NRSV reads "peoples," as do the commentaries by Heinrich Kraft, Leon Morris, Robert Mounce, and G. K. Beale.

So Jesus is saying that his commission to take the message of repentance and forgiveness to all nations "is written" in the Old Testament "Scriptures." This is one of the things he opened their minds to understand. But what is the Old Testament conception of the worldwide purpose of God (which we saw above)? It is just what Paul saw: a purpose to bless all the families of the earth and win a worshiping people from "all nations."[25]

Therefore, we have strong evidence that the *panta ta ethnē* in Luke 24:47 was understood by Jesus not merely as Gentile individuals but also as an array of world peoples who must hear the message of repentance for the forgiveness of sin.

Luke's other account of Jesus' commission in Acts 1:8 points in the same direction. Jesus says to his apostles just before his ascension, "You will receive power when the Holy Spirit has come upon you, and you will be my witnesses in Jerusalem and in all Judea and Samaria, and to the end of the earth." This commission suggests that getting to all the unreached areas (if not explicitly people groups) is the special task of missions. There is a pressure to keep moving, not just to unconverted individuals nearby but also to places beyond, even to the end of the world. Not only that, but the phrase "end of the earth" is sometimes in the Old Testament closely associated with all the peoples of the earth. For example, Psalm 22:27: "All the ends of the earth shall remember and turn to the LORD, and all the families of the nations shall worship before you."

This parallel shows that "end of the earth" sometimes carried the association of distant peoples.[26] The apostles would probably not have heard the commission of Acts 1:8 as significantly different from the commission of Luke 24:47.

A House of Prayer for All Nations

Another pointer to the way Jesus thought about the worldwide missionary purposes of God comes from Mark 11:17. When Jesus cleanses the temple, he quotes Isaiah 56:7: "Is it not written, 'My house shall be called a house of prayer for all the nations [*pasin tois ethnesin*]'"?

25. From all the uses of *panta ta ethnē* in the Old Testament that Jesus may be alluding to, at least these relate to the missionary vision of the people of God: Gen. 18:18; 22:18; 26:4; Pss. 48:2; 71:11, 17; 81:8; 85:9; 116:1; Isa. 2:2; 25:7; 52:10; 56:7; 61:11; 66:18–20 (all references are to the LXX verse and chapter divisions).

26. Similar associations are found in Pss. 2:8; 67:5–7; 98:2–3; Isa. 52:10; Jer. 16:19; Zech. 9:10. But four different Greek expressions are used in these texts, only one of which (Jer. 16:19) is the exact wording of the phrase in Acts 1:8.

This is important because it shows Jesus reaching back to the Old Testament (just as he does in Luke 24:45–47) to interpret the worldwide purposes of God. He quotes Isaiah 56:7, which in Hebrew explicitly says, "My house shall be called a house of prayer for all peoples [*kol ha'ammim*]."

The people-group meaning is unmistakable. Isaiah's point is not that every individual Gentile will have a right to dwell in the presence of God but that there will be converts from "all peoples" who will enter the temple to worship. The fact that Jesus was familiar with this Old Testament hope, and that he based his worldwide expectations on references to it (Mark 11:17; Luke 24:45–47), suggests that we should interpret his Great Commission along this line—the very same line found in the writings of Paul and John.

Back to the Great Commission in Matthew

We come back now to our earlier effort to understand what Jesus meant in Matthew 28:19 when he said, "Go and make disciples of *panta ta ethnē*." This command has its corresponding promise of success in Matthew 24:14: "And this gospel of the kingdom will be proclaimed throughout the whole world as a testimony to all nations [*pasin tois ethnesin*], and then the end will come." The scope of the command and the scope of the promise hang on the meaning of *panta ta ethnē*.

My conclusion from what we have seen in this chapter is that one would have to go against the flow of the evidence to interpret the phrase *panta ta ethnē* as "all Gentile individuals" (or "all countries"). Rather, the focus of the command is the discipling of all the people groups of the world. This conclusion comes from the following summary of our biblical investigation:

1. In the New Testament, the singular use of *ethnos* never means Gentile individuals but always people group or nation.
2. The plural *ethnē* can mean either Gentile individuals or people groups. Sometimes the context demands that it mean one or the other, but in most instances it could carry either meaning.
3. The phrase *panta ta ethnē* occurs eighteen times in the New Testament. Only once must it mean Gentile individuals. Nine times it must mean people groups. The other eight times are ambiguous.
4. Virtually all of the nearly one hundred uses of *panta ta ethnē* in the Greek Old Testament refer to nations in distinction from the nation of Israel. See note 15.

5. The promise made to Abraham that in him "all the families of the earth" would be blessed and that he would be "the father of many nations" is taken up in the New Testament and gives the mission of the church a people-group focus because of this Old Testament emphasis.

6. The Old Testament missionary hope is expressed repeatedly as exhortations, promises, prayers, and plans for God's glory to be declared among the peoples and his salvation to be known by all the nations.

7. Paul understood his specifically missionary task in terms of this Old Testament hope and made the promises concerning peoples the foundation of his mission. He was devoted to reaching more and more people groups, not simply more and more individuals. He interpreted Christ's commission to him in these terms.

8. The apostle John envisioned the task of missions as the ingathering of "the children of God" or the "other sheep" out of "every tribe, tongue, people, and nation."

9. The Old Testament context of Jesus' missionary commission in Luke 24:46–47 shows that *panta ta ethnē* would most naturally mean all the peoples or nations.

10. Mark 11:17 shows that Jesus probably thinks in terms of people groups when he envisions the worldwide purpose of God.

Therefore, in all likelihood, Jesus did not send his apostles out with a general mission merely to win as many individuals as they could but rather to reach all the peoples of the world and thus to gather the "sons of God" who are scattered (John 11:52) and to call all the "ransomed from every tongue and tribe and people and nation" (Rev. 5:9), until redeemed persons from "all the peoples praise him" (Rom. 15:11).

Thus, when Jesus says in Mark 13:10 that "the gospel must first be proclaimed to all nations [*panta ta ethnē*]," there is no good reason for construing this to mean anything other than that the gospel must reach all the peoples of the world before the end comes. And when Jesus says, "Go and make disciples of all the nations [*panta ta ethnē*]," there is no good reason for construing this to mean anything other than that the missionary task of the church is to press on to all the unreached peoples until the Lord comes. Jesus commands it, and he assures us that it will be done before he comes again. He can make that promise because he himself is building his church from all the peoples. All authority in heaven and on earth has been given to him for this very thing (Matt. 28:18).

What Is a People Group?

We have tried to establish that the special missionary task of the New Testament is to reach all the people groups of the world. But we have not defined precisely what a people group is. What we have found, in fact, is that a precise definition is probably not possible to give on the basis of what God has chosen to reveal in the Bible. God probably did not intend for us to use a precise definition of people groups. That way we can never stop doing pioneer missionary work just because we conclude that all the groups with our definition have been reached.

For example, the point of Matthew 24:14 ("This gospel of the kingdom will be proclaimed throughout the whole world as a testimony to all nations, and then the end will come") is not that we should reach all the nations as we understand them and then stop. The point rather is that as long as the Lord has not returned, there must be more people groups to reach, and we should keep on reaching them.

There are biblical pointers to the nature of a people group. For example, Revelation 5:9 uses four terms to describe the people groups that will be represented at the throne of God: "By your blood you ransomed people for God from every tribe and language and people and nation." To these four the promise to Abraham adds another: "In you all the families[27] of the earth shall be blessed."

What Is a Language?

From this we can say, for example, that at least every *language group* ("language" in Rev. 5:9) should be sought out in the missionary task. But when does a dialect become so distinct that it is a different language? Questions such as this show why there is such difficulty and disagreement concerning the definition of a people group. For years, Ralph Winter put forward the number twenty-four thousand as the total number of people groups in the world. However, Patrick Johnstone observes in the 2001 edition of *Operation World*: "It was only during the 1990s that a reasonably complete listing of the world's peoples and languages was developed. For the first

---

27. The Greek Old Testament translates the Hebrew *mishpehot* (families or clans) with *phylai*, which is translated "tribes" in Revelation 5:9. So it may look as though this is not a different category of group. But in fact *phylai* is usually the translation of the Hebrew *shebet*, and the Hebrew *mishpehot* is usually translated *suggeneia*. Therefore, we should take seriously the difference between *mishpehot* and "tribe," especially since it is clearly a smaller unit according to Exodus 6:14f.

time in history we have a reasonably clear picture of the remaining task for us to disciple the nations."[28] He refers to a total of "the world's twelve thousand ethnolinguistic peoples."

In harmony with Johnstone, David Barrett, in his 2001 revision of the *World Christian Encyclopedia*, defines an ethnolinguistic people as follows: "A distinct homogenous ethnic or racial group within a single country, speaking its own language (one single mother tongue). A large people spread across two, three, four, or several countries is treated here as being two, three, four, or several distinct ethnolinguistic peoples."[29] The total number of ethnolinguistic peoples, as Barrett reckons it, is 12,600.[30]

There is good reason for the discrepancy between the Winter number and the Barrett/Johnstone number, and this reason highlights the difficulty of defining precisely the biblical meaning of "language" in Revelation 5:9. Winter illustrates the problem. He observes the difference between his 24,000 estimate and Barrett's earlier estimate of 8,990 peoples in the 1982 edition of the *World Christian Encyclopedia*. Then he says:

> It is clear in [Barrett's] table that his listing is almost identical to the number of languages which in his opinion need translations [of the Bible]. Now let's see where that leads us. Wycliffe Bible Translators, for example, go into South Sudan and count how many languages there are into which the Bible must be translated, and presented in printed form, in order to reach everybody in that area. Wycliffe's answer is 50 distinct translations. What does "50" mean in this instance? Does it mean 50 groups of people? Certainly not, if we are speaking of unreached peoples, because in many cases quite alien groups can read the same translation.
>
> How do I know this? Gospel Recordings also goes into South Sudan and counts the number of languages. Their personnel, however, come up with 130. Why? Because they put the gospel out in cassette form, and those cassettes represent a more embarrassingly precise language communication than does the written language. Different authors for different reasons, and different organizations for different purposes, are counting different things.[31]

28. Patrick Johnstone and Jason Mandryk, *Operation World: When We Pray God Works* (Carlisle, U.K.: Paternoster, 2001), 15.

29. David Barrett, George T. Kurian, and Todd M. Johnson, *World Christian Encyclopedia: A Comparative Survey of Churches and Religions—AD 30 to 2200*, vol. 2 (Oxford: Oxford University Press, 2001), 27–28.

30. Ibid., 16.

31. Ralph Winter, "Unreached Peoples: What, Where, and Why?" in *New Frontiers in Mission*, ed. Patrick Sookhedeo (Grand Rapids: Baker, 1987), 154.

So we can see that the reference to "languages" in Revelation 5:9 will not yield a precise definition of people groups. Neither will the other designations for people groups in that verse.

"People" (*laou*) and "nation" (*ethnous*), for example, are virtually synonymous and interchangeable in Genesis 25:23 ("Two nations are in your womb, and two peoples from within you shall be divided"). Sometimes Israel as a whole is called a "people," but in Acts 4:27 we read about the "peoples (*laois*) of Israel." Nevertheless, in Revelation 21:3, "peoples" (*laoi*)[32] refers to all the groups and individuals in the new earth. These facts prevent us from forming precise definitions of the people groups missionaries are to reach.

How Small Is a Family?

The fact that all the families of the earth will be blessed alerts us to the fact that the groupings God intends to reach with his gospel may be relatively small. The modern nuclear family is not in view but rather something like a clan. For example, Exodus 6:14–15 reveals the sort of grouping that is probably in mind:

> These are the heads of their fathers' houses: the sons of Reuben, the firstborn of Israel: Hanoch, Pallu, Hezron, and Carmi; these are the clans ["families" in RSV and NASB] of Reuben. The sons of Simeon: Jemuel, Jamin, Ohad, Jachin, Zohar, and Shaul, the son of a Canaanite woman; these are the *clans* ["families" in RSV and NASB] of Simeon.

Thus, "families" are smaller than the tribes of Israel (cf. also 1 Sam. 10:20–21). But they are not as small as households. The case of Achan in Joshua 7 shows this. After Achan had sinned and was to be found out, Joshua said that there would be a test of all the people to find out who the culprit was.

> In the morning therefore you shall be brought near *by your tribes*. And the tribe that the LORD takes by lot shall come near *by clans* [*mishpehot* ("families" in RSV and NASB)]. And the clan that the LORD takes shall come near *by households*. And the household that the LORD takes shall come near man by man.
>
> Joshua 7:14

---

32. See note 24.

What this shows is that the "family" of the Old Testament is better thought of as a "clan" (which is why the ESV has translated it this way). Its size is between the size of a tribe and a household.

Thus, the missionary task of the New Testament is to reach not only every people the size of Israel and every tribe the size of Reuben or Simeon or Judah but also all the clans, such as those of Hanoch, Pallu, Hezron, Carmi, and Achan.

The fact that *ethnē* is used so often in the Old Testament and the New Testament to designate the focus of missions should not limit our focus to the larger groupings. The word is flexible enough to provide an inclusive designation for groups of various sizes. In fact, Karl Ludwig Schmidt concludes his study of *ethnos* in the *Theological Dictionary of the New Testament* by contrasting it with *laos*, *glōssa*, and *phylē*: "*Ethnos* is the most general and therefore the weakest of these terms, having simply an ethnographical sense and denoting the natural cohesion of a people in general."[33] Thus, *panta ta ethnē* would be the most suitable term for including the others, which is in fact what we find in Revelation 22:2. Here *ethnē* refers to all the people in the new earth, including the "languages" and "peoples" and "tribes." So *panta ta ethnē* is probably the simplest way of giving a summary designation not only to the larger but also to the smaller groupings.

What Do "Reached" and "Unreached" Mean?

If the task of missions is to reach all the unreached people groups of the world,[34] we need to have some idea what "reached" means so that the

33. Kittel, *Theological Dictionary of the New Testament*, vol. 2, 369.
34. I will deal with two problems only briefly here in a note because they are not part of biblical revelation and do not seem to have much bearing on the missionary task: (1) One is whether all the peoples will be represented at the throne of God even without missions because infants in each of these peoples have died and presumably will go to heaven and come to maturity for the praise of God. (2) The other problem is whether all clans and tribes will in fact be represented at the throne of God since many clans and tribes no doubt died out before they were evangelized. With regard to the first problem, I do believe that infants who die will be in the kingdom. I base this on the principle that we are judged according to the knowledge available to us (Rom. 1:19–20), and infants have no knowledge available to them since the faculty of knowing is not developed. However, God does not ever mention this or relate it in any way to the missionary enterprise or to the promise that all the families of the earth will be blessed. Rather, it appears to be his purpose to be glorified through the conversion of people who recognize his beauty and greatness and come to love him above all gods. God would not be honored so greatly if the only way he got worshipers from all the nations was by the natural mortality of infants. With regard to the other problem, it may be true that some clans and tribes disappear from history

people called to the missionary task of the church will know which people groups to enter and which to leave. Paul must have had some idea of what "reached" means when he said in Romans 15:23, "I no longer have any room for work in these regions." He must have known what it means to complete the missionary task when he said in Romans 15:19, "From Jerusalem and all the way around to Illyricum I have fulfilled the ministry of the gospel of Christ." He knew his work was done in that region. That is why he headed for Spain. The 1982 Unreached Peoples Meeting, referred to earlier, defined an "unreached" people group as "a people group within which there is no indigenous community of believing Christians able to evangelize this people group."[35] Thus, a group is reached when mission efforts have established an indigenous church that has the strength and resources to evangelize the rest of the group.

Patrick Johnstone points out that in a strict sense "reaching has nothing to do with response. . . . Reaching is really an indication of the quality and extent of the effort to evangelize a people or region, not of discipling and church planting." But he admits that "because of popular usage, we have to extend [the meaning of] reachedness."[36]

Both the narrow and broader meaning are warranted from Scripture. For example, Mark 16:15 renders the missions mandate as, "[Jesus] said to them, 'Go into all the world and proclaim the gospel to the whole creation.'"[37] This does not say anything about response. If we had only this word, the missions mandate would be fulfilled if the message were universally proclaimed. Similarly, Matthew 24:14 says, "And this gospel of the kingdom will be proclaimed throughout the whole world as a testimony to all nations, and then the end will come." Again, there is no mention of

---

with none of their members being saved. The Bible does not reflect on this issue. We would be speculating beyond the warrant of Scripture if we said that there had to be another way of salvation for such tribes besides the way of hearing and believing the gospel of Jesus. (See the support for this in chapter 4.) Rather, we would do well to assume, in the absence of specific revelation, that the meaning of the promise and the command concerning the nations is that "all the nations" refers to all those who exist at the consummation of the age. When the end comes, there will be no existing people group that is left out of the blessing.

35. Winter, "Unreached Peoples," 12.

36. "What Does Reached Mean? An EMQ Survey," *Evangelical Missions Quarterly* 26, no. 3 (July 1990): 316.

37. The KJV translates, "Go ye into all the world, and preach the gospel to every creature." But "the whole creation" is more likely. The closest parallel to this Greek expression (*pasē tē ktisei*) is found in Romans 8:22: "We know that the whole creation [*pasa hē ktisis*] has been groaning together in the pains of childbirth until now." The words and word order are identical; only the case is different, dative in Mark 16 and nominative in Romans 8. For my purposes here, we do not need to settle whether Mark 16:9ff. is an early addition to the Gospel of Mark. Verse 15 represents one biblical way of expressing the Great Commission.

response (cf. Luke 24:47; Acts 1:8). In this limited sense, therefore, a people group is reached if the message is proclaimed in it as an understandable testimony.

But this is *not* the only way the missions mandate is expressed in Scripture. Matthew 28:19 says, "Go therefore and make disciples of all nations." Here the mandate clearly includes a response. The missions task is not complete until at least some individuals in a people group have become disciples.[38] This is also the implication of Revelation 5:9 and 7:9, which portray the final company of the redeemed as coming "from every tribe and language and people and nation." If there are converts from all the peoples, then the missions mandate must include making converts, not just proclamation.

Most missions leaders define a people group as "reached" when there is an indigenous church able to evangelize the group. This is because the New Testament clearly teaches that a people must continue to be evangelized once the missions task is complete. For example, when Paul finished his missionary work among the peoples of Ephesus, he nevertheless left Timothy there and told him to "do the work of an evangelist" (2 Tim. 4:5). Paul's specific missionary task was evidently to plant the church, which would then be able to go on with the task of evangelism (cf. 1 Cor. 3:6–10). But the task of evangelism is not the same as missions. Missions is what moved Paul away from the peoples of Asia Minor and Greece (even from those who were still unconverted!) and pressed him toward the unreached peoples of Spain (Rom. 15:24, 28).

There is a difficulty with defining the specific task of missions as planting an indigenous church in every people group. The difficulty is that our *biblical* definition of people groups includes groups that may be so small and so closely related to another group that such a church would be unnecessary. How large was the family or clan of Carmi in the tribe of Reuben, or the family of Achan in the tribe of Judah? And are we sure that the families

---

38. "Make disciples of all nations" might be taken to mean: make the whole nation into disciples. But the wording of verses 19 and 20 points in another direction. The word "nations" (*ethnē*) is neuter in Greek. But the word for "them" in the following clauses is masculine: "baptizing them [*autous*] in the name of the Father and of the Son and of the Holy Spirit, teaching them [*autous*] to observe all that I have commanded you." This suggests that the discipling in view is the winning of individual disciples from the nations, rather than treating the nation as a whole as the object of conversion and discipleship. This was affirmed strongly by Karl Barth, who lamented that the interpretation that took *ethnē* in the sense of corporate discipling "once infested missionary thinking and was connected with the painful fantasies of the German Christians. It is worthless." Karl Barth, "An Exegetical Study of Matthew 28:16–20," in *Classics of Christian Missions*, ed. Francis M. DuBose (Nashville: Broadman, 1979), 46.

in Genesis 12:3 are so distinct that each must have its own church? When Paul said that his special missionary work was completed from Jerusalem to Illyricum, had he in fact planted a church in every family or clan?

These questions show that there will always be some ambiguity in the definition of "reached" and in the aim of missionary work.[39] For some families or clans, "reached" may mean that there are converts among them and that the church in an adjacent kindred clan suffices as an effective ministry of worship, fellowship, and equipping. The task of missions with regard to such near-kinship families may not be to plant a church among each one but to plant a church close enough in culture and language that they can be effectively evangelized. It seems that this must have been what Paul had done when he said that he no longer had room for work in that vast territory. Surely there were some families or clans that had not yet been touched. He would probably have said, "This is the work of the nearby churches."

What this implies is that the dividing line between missionary tasks and the tasks of near-neighbor evangelism are sometimes unclear. This is why the terms "E-1," "E-2," and "E-3" evangelism have been invented.[40] They show that there are not two clearly distinct tasks (domestic evangelism vs. frontier missions) but rather gradations of cultural distance from the Christian community. Where that distance becomes so great that we start calling its penetration "missions" is not always clear.[41]

39. This problem, of course, does not exist by definition for Ralph Winter and other missiologists who define a people group as "the largest group within which the Gospel can spread as a church planting movement without encountering barriers of understanding or acceptance." Winter, "Unreached Peoples," 12. In other words, if an unevangelized "family" is culturally near enough to another evangelized "family" that the gospel can move without significant barriers, then by definition this unevangelized family, according to Winter, is not an "unreached people group." It is simply part of a larger reached group that needs to evangelize its members. The difference between Winter's approach and mine is that I am simply trying to come to terms with the *biblical* meaning of "families" in Genesis 12:3, while he is defining people groups in terms of what missionary efforts are needed. The two approaches are not at odds, but the difference may result in my calling a "family" or clan an unreached people group in biblical terms (one of the *panta ta ethnē* to be discipled), which Winter, however, would say is not "unreached" for specifically missionary purposes.

40. These terms are not as frequent in the literature as they were when the first edition of this book was published in 1993, but some churches (including the one I serve) and organizations still use them as helpful tactical guides. The "E" stands for evangelize: E-1—people basically "like us"; E-2—people who are not like us but speak the same language and overlap significantly in culture (e.g., a suburban white church in relation to a black urban center); E-3—people who speak a different language and have a very different culture (regardless of how near or far away they live).

41. *Biblically*, reaching every clan in a region is a missionary task regardless of its cultural nearness to other reached clans. But *missiologically*, this effort may not be seen as part of the missionary task. What is needed perhaps is more refined distinctions in our language. Paul certainly

Implications

But the fact that there is a distinct calling on the church to do frontier missionary work among all the remaining unreached people groups is crystal clear from the New Testament. Our question today should be: What persons or agencies in the various churches and denominations should pick up this unique Paul-type mission? It is not the *only* work of the church. Timothy-type ministries are also important. He was a foreigner working at Ephesus, continuing what Paul had begun. But Paul had to move on because he was driven by a special commission[42] and by a grasp of God's worldwide mission purpose revealed in the Old Testament. There is no reason to think that God's purpose has changed today.

Who then is to pick up the mantle of the apostle's unique missionary task of reaching more and more peoples? Shouldn't every denomination and church have some vital group that is recruiting, equipping, sending, and supporting Paul-type missionaries to more and more unreached peoples? Shouldn't every church and denomination have a group of people (a missions agency or board) who sees its special and primary task as not merely to win as many individuals to Christ as possible but to win some individuals (i.e., plant a church) among all the unreached peoples of the earth?

The Supremacy of God in the Worship of the Nations

What does this chapter have to do with the supremacy of God? God's great goal in all of history is to uphold and display the glory of his name for the enjoyment of his people from all the nations.[43] The question now is: Why does God pursue the goal of displaying his glory by focusing the missionary task on *all the peoples* of the world? How does this missionary aim serve best to achieve God's goal?

The first thing we notice in pondering this question is how the ultimate goal of God's glory is confirmed in the cluster of texts that focus missionary attention on the people groups of the world. For example,

---

saw his missionary work as finished before every clan in Asia was evangelized. Yet if the Great Commission of Matthew 28:19 includes "all the families of the earth" in *panta ta ethnē*, then the missionary task *in that sense* is not complete until all the clans are represented in the kingdom. Practically, it is probably wise to emphasize the Pauline strategy as the essence of missions.

42. "Go, for I will send you far away to the *ethnē*" (Acts 22:21).

43. I have labored to demonstrate this from Scripture in chapter 1 and in *Desiring God: Meditations of a Christian Hedonist* (Sisters, Ore.: Multnomah, 1996), 255–66; and *The Pleasures of God: Meditations on God's Delight in Being God* (Sisters, Ore.: Multnomah, 2000), 97–119.

Paul said that his apostleship was given "to bring about the obedience of faith *for the sake of* [*Christ's*] *name* among all the nations" (Rom. 1:5). Missions is for the glory of Christ. Its goal is to reestablish the supremacy of Christ among the peoples of the world. Similarly, in Romans 15:9, Paul says that Christ did his own missionary work and inspired Paul's "in order that the Gentiles [or nations] *might glorify God* for his mercy." The goal of Christ's mission and ours is that God might be glorified by the nations as they experience his mercy. Accordingly, the consummation of missions is described in Revelation 5:9 as persons from "every tribe and language and people and nation" worshiping the Lamb and declaring the infinite worth of his glory. All of this is in accord with the repeated Old Testament calls: "Declare his *glory* among the nations, his *marvelous works* among all the peoples!" (Ps. 96:3). The goal of missions is the glory of God.

Diversity: Intended and Eternal

Another thing we notice as we ponder this question is that the diversity of the nations has its creation and consummation in the will of God. Its origin was neither accidental nor evil.[44] And its future is eternal: The diversity will never be replaced by uniformity. The evidence for this is found in Acts 17:26 and Revelation 21:3.

To the Athenians Paul said, "[God] made from one man every nation of mankind to live on all the face of the earth, having determined allotted periods and the boundaries of their dwelling place" (Acts 17:26). This means that the origin of peoples is not in spite of but because of God's will and plan. He *made* the nations. He set them in their place. And he determines the duration of their existence. The diversity of the nations

44. The story of the tower of Babel in Genesis 11 does not mean that God disapproves of the diversity of languages in the world. We are not told that apart from the tower of Babel God would not have created different languages in the world. Blocking an act of pride (Gen. 11:4) was the occasion when God initiated the diversity of languages in the world. But that does not mean that the diversity of languages was a curse that would need to be reversed in the age to come. In fact, the diversity of languages is reported in Genesis 10:5, 20, 31 before the tower of Babel is mentioned in Genesis 11. What we learn is that God's plan of a common origin for all peoples on the one hand and his plan for diversified languages on the other hand restrains the pride of man on two sides: Diversity restrains the temptation to unite against God (as at Babel), and unified origin restrains the temptation to boast in ethnic uniqueness (as, we will see, in Athens). The miracle and the blessing of "tongues" at Pentecost was not a declaration that in the age of promise the languages of the world would disappear but rather a declaration that in the age of promise every obstacle to humble, God-glorifying unity in faith would be overcome.

is God's idea. Therefore, for whatever reason, he focuses the missionary task on all the nations; it is not a response to an accident of history. It is rooted in the purpose he had when he determined to make the nations in the first place.

God's purpose to have diversity among nations is not a temporary one only for this age. In spite of the resistance of most English versions, the standard Greek texts of the New Testament[45] now agree that the original wording of Revelation 21:3 requires the translation: "And I heard a loud voice from the throne saying, 'Behold, the dwelling place of God is with man. He will dwell with them, and they will be his *peoples*." Most versions translate: "They will be his *people*." But what John is saying is that in the new heavens and the new earth the humanity described in Revelation 5:9 will be preserved: persons ransomed by the blood of Christ "from every tribe and language and people and nation." This diversity will not disappear in the new heavens and the new earth. God willed it from the beginning. It has a permanent place in his plan.

How Diversity Magnifies the Glory of God

Now, we return to the question, How does God's focus on the diversity of the peoples advance his purpose to be glorified in his creation?[46] As I have tried to reflect biblically on this question, at least[47] four answers have emerged.

45. See note 24.

46. One of the questions raised by those of us who believe God means to pursue worshipers from all the peoples of the world is, "What about peoples who exist and then die out before any gospel witness comes? If you believe that these people are lost, as you have argued, then none of them will be represented in the worshiping host of heaven." I have three responses to this question: (1) I do not know for sure that the biblical assurance that Christ has "ransomed people for God from every tribe and language and people and nation" must include those who live and die out before any can believe. (2) While the biblical teaching on the final state of those who die in infancy is not explicit, I hold the view that infants who die do not perish but prove to be elect and are brought to faith in Christ and eternal life in a way we are not told. (See chapter 4, note 27.) Therefore, those who have died as infants in the vanishing tribes would be represented among the redeemed. (3) But the way I argue in this closing section as to *why* diversity glorifies God points in another direction for the decisive answer. Among the main reasons diversity glorifies God is that conscious allegiance to one leader from a greatly diverse group magnifies the unique glory of the leader. See below. But this would suggest then that perhaps the decisive aim of God in commanding our pursuit of *living* peoples is that only those who hear of Jesus and consciously follow him will glorify him in this way. This may suggest then that the issue of vanished peoples is simply not in view when the "every" of Revelation 5:9 is contemplated.

47. I omit discussing the real possibility that there are mysterious correlations between the numbers and the purposes of the peoples and the numbers of the saints or the angels. Deuter-

1. First, there is a beauty and power of praise that comes from unity in diversity that is greater than that which comes from unity alone. Psalm 96:3–4 connects the evangelizing of the peoples with the quality of praise that God deserves. "Declare his glory among the nations, his marvelous works among all the peoples! *For great is the* LORD, *and greatly to be praised*; he is to be feared above all gods." Notice the word "for." The extraordinary greatness of the praise that the Lord should receive is the ground and impetus of our mission to the nations.

I infer from this that the beauty and power of praise that will come to the Lord from the diversity of the nations are greater than the beauty and power that would come to him if the chorus of the redeemed were culturally uniform. The reason for this can be seen in the analogy of a choir. More depth of beauty is felt from a choir that sings in parts than from a choir that sings only in unison. Unity in diversity is more beautiful and more powerful than the unity of uniformity. This carries over to the untold differences that exist between the peoples of the world. When their diversity unites in worship to God, the beauty of their praise will echo the depth and greatness of God's beauty far more than if the redeemed were from only a few different people groups.

2. Second, the fame and greatness and worth of an object of beauty increases in proportion to the diversity of those who recognize its beauty. If a work of art is regarded as great among a small and like-minded group of people but not by anyone else, the art is probably not truly great. Its qualities are such that it does not appeal to the deep universals in our hearts but only to provincial biases. But if a work of art continues to win more and more admirers not only across cultures but also across decades and centuries, then its greatness is irresistibly manifested.

Thus, when Paul says, "Praise the Lord all you nations, and let all the peoples extol him" (Rom. 15:11, author's translation), he is saying that there is something about God that is so universally praiseworthy and so profoundly beautiful and so comprehensively worthy and so deeply satisfying that God will find passionate admirers in every diverse people group in the world. His true greatness will be manifest in the breadth of the diversity of those who perceive and cherish his beauty. His excellence will be shown

---

onomy 32:8 says, "When the Most High gave to the nations their inheritance, when He separated the sons of man, He set the boundaries of the peoples *according to the number of the sons of Israel*" (NASB). The Greek Old Testament contains the strange rendering: ". . . according to the number of the *angels of God*," which the ESV follows, by translating, ". . . according to the number of the sons of God." Making much of this would be speculation, but it does remind us that God has reasons that are often high and hidden.

to be higher and deeper than the parochial preferences that make us happy most of the time. His appeal will be to the deepest, highest, largest capacities of the human soul. Thus, the diversity of the source of admiration will testify to his incomparable glory.

3. Third, the strength and wisdom and love of a leader is magnified in proportion to the diversity of people he can inspire to follow him with joy. If you can lead only a small, uniform group of people, your leadership qualities are not as great as they would be if you could win a following from a large group of very diverse people.

Paul's understanding of what is happening in his missionary work among the nations is that Christ is demonstrating his greatness in winning obedience from all the peoples of the world: "I will not venture to speak of anything except what *Christ has accomplished through me to bring the Gentiles* [*or nations*] *to obedience* (Rom. 15:18). It is not Paul's missionary expertise that is being magnified as more and more diverse peoples choose to follow Christ. It is the greatness of Christ. He is showing himself superior to all other leaders.

The last phrase of Psalm 96:3–4 shows the leadership competition that is going on in world missions. "Declare his glory among the nations. . . . *He is to be feared above all gods.*" We should declare the glory of God among the nations because in this way he will show his superiority over all other gods that make pretentious claims to lead the peoples. The more diverse the people groups who forsake their gods to follow the true God, the more visible is God's superiority over all his competitors.

4. By focusing on all the people groups of the world, God undercuts ethnocentric pride and throws all peoples back upon his free grace rather than any distinctive of their own. This is what Paul emphasizes in Acts 17:26 when he says to the proud citizens of Athens, "[God] made from one man every nation of mankind to live on all the face of the earth, having determined allotted periods and the boundaries of their dwelling place." F. F. Bruce points out that "the Athenians . . . pride themselves on being . . . sprung from the soil of their native Attica. . . . They were the only Greeks on the European mainland who had no tradition of their ancestors coming into Greece; they belonged to the earliest wave of Greek immigration."[48]

Against this boast Paul countered: You and the Barbarians and the Jews and the Romans all came from the same origin. And you came by God's will, not your own; and the time and place of your existence is in God's hand. Every time God expresses his missionary focus for *all* the nations,

48. Bruce, *Commentary on the Book of Acts*, 357–58.

he cuts the nerve of ethnocentric pride. It's a humbling thing to discover that God does not choose our people group because of any distinctives of worth but rather that we might double our joy in him by being a means of bringing all the other groups into the same joy.

Humility is the flip side of giving God all the glory. Humility means reveling in his grace, not our goodness. In pressing us on to all the peoples, God is pressing us further into the humblest and deepest experience of his grace and weaning us more and more from our ingrained pride. In doing this he is preparing for himself a people—from all the peoples—who will be able to worship him with free and white-hot admiration.

PART 3

MAKING GOD SUPREME IN MISSIONS

THE PRACTICAL OUTWORKING OF COMPASSION AND WORSHIP

6

A Passion for God's Supremacy and Compassion for Man's Soul

Jonathan Edwards on the Unity of Motives for World Missions

Missions is not the ultimate goal of the church. Worship is. Missions exists because worship doesn't. Worship is ultimate, not missions, because God is ultimate, not man. When this age is over, and the countless millions of the redeemed fall on their faces before the throne of God, missions will be no more. It is a temporary necessity. But worship abides forever.

With those words I began this book on the supremacy of God in missions. There are deep roots to those sentences, and I owe more debts than I can ever pay. The person most responsible for my views and for my articulation of those views (under God and after the Bible) is Jonathan Edwards, the eighteenth-century pastor and theologian whose God-entranced worldview sheds its light across all the pages of this book. The impact that Edwards has had on my thinking as it relates to worship and missions (and almost everything else) is incalculable. This chapter is another tribute that I pay to him and to his God on the occasion of this three-hundredth anniversary of his birth.

The Pervasive Influence of Jonathan Edwards

You can hear his influence in the questions behind the first sentence: What is the ultimate goal of the church? What is the ultimate goal of redemption and of history and of creation? Edwards was always asking about the ultimate end of things, because once we know and embrace the final and highest reason that we and the church and the nations exist, then all our thinking and all our feeling and all our acting will be governed by that aim. It continually amazes me how few people ask and answer with conviction and passion the most important questions—the ultimate questions.

But that is what Edwards cared about most. Edwards was absolutely clear on the ultimate question of why all things exist, including you and me and the church universal and the nations and history. He was absolutely clear on it because God was absolutely clear on it. Edwards wrote a book called *The End for Which God Created the World*.[1] In my own thinking, it is the most important thing he ever wrote. Once we understand what he wrote there, everything—absolutely everything—changes. His answer to the question, What is the ultimate goal of creation and history and redemption and your life and everything else? is this: "All that is ever spoken of in the Scripture as an ultimate end of God's works, is included in that one phrase, the glory of God."[2]

Edwards's Biblically Saturated Argumentation

Edwards is sure of this because the Bible is clear about this. For nearly seventy pages[3] Edwards piles text upon text from the Scriptures to show the radical God-centeredness of God. He puts it like this:

> God had respect to *himself*, as his highest end [or goal], in this work [of creation]; because he is *worthy* in himself to be so, being infinitely the greatest

1. Jonathan Edwards, *The End for Which God Created the World* is published in its entirety in John Piper, *God's Passion for His Glory: Living the Vision of Jonathan Edwards* (Wheaton: Crossway, 1998).
2. Ibid., 242.
3. Ibid., 183–251.

and best of beings. All things else, with regard to worthiness, importance, and excellence, are perfectly as nothing in comparison [to] him."[4]

He cites Romans 11:36: "For from him and through him and *to him* are all things. To him be glory forever." And Colossians 1:16: "All things were created through him and *for him.*" And Hebrews 2:10: "For it was fitting that he, *for whom* and by whom all things exist, in bringing many sons to glory, should make the founder of their salvation perfect through suffering." And Proverbs 16:4: "The Lord hath made all things *for himself*" (KJV).[5]

The point of these texts—and dozens more[6]—is not that God has deficiencies he is trying to remedy but that he has perfections he wants to display. God's aim in creation is to put himself on display. "The heavens declare the glory of God," Psalm 19:1 says. Who set it up that way? God did. This is *his* aim in creation. To make himself known as glorious. And the same thing is true of the history of redemption. Isaiah 48:9–11 is like a banner not just over God's rescue of Israel from exile but over all his acts of rescue, especially the cross:

> For my name's sake I defer my anger, for the sake of my praise I restrain it for you, that I may not cut you off. Behold, I have refined you. . . . I have tried you in the furnace of affliction. For my own sake, for my own sake, I do it, for how should my name be profaned? My glory I will not give to another.

All of creation, all of redemption, all of history is designed by God to display God. That is the ultimate goal of the church.

Why Did I Put "Worship" Where the Glory of God Belongs?

But that is not what I said in the first sentence of this book on missions. I said, "Missions is not the ultimate goal of the church. *Worship* is." Why the substitution of "worship" for "the glory of God"? Why not say, "Missions

---

4. Ibid., 140 (italics in original).
5. Emphasis added. Most modern versions translate this verse so that "for himself" is rendered "for its own purpose": "The Lord has made everything *for its own purpose*, even the wicked for the day of evil" (NASB). But this is a contextual judgment call, not a necessary grammatical feature of the text. The Hebrew *lamma'anehu* can be properly translated "for himself."
6. Some of these are gathered in chapter 1 of this book.

is not the ultimate goal of the church. The *glory of God* is"? The reason is that missions is demanded not by God's failure to show glory but by man's failure to savor the glory. Creation is telling the glory of God, but the peoples are not treasuring it.

> His invisible attributes, namely, his eternal power and divine nature, have been clearly perceived, ever since the creation of the world, in the things that have been made. So they are without excuse. For although they knew God, they did not honor him as God or give thanks to him.
>
> Romans 1:20–21

Natural revelation is not getting through. Honor and thanks to God are not welling up in the hearts of the peoples when they see his glory manifest in nature. They are not worshiping the true God. That's why missions is necessary.

Missions exists because *worship* doesn't. The ultimate issue addressed by missions is that God's glory is dishonored among the peoples of the world. When Paul brought his indictment of his own people to a climax in Romans 2:24, he said, "The name of God is blasphemed among the Gentiles because of you." That is the ultimate problem in the world. That is the ultimate outrage.

The glory of God is not honored.
The holiness of God is not reverenced.
The greatness of God is not admired.
The power of God is not praised.
The truth of God is not sought.
The wisdom of God is not esteemed.
The beauty of God is not treasured.
The goodness of God is not savored.
The faithfulness of God is not trusted.
The commandments of God are not obeyed.
The justice of God is not respected.
The wrath of God is not feared.
The grace of God is not cherished.
The presence of God is not prized.
The person of God is not loved.

A Passion for God's Supremacy and Compassion for Man's Soul   231

The infinite, all-glorious Creator of the universe, by whom and for whom all things exist—who holds every person's life in being at every moment (Acts 17:25)—is disregarded, disbelieved, disobeyed, and dishonored among the peoples of the world. That is the ultimate reason for missions.

The opposite of this disrespect is worship. Worship is not a gathering. It is not essentially a song service or sitting under preaching. Worship is not essentially any form of outward act. Worship is essentially an inner stirring of the heart to treasure God above all the treasures of the world—

a valuing of God above all else that is valuable

a loving of God above all else that is lovely

a savoring of God above all else that is sweet

an admiring of God above all else that is admirable

a fearing of God above all else that is fearful

a respecting of God above all else that is respectable

a prizing of God above all else that is precious

Worship from the Inside Out

In other words, worship is right affections in the heart toward God, rooted in right thoughts in the head about God, becoming visible in right actions of the body reflecting God. These three stages of worship from inner essence to outward display can be seen in three texts.

- First, Matthew 15:8–9: "This people honors me with their lips, but *their heart* is far from me; in vain do they worship me." So if worship is not from the heart, it is vain and empty, meaning it is *not* worship. That means the essence can't be outward. The essence of worship is affection, not action.
- Second, John 4:23: "The hour is coming, and is now here, when the true worshipers will worship the Father in spirit *and truth*, for the Father is seeking such people to worship him." Notice, the Father seeks worship in spirit *and* truth—right affections rising for God, rooted in right thinking about God.
- Third, Matthew 5:16: "Let your light shine before others, so that they may see your *good works* and give glory to your Father who is in heaven." God intends for his glory to be public. He did not create the world so that his glory would remain incognito. And he does

not redeem people so that they will have merely private experiences of his preciousness. His aim is that his glory be openly reflected in the *deeds* of his people, whose *thoughts* reflect his truth and whose *affections* reflect his worth. Worship is seeing, savoring, and showing the glory of all that God is for us in Jesus Christ.

The first and ultimate goal of missions is that this worship happens among all the nations of the world—that God's glory and greatness find a fitting reflection among the peoples.

Not Just More People but People from All Peoples

Note that I said "peoples," not people. The aim of missions (as distinct from local evangelism where the church already exists) is that there be a church who worships God through Jesus Christ in all the peoples and tribes and languages and ethnic groups of the world. We have seen this goal of missions most clearly in the result of missions in Revelation 5:9. The song to Christ in heaven will be, "Worthy are you to take the scroll and to open its seals, for you were slain, and by your blood you ransomed people for God from every tribe and language and people and nation." Jesus Christ, the Son of God, died to redeem a worshiping people for his Father from all the peoples, tribes, languages, and nations. Missions exists to plant Christ-purchased, God-exalting worshiping communities of the redeemed in all the peoples of the world.

The passion of a missionary—as distinct from that of an evangelist—is to plant a worshiping community of Christians in a people group who has no access to the gospel because of language or cultural barriers. Paul was one of these "frontier" missionaries: "I make it my ambition to preach the gospel, not where Christ has already been named. . . . But now, since I no longer have any room for work in these regions . . . I go to Spain" (Rom. 15:20, 23–24).

The first great passion of missions, therefore, is to honor the glory of God by restoring the rightful place of God in the hearts of people who presently think, feel, and act in ways that dishonor God every day, and in particular, to do this by bringing forth a worshiping people from among all the unreached peoples of the world. If you love the glory of God, you cannot be indifferent to missions. This is the ultimate reason Jesus Christ came into the world. Romans 15:8–9 says, "Christ became a servant to the circumcised . . . *in order that the Gentiles might glorify God for his mercy.*" Christ came to get glory for his Father among the nations. If you love what Jesus Christ came to accomplish, you love missions.

Compassion for People, Not Just Passion for God

But now comes the question this chapter is mainly designed to answer: How does the motive of compassion for people relate to this primary motive of a passion for the glory of God? Most of us would agree that Jesus came not only to vindicate God's righteousness and uphold God's glory but also to rescue sinners from everlasting misery.

Alongside the truth that we are all guilty of treason and have dishonored our King, we must now put forward the truth that we are therefore worthy of execution and everlasting punishment. With mutiny comes misery. Unbelief not only dishonors God but also destroys the soul. Everything that discredits God damages man. Every assault on God's holiness is an assault on human happiness. Every thought or feeling or action that makes God look wrong or irrelevant increases humanity's ruin. Everything that decreases God's reputation increases our suffering.

And so missions is driven by a passion not only to restore the glory of God to its rightful place in the worshiping soul but also to rescue sinners from everlasting pain. If there is one thing that almost everyone knows about Jonathan Edwards, it is that he believed in the reality and eternality of hell.

Edwards Wanted to Honor God *and* Rescue People from Hell

In his most famous sermon, "Sinners in the Hands of an Angry God," Edwards was not a cool, detached observer of perishing people. He was a passionate evangelist pleading for people to receive mercy while there was still time. After referring to Revelation 14:20, which speaks of "the winepress of the fierceness and wrath of Almighty God," he says:

> The words are exceeding terrible. . . . "The fierceness and wrath of God." The fury of God! The fierceness of Jehovah! O how dreadful must that be! Who can utter or conceive what such expressions carry in them? . . . Consider this, you who are here present, that yet remain in an unregenerate state. . . . Now God stands ready to pity you; this is a day of mercy.[7]

7. Jonathan Edwards, "Sinners in the Hands of an Angry God," in *The Works of Jonathan Edwards*, vol. 2 (Edinburgh: Banner of Truth Trust, 1974), 10.

And Edwards believed not only that hell would be horrible and conscious but also that it would be never ending. He would have been appalled at the number of so-called evangelicals today who have abandoned the biblical teaching on hell as eternal, conscious torment in favor of a view of annihilation (Matt. 25:41, 46; Mark 9:42–48; 2 Thess. 1:5–10; Rev. 14:9–11; 20:10, 14–15).[8] In response to the annihilationists of his own day, Edwards preached a message on April 2, 1739, with the stated doctrine, "The misery of the wicked in hell will be absolutely eternal." In another sermon, he makes the point that annihilation is not the form of punishment that unbelievers receive but the relief from punishment that they desire and don't receive. "Wicked men will hereafter earnestly wish to be turned to nothing and forever cease to be that they may escape the wrath of God."[9] I believe Edwards is right, and we should tremble and fly to Christ, our only hope.[10]

So I say again, missions is driven not only by a passion for the supremacy of God in all things but also by a compassion for perishing people, whom we all once were.

Edwards preached a series of fifteen sermons on the "love chapter," 1 Corinthians 13 ("Charity and Its Fruits") and said in sermon four, on verse 4 ("Love suffers long and is kind"), "A Christian spirit disposes persons meekly to bear ill that is received from others, and cheerfully and freely to do good to others."[11] One of his applications was:

> Men may do good to the souls of vicious persons by being the instruments of reclaiming them from their vicious courses. They may do good to the souls of secure and senseless sinners by putting them in mind of their misery and danger and so being the instruments of awakening them. And persons may be the instruments of others' conversion, of bringing them home to Christ. We read in Daniel 12:3 of those that turn many to righteousness.[12]

The motive of love toward sinners and the desire to do good to them are essential to the Christian spirit. It is the spirit of Christ himself.

8. See my response to this abandonment in chapter 4.
9. Quoted in John Gerstner, *Jonathan Edwards on Heaven and Hell* (Grand Rapids: Baker, 1980), 75.
10. For a fuller treatment of Edwards's argument about the justice of hell, see chapter 4, note 19.
11. Jonathan Edwards, "Charity and Its Fruits," in *The Works of Jonathan Edwards*, vol. 8, *Ethical Writings*, ed. Paul Ramsey (New Haven: Yale University Press, 1989), 185.
12. Ibid., 207–8. Daniel 12:3 says, "And those who are wise shall shine like the brightness of the sky above; and those who turn many to righteousness, like the stars forever and ever."

Mark 6:34 says, "When [Jesus] went ashore he saw a great crowd, and he had *compassion* on them, because they were like sheep without a shepherd. And he began to teach them many things." In Luke 15:20, in the parable of the prodigal son, Jesus portrays the heart of his Father in the same way: "[His son] arose and came to his father. But while he was still a long way off, his father saw him and felt *compassion*, and ran and embraced him and kissed him." "For God so loved the world, that he gave his only Son, that whoever believes in him should not perish but have eternal life" (John 3:16). The love of God for perishing sinners moved him to provide at great cost a way to rescue them from everlasting destruction, and missions is the extension of that love to the unreached peoples of the world.

How Does Compassion for People Relate to Passion for God?

Here is the main question I am pursuing: What is the relationship between our passion for the supremacy of God—the glory of God, the honor of God and of his Son among the nations—and our compassion for perishing sinners whose end is everlasting misery if they do not hear the gospel and believe? I wonder if you've ever experienced a tension in your own soul between these two motives. I have. That's why this question matters so much to me. I want to be utterly devoted to the cause of world evangelization, and I want it to be from God-exalting, person-loving motives. And these two do not always feel emotionally compatible. Are they? How are they? Does Jonathan Edwards provide a key? I will try to unfold the answer in five steps:

1. *Compassion pursues the rescue of perishing sinners.* Compassion moves us to work for the rescue of unbelievers from the coming wrath of God in hell (1 Thess. 1:10). The biggest problem in the world for every human being—from the poorest to the richest, from the sickest to the healthiest—is the same: how to escape the wrath of God that hangs over all humans because of our sin. Love demands that we work to rescue people from the wrath of God.

2. *Fear of hell by itself saves nobody.* Edwards never tired of warning people to flee from the wrath to come.[13] But he knew that mere fear of the consequences of sin is not a saving fear. People who love sin fear and

13. Gerstner, *Jonathan Edwards on Heaven and Hell.* See page 51 for a 1747 sermon in which he comments on how frequently he warned his people about the dangers of hell.

sometimes weep over the consequences of sin.[14] It is natural to hate pain. It is supernatural to hate sin. It is natural to love sin and supernatural to love Christ.

What this implies is that you can scare people toward heaven, but you can't scare anybody into heaven. Saving faith means receiving Christ as your treasure, not just as a deliverer from pain. It is possible to claim faith in Christ as merely a rescuer from hell. Such faith saves no one. Jesus said, "I am the bread of life; whoever comes to me shall not hunger, and whoever believes in me shall never thirst" (John 6:35). Saving faith is a coming to Jesus for the satisfaction of your soul thirst.[15]

Until your soul has a thirst for Christ as the bread of life and the living water, you will use Christ for what your soul thirsts after. Many people who claim to have saving faith simply use Christ to get what they really want, which is not Christ but his gifts (escape from hell, peace of mind, health of body, a better marriage, a social network, etc.). We are saved by coming to Christ not only as our deliverer but also as our treasure—coming for all that God is for us in Jesus. Test yourself: Would you want to go to heaven if Christ were not there? Is he or his gifts your treasure?

3. *Therefore, compassion must not merely warn people about the pains of going to hell but must also lure people to the pleasures of knowing Christ.* The only way to get to heaven is by wanting to be with Christ and by trusting his work to get you there. Wanting to avoid hell is not the same as wanting to be with Christ. And so it would not be compassionate merely to warn people about hell. We must display to them the beauties of Christ. Compassion does not merely warn people; it woos people. Compassion aims to awaken in people a delight in Christ, not just a dread of hell. No one goes to heaven who does not love Christ. Paul said, "If any one does not love the Lord, let him be accursed" (1 Cor. 16:22 NASB). Compassion seeks, with prayer and preaching and serving in the power of the Holy Spirit, to create joy in who Christ is. Compassion stirs up satisfaction in Christ. At its heart, that is what saving faith is: being satisfied with all that God is for us in Jesus.

4. *The key from Jonathan Edwards: It is precisely this satisfaction in Christ himself that magnifies Christ and glorifies God.* The key to the coherence between passion for God's glory and compassion for perishing

14. Note the contrast in 2 Corinthians 7:10 between "godly grief" and "worldly grief": "For *godly grief* produces a repentance that leads to salvation without regret, whereas *worldly grief* produces death."

15. For an extended exposition of this sentence, see John Piper, *The Purifying Power of Living by Faith in Future Grace* (Sisters, Ore.: Multnomah, 1995).

humans is that rejoicing in God himself, through Christ, glorifies God. The pleasure you take in God is the measure of the treasure you find in him. You make much of him and show him to be great when you find your joy in him, especially when the taste and lure of this joy enables you to leave comforts and risk your life in the cause of missions. Here is the key quotation from Edwards:

> So God glorifies Himself toward the creatures also in two ways: 1. By ap-pearing to . . . their understanding. 2. In communicating Himself to their hearts, and in their rejoicing and delighting in, and enjoying, the manifesta-tions which He makes of Himself. . . . *God is glorified not only by His glory's being seen, but by its being rejoiced in.* When those that see it delight in it, God is more glorified than if they only see it. His glory is then received by the whole soul, both by the understanding and by the heart. God made the world that He might communicate, and the creature receive, His glory; and that it might [be] received both by the mind and heart. He that testifies his idea of God's glory [doesn't] glorify God so much as he that testifies also his approbation of it and his delight in it.[16]

My way of saying this is, "God is most glorified in us when we are most satisfied in him."[17]

With this profound insight from Jonathan Edwards into God's pur-pose in creation and redemption, we see the unity of our two motives in missions:

5. *The aim of compassion to rescue sinners from everlasting pain and the aim of passion to see God honored are not in conflict.* Sinners escape hell and honor God with the same act: treasuring all that God is for them in Christ, being satisfied with all that God is for them in Christ. God does not get the honor he should, and man does not escape the pain he would, if Christ himself is not our treasure. But if, by the mercy of God, Christ becomes the treasure of the nations and God becomes their delight, then he is honored and we are saved.

And that's the goal of missions. Therefore, the twofold motive of mis-sions, mercy for man and glory for God, is one coherent goal. So let us

16. Jonathan Edwards, *The "Miscellanies,"* in *The Works of Jonathan Edwards,* vol. 13, ed. Thomas Schafer (New Haven: Yale University Press, 1994), 495, emphasis added. Miscellany #448; see also #87, 251–52; #332, 410; #679 (not in the New Haven volume).
17. For an exposition of this statement, see John Piper, *Desiring God: Mediations of a Christian Hedonist* (Sisters, Ore.: Multnomah, 1996); and John Piper, *The Dangerous Duty of Delight: The Glorified God and the Satisfied Soul* (Sisters, Ore.: Multnomah, 2001).

take up our cross and, for the joy set before us, be willing to lay down our lives to make the nations glad in God.

> Let the peoples praise you, O God;
> let all the peoples praise you!
> Let the nations be glad and sing for joy.
>
> Psalm 67:3–4

7

The Inner Simplicity and Outer Freedom of Worldwide Worship

I write this final chapter[1] to clarify the first two sentences of chapter 1: "Missions is not the ultimate goal of the church. Worship is." I want to clarify what I mean by "worship," lest any take me to mean merely the gathering of Christians for corporate worship or (still more limiting) that part of the gathering for singing songs and hymns. I love those times and meet God powerfully in them. But to say that missions exists for *that* would be too narrow and far from my meaning. I mean something much more radical and soul-gripping and life-encompassing when I speak of worship as the goal of missions.

A Stunning Degree of Indifference to Outward Form

My thesis is that worship in the New Testament moved toward something radically simple and inward, with manifold external expressions in life and liturgy. One of the reasons for this is that the New Testament is a vision for missions that is usable across thousands of cultures and therefore could not be laden with externals. I would even dare to claim (not that every reader will be as excited about this as I am) that this radical simplification and internalization is in line with the Reformed tradition. In short, what

1. This chapter is an adaptation of material first published in John Piper, *Brothers, We Are Not Professionals* (Nashville: Broadman & Holman, 2002), chap. 28.

239

we find in the New Testament is an utterly stunning degree of indifference to worship as an outward form and an utterly radical intensification of worship as an inward experience of the heart.

Little Explicit Teaching in the New Testament about Corporate Worship

Let's begin with a startling fact, namely, that the epistles of the New Testament contain very little instruction that deals explicitly with corporate worship—what we call worship services. Not that there were no corporate gatherings for worship. First Corinthians 14:23 speaks of "the whole church" assembling together, Acts 2:46 speaks of the early church "attending the temple together and breaking bread in their homes," and Hebrews 10:25 speaks of "not neglecting to meet together." But this is not much, and the remarkable thing is that even when the gatherings are in view, the apostles do not speak of them explicitly as worship.

Let me illustrate this so we can feel its full force. In the Old Testament, the most common word for worship is the Hebrew word *hishtahavah* (or a related form of that word). Its basic meaning is "bow down," with the sense of reverence, respect, and honor. It occurs 171 times. In the Greek Old Testament, 164 of those instances of this Hebrew word are translated by the Greek *proskyneō*. In the Greek New Testament, this is the main word for worship. But when we look at its use, we notice something astonishing.[2] It is common in the Gospels (twenty-six times)—people would often bow down worshipfully before Jesus. And it is common in the Book of Revelation (twenty-one times) because the angels and elders in heaven often bow down before God. But in the epistles of Paul, it occurs only once, namely, in 1 Corinthians 14:25, where the unbeliever falls down at the power of prophecy and confesses that God is in the assembly. And it doesn't occur at all in the letters of Peter, James, or John.

2. Heinrich Greeven in *Theological Dictionary of the New Testament*, ed. Gerhard Friedrich, trans. Geoffrey Bromiley, vol. 6 (Grand Rapids: Eerdmans, 1968), 765, observes the "astonishing fact" that while *proskyneō* is abundant in the Gospels (twenty-six times) and Acts (four times) and Revelation (twenty-one times), it is almost completely absent in the epistles (Heb. 1:6 and 11:21 are Old Testament quotations). Apart from Acts 24:11, where *proskynein* is a technical term for worship in the temple, the only instance of *proskynēsis* in the primitive Christian community is in 1 Corinthians 14:25, where there appears to be an actual falling down. Elsewhere there is reference to kneeling in prayer (Acts 9:40; 20:36) and lifting the hands (1 Tim. 2:8), but the word *proskynein* is not used. Greeven concludes: "This is, however, a further proof of the concreteness of the term. *Proskynēsis* demands visible majesty before which the worshipper bows. The Son of God was visible to all on earth (the Gospels) and the exalted Lord will again be visible to His own when faith gives way to sight (Revelation)."

This is remarkable. The main word for worship in the Old Testament is virtually absent from the letters of the New Testament.[3] Why is this? Why are the very epistles that were written to help the church be what it ought to be in this age almost totally devoid of this word and of explicit teaching on the specifics of corporate worship?

Jesus Is the New "Place" of Worship

I think the reason is found in the way Jesus treated worship in his life and teaching. His main statement is found in John 4:20–24. But before we look at this text, consider a few other things he said. For example, his attitude toward the temple, the main place of Jewish worship, was not at all what the Jewish leaders thought it should be.

When he wove a whip and drove out the moneychangers, he said he did so not for the sake of proper sacrifices but for the sake of prayer—in fact, prayer for *all the nations*. "My house shall be called a house of prayer for all the nations" (Mark 11:17). In other words, he focused attention away from the outward acts of Jewish sacrifices to the personal act of communion with God for all peoples.

Then he said two other things about the temple that pointed to a radically altered view of worship. He said, "Something greater than the temple is here," referring to himself (Matt. 12:6), and, "Destroy this temple, and in three days I will raise it up" (John 2:19). This attitude toward the temple got not only him killed (Mark 14:58; 15:29) but also Stephen (Acts 6:14). That's how important it was.

Jesus identified himself as the true temple. "Something greater than the temple is here." In himself he would fulfill everything the temple stood for, especially the "place" where believers meet God. He diverted attention away from worship as a localized activity with outward forms and pointed toward a personal, spiritual experience with himself at the center. Worship does not have to have a building, a priesthood, and a sacrificial system. It has to have the risen Jesus.

Jesus Loosens Worship from Place and Form

What Jesus did to worship in the way he related to the temple is made explicit in John 4:20–24. Here he uses the word *proskyneō*—the dominant

---

3. See note 2 for the few apparent exceptions in Hebrews.

242   Making God Supreme in Missions

Old Testament word for worship—and shows that it is laden with outward
and localized meaning. Then he transforms it into a concept that is mainly
inward rather than outward and mainly pervasive rather than localized.

The woman at the well said:

> Our fathers worshiped on this mountain, but you say that in Jerusalem
> is the place where people ought to worship." [The word for worship used
> here is the common Old Testament word *proskyneō*. Note the localized
> emphasis in her mind.] Jesus said to her, "Woman, believe me, an hour is
> coming when neither on this mountain nor in Jerusalem will you worship
> the Father."
>
> John 4:20–21

Here Jesus loosens worship from its outward and localized connotations. Place is not the issue: "neither on this mountain nor in Jerusalem."
He goes on:

> But the hour is coming, and is now here, when the true worshipers will
> worship the Father in spirit and truth, for the Father is seeking such people
> to worship him. God is spirit, and those who worship him must worship
> in spirit and truth."
>
> John 4:23–24

Here is the key sentence: True worship, which was anticipated for the
age to come, has arrived: "The hour *is coming* [in the age to come] and is
now here [in me!]." What marks this true future worship, which has broken
into the present from the glorious age to come, is that it is not bound by
localized place or outward form. Instead of being on this mountain or in
Jerusalem, it is "in spirit and truth."[4]

Jesus strips *proskyneō* of its last vestiges of localized and outward
connotations.[5] It will not be wrong for worship to be in a place or to use
outward forms, but he makes explicit and central that this is *not* what

4. In line with what we saw in note 2, Heinrich Greeven remarks that "if instead of naming
a place to which the pilgrims should go to worship, Jesus says that the true place of worship is
in the spirit and in truth: this is an oxymoron. Undiluted *proskynein*, the act of worship which
is concrete in place and gesture, is lifted up to a new dimension: 'spirit and truth.'" *Theological
Dictionary of the New Testament*, 6:764.

5. I am aware that Jesus may not have spoken Greek with this woman at the well and so
may not have actually used the word *proskyneō*. But I take it that John's rendering of Jesus'
intention is accurate and that John's use of *proskyneō* faithfully captures what Jesus wanted
to communicate about the meaning of worship carried by that word.

makes worship worship. What makes worship worship is what happens "in spirit and truth"—with or without a place and with or without outward forms.

What do those two phrases mean: "in spirit" and "in truth"?

> I take "in spirit" to mean that this true worship is carried along by the Holy Spirit and is happening mainly as an inward, spiritual event, not mainly as an outward, bodily event. And I take "in truth" to mean that this true worship is a response to true views of God and is shaped and guided by true views of God.[6]

Jesus, therefore, broke decisively any necessary connection between worship and its outward and localized associations. It is mainly something inward and free from locality. This is what he meant when he said, "This people honors me with their lips, but their heart is far from me; in vain do they worship me" (Matt. 15:8–9). When the heart is far from God, worship is vain, empty, nonexistent. The experience of the heart is the defining, vital, indispensable essence of worship.

Why Is the Main Old Testament Word for Worship Boycotted?

Let's go back to our earlier question: Why is the central Old Testament word for worship, *proskyneō*, virtually boycotted by Peter, James, John, and Paul in the letters they write to the churches?[7] I think the reason is that the word did not make clear enough the inward, spiritual nature of true worship. It carried significant connotations of place and form. The word was associated with bodily bowing down and with the actual presence of a visible manifestation to bow down before.

In the Gospels, Jesus was present in *visible* form to fall before, so the word *proskyneō* is used often. In the Book of Revelation, the act of bowing down usually happens before God's manifestation in heaven or before false gods on the earth. Therefore, the word *proskyneō* is widely used in Revelation too. But in the epistles something very different is happening.

---

6. See John Piper, *Desiring God: Meditations of a Christian Hedonist* (Sisters, Ore.: Multnomah, 1996), 73–95, for a fuller treatment of the context of John 4 and its relationship to worship in spirit and truth.

7. Another important word for worship, *sebomai*, is used twice in the Gospels ("In vain do they *worship* me" [Matt. 15:9 = Mark 7:7]) and eight times in Acts, always for God-fearing Gentiles except once for pagan worship (Acts 19:27). The absence of this word in the epistles is again remarkable. It is as if the apostles, in their letters, avoided words that were current for synagogue worship, both *proskyneō* and *sebomai*.

Jesus is not present in visible glory to fall before. As a result, the tendency of the early church was to deal with worship as primarily inward and spiritual rather than outward and bodily, and primarily pervasive rather than localized.

Unlocalizing and Unformalizing Words for Worship

To confirm this and to see even more clearly how radically non-place and non-event oriented the New Testament view of worship is, consider what Paul does to some of the other words related to Old Testament worship. For example, the next most frequent word for worship in the Greek translation of the Old Testament (after *proskyneō*) is the word *latreuō*[8] (over ninety times, almost always translating the Hebrew *'abad*), which is usually rendered "serve," as in Exodus 23:24: "You shall not bow to their gods or *serve [latreusēs]* them."

When Paul uses it for Christian worship, he goes out of his way to make sure that we know he does not mean a localized or outward form for worship practice but a nonlocalized, spiritual experience. In fact, he treats virtually all of life as worship when lived in the right spirit. For example, in Romans 1:9, he says, "I *serve* [or worship, *latreuō*] [God] *with my spirit* in the gospel of his Son." In Philippians 3:3, Paul says that true Christians "worship *by the Spirit* of God . . . and put no confidence in the flesh." And in Romans 12:1, Paul urges Christians, "Present your bodies as a living sacrifice, holy and acceptable to God, which is your *spiritual* worship."

Even when Paul uses an Old Testament word for worship, he takes pains to convey that what he has in mind is not mainly a localized or external event of worship but an internal, spiritual experience—so much so that he sees all of life and ministry as an expression of that inner experience of worship.

The same thing can be seen in the New Testament use of the Old Testament language for temple sacrifices and priestly service. The praise and thanks of the lips is called a sacrifice to God (Heb. 13:15). But so are the good works in everyday life (Heb. 13:16). Paul calls his own ministry a "priestly service [of worship]," and he calls the converts themselves an "acceptable offering [in worship]" to God (Rom. 15:16; see also Phil.

---

8. The noun of this verb is *latreia* and is used to translate the noun *'abodah* five times in the Greek Old Testament. Paul uses it twice, once for the Old Testament worship (Rom. 9:4) and once for the Christian life (Rom. 12:1).

2:17). He even calls the money that the churches send him "a fragrant offering, a sacrifice acceptable and pleasing to God [in worship]" (Phil. 4:18). And his own death for Christ he calls a "drink offering" to God (2 Tim. 4:6).[9]

Making Worship Radically Inward So That It Permeates All of Life Outwardly

In the New Testament, worship is significantly de-institutionalized, de-localized, de-externalized. The entire thrust is taken off ceremony and seasons and places and forms and is shifted to what is happening in the heart—not just on Sunday but on every day, and all the time in all of life.

This is what is meant when we read things such as, "Whether you eat or drink, or whatever you do, do all to the glory of God" (1 Cor. 10:31). And "whatever you do, in word or deed, do everything in the name of the Lord Jesus, giving thanks to God the Father through him" (Col. 3:17). This is the essence of worship: to act in a way that reflects the heart's valuing of the glory of God. But the New Testament uses those greatest of all worship sentences without any reference to worship services. They describe life.

Even when Paul calls us to "be filled with the Spirit, addressing one another in psalms and hymns and spiritual songs, singing and making melody to the Lord with all your heart, giving thanks always and for everything to God the Father in the name of our Lord Jesus Christ" (Eph. 5:18–20), he makes no reference to a time or a place or a service. In fact, the keys words are "always" and "for everything"—"giving thanks *always* and for *everything*" (cf. Col. 3:16). This may in fact be what we should do in a worship service, but it is not Paul's burden to tell us that. His burden is to call for a radical, inward authenticity of worship and an all-encompassing pervasiveness of worship in all of life. Place and form are not of the essence. Spirit and truth are all-important.

9. The same thrust is seen in the imagery of the people of God (body of Christ) as the New Testament "temple" where spiritual sacrifices are offered (1 Peter 2:5), where God dwells by his Spirit (Eph. 2:21–22), and where all the people are seen as the holy priesthood (1 Peter 2:5, 9). Second Corinthians 6:16 shows that the New Covenant hope of God's presence is being fulfilled even now in the church as a people, not in any particular service: "We are the temple of the living God; as God said, 'I will make my dwelling among them and walk among them, and I will be their God, and they shall be my people.'"

The Reformed and Puritan Impulse

This is what gripped and shaped the Reformed tradition, especially the Puritans and their heirs. Worship is radically oriented on the experience of the heart and freed from form and place. John Calvin expresses the freedom of worship from traditional form in the following way:

> [The Master] did not will in outward discipline and ceremonies to prescribe in detail what we ought to do (because he foresaw that this depended on the state of the times, and he did not deem one form suitable for all ages). . . . Because he has taught nothing specifically, and because these things are not necessary to salvation, and for the upbuilding of the church ought to be variously accommodated to the customs of each nation and age, it will be fitting (as the advantage of the church will require) to change and abrogate traditional practices and to establish new ones. Indeed, I admit that we ought not to charge into innovation rashly, suddenly, for insufficient cause. But love will best judge what may hurt or edify; and if we let love be our guide, all will be safe.[10]

Luther expresses the freedom of worship from place: "The worship of God . . . should be free at table, in private rooms, downstairs, upstairs, at home, abroad, in all places, by all people, at all times. Whoever tells you anything else is lying as badly as the pope and the devil himself."[11] The Puritans carried through the simplification and freedom of worship in music, liturgy, and architecture. Patrick Collinson summarizes Puritan theory and practice by saying that "the life of the Puritan was in one sense a continuous act of worship, pursued under an unremitting and lively sense of God's providential purposes and constantly refreshed by religious activity, personal, domestic and public."[12] One of the reasons Puritans called their churches "meeting houses" and kept them very simple was to divert attention from the physical place to the inward, spiritual nature of worship through the Word.

A Radical Intensification of Worship as Inward, Spiritual Experience

My conclusion, then, is that in the New Testament there is a stunning indifference to the outward forms and places of worship. At the same

10. John Calvin, *Institutes of the Christian Religion*, vol. 2 (Philadelphia: Westminster, 1960), IV, 10, 30, 1208.
11. Quoted in Ewald M. Plass, ed., *What Luther Says*, vol. 3 (St. Louis: Concordia, 1959), 1546.
12. Quoted in Leland Ryken, *Worldly Saints: The Puritans as They Really Were* (Grand Rapids: Zondervan, 1986), 116.

time, there is a radical intensification of worship as an inward, spiritual experience that has no bounds and pervades all of life. These emphases were recaptured in the Reformation and came to clear expression in the Puritan wing of the Reformed tradition. One of the reasons for this development in the New Testament is that the New Testament is not a manual for worship services. Rather, it is a vision for missions in thousands of diverse people groups around the world. In such groups, outward forms of worship will vary drastically, but the inner reality of treasuring Christ in spirit and truth is common ground.

What Is the Essence of This Radical, Inward Experience of Worship?

What begs for attention now is the question, What is the essence of this radical, authentic, inward, unifying experience called worship, and how is it that this experience comes to expression in gathered congregations and in everyday life? My answer in advance is that the essential, vital, indispensable, defining heart of worship is the experience of *being satisfied with God*. And the reason this worship pervades all of life is that all Christian behavior is properly motivated by a thirst for more and more satisfaction in God.

In other words, the basic reason why the apostle Paul makes so little distinction between worship as a congregational service, on the one hand, and worship as a pattern of daily life, on the other hand, is that they are united with the same root—a radical valuing, cherishing, esteeming, treasuring of God in Christ and a passion for more of him. The impulse for singing a hymn and the impulse for visiting a prisoner are the same: a freeing contentment in God and a thirst for more of God—a desire to experience as much satisfaction in God as we can.

I have written for some years on these things and have tried to unfold them and defend them biblically, especially in *Desiring God*,[13] *Future Grace*,[14] *The Pleasures of God*,[15] and *God's Passion for His Glory*.[16] So here I will give just a brief explanation to show the biblical root of my thesis, which is so crucial for the missionary enterprise.

13. See note 6.
14. John Piper, *The Purifying Power of Living by Faith in Future Grace* (Sisters, Ore.: Multnomah, 1995).
15. John Piper, *The Pleasures of God: Meditations on God's Delight in Being God* (Sisters, Ore.: Multnomah, 2000).
16. John Piper, *God's Passion for His Glory: Living the Vision of Jonathan Edwards* (Wheaton: Crossway, 1998).

I start with God. The root of our passion and thirst for God is God's own infinite exuberance for God. The root of our quest for satisfaction in God's glory is God's jealousy that his own satisfaction in his own glory be known and shared by his people. God is infinitely committed to preserving and displaying his glory in all that he does from creation to consummation. And in this commitment, we see his zeal and love and satisfaction in his glory (as we saw in chapter 1 and chapter 6). God has purposed and worked so that predestination (Eph. 1:4–6), creation (Isa. 43:6–7), incarnation (Rom. 15:8–9), propitiation (Rom. 3:25–26), sanctification (Phil. 1:10–11), and consummation (2 Thess. 1:10) are all designed to magnify his own worth and glory in the world.

In other words, God is so overflowingly, unashamedly satisfied with his own glory that he devotes all his energies to making this glory known. The creation of the universe, the history of redemption, and the consummation of all things are driven ultimately by this great passion in the heart of God—to exult fully in his own glory by making it known and praised among all the nations.

But if God is so satisfied with his glory that he makes its display the goal of all that he does, then is not his own satisfaction in himself the root of our satisfaction in him? But putting it that way doesn't quite get to the heart of the matter. To get to the heart of the matter we need to ask, Why is it a loving thing for God to be so self-exalting, and why, if we come to share his satisfaction in himself, is it the essence and heart of worship?

How C. S. Lewis Helped Me See the Obvious

The answer to the first question—Why is it loving of God to be so self-exalting that he does all that he does for his own glory?—came to me with the help of C. S. Lewis. When I was pondering the fact that in Ephesians 1:6, 12, 14 Paul says that God performs all the acts of redemption so that we might praise his glory, I discovered that in his early days as a Christian, Lewis was bothered by the commands of God to praise God. They seemed vain.

But then he discovered why this is not vain but profoundly loving of God to do. Here is his all-important insight:

> The most obvious fact about praise . . . strangely escaped me. . . . I had never noticed that all enjoyment spontaneously overflows into praise. . . . The world rings with praise—lovers praising their mistresses, readers their favorite poet, walkers praising the countryside, players praising their favorite game—praise of weather, wines, dishes, actors, horses, colleges, countries, historical personages, children, flowers, mountains, rare stamps,

rare beetles, even sometimes politicians and scholars. . . . My whole, more general difficulty about praise of God depended on my absurdly denying to us, as regards the supremely Valuable, what we delight to do, what indeed we can't help doing, about everything else we value.

I think we delight to praise what we enjoy because the praise not merely expresses but completes the enjoyment; it is its appointed consummation. It is not out of compliment that lovers keep on telling one another how beautiful they are, the delight is incomplete till it is expressed.[17]

In other words, genuine, heartfelt praise is not artificially tacked on to joy. It is the consummation of joy. Joy in some beauty or some value is not complete until it is expressed in a kind of praise.

Now, if God loves us the way the Bible says he does, then he would surely give us what is best for us. And what is best for us is *himself*. So if God loves us, God must give us God, for our enjoyment, and nothing less. But if our enjoyment—if our satisfaction in God—is incomplete until it comes to completion in praise, then God would not be loving if he were indifferent to our praise. If he didn't command us to praise him, he would not be commanding us to be as satisfied as we could be, and that would not be loving.

So what emerges on reflection is that God's self-exaltation—his doing everything to display his glory and to win our praise—is not unloving; it is the only way that an infinitely all-glorious God can love. His greatest gift of love is to give us a share in the very satisfaction that he has in himself and then to call that satisfaction to its fullest consummation in the expression of praise.

The love of God is expressed by the repeated biblical commands that we rejoice in the Lord (Phil. 4:4), that we delight ourselves in the Lord (Ps. 37:4), that we serve the Lord with gladness (Ps. 100:2), that we be glad in the Lord (Ps. 32:11) and by the manifold promise that "in your presence there is fullness of joy; at your right hand are pleasures forevermore" (Ps. 16:11).

Joy in God Is Itself a Tribute to His All-Satisfying Worth, Even before Praise

There is one more component of this argument, leading to the conclusion that overflowing satisfaction in God is the essence (not the entirety) of worship. I will state it logically and then exegetically. Logically, if our

---

17. C. S. Lewis, *Reflections on the Psalms* (New York: Harcourt Brace and World, 1958), 93–95.

praise is the consummation of our joy in God and not a mere add-on, then our joy in God must itself be a tribute to God. This joy, even before it overflows in praise, is a reflection (if we could see into the heart) of God's all-satisfying worth. That is, he is honored by our delight in him. We know this from experience; to enjoy someone's presence is to honor that person. To feel constrained to be around someone out of duty does not honor the person very much. This, then, is our conclusion: God is glorified in us when we are satisfied in him. And since worship is essentially the experience of magnifying the glory of God, the essence of worship is being satisfied in God.

Now, we must see how this is rooted in Scripture. Consider Philippians 1:20–21. Paul says, "It is my eager expectation and hope that . . . Christ will be honored in my body, whether by life or by death. For to me to live is Christ, and to die is gain." The issue is, How shall Christ be honored in Paul's body? That is a worship question. How shall Paul show the worth of Christ with his body? He says he wants to honor Christ "whether by life or by death," so there is a way to honor Christ in the body by dying. The question is, What is it? How do we honor Christ in death?

Paul answers in verse 21. He says in sum, "I expect and hope to honor Christ in my body in death . . . *for* to me to die is gain." In other words, if I can experience death as gain, my death will honor Christ. We can see here how Paul's mind is working. The honor and all-satisfying worth of Christ is reflected in my dying to the degree that in my soul I am not begrudging the loss of all my earthly things and relations but am counting Christ as so superior that death is all gain. The assumption—which he makes clear in verse 23—is that death means a closer intimacy with Christ. In verse 23, he says, "My desire is to depart and be with Christ, for that is far better." So the reason death is gain is that it brings a better experience of Christ. The exegetical conclusion then is that savoring Christ above all that we lose in death magnifies the worth of Christ. The degree to which we are satisfied in him as we die is the degree to which he is honored as we die. He is most glorified in us when we are most satisfied in him—in life and death.

What Then Is the Essence of Worship?

From all this I conclude (logically and exegetically) that the essential, vital, indispensable, defining heart of worship is the experience of *being satisfied with God in Christ*. This experience magnifies his worth, and such magnifying is what worship is. This is why Jesus and the apostles were so stunningly indifferent to external forms and so radically intent on inward, spiritual, authentic worship. Without the experience of heartfelt satisfaction in God, praises are vain. If genuine praise can flow from a heart without satisfaction in God, then the word "hypocrisy" has no meaning, and Jesus' words are pointless when he says, "This people honors me with their lips [that is, with verbal praises], but their heart [that is, their heartfelt treasuring and satisfaction] is far from me" (Matt. 15:8).

So when I say, "Missions is not the ultimate goal of the church. Worship is," I do not mean "worship services." I do not mean "worship singing." Those are part of the *expression* of the essence of worship, but those things can happen and *not* be worship. Worship is not first an outward act; it is an inner spiritual treasuring of the character and the ways of God in Christ. It is a cherishing of Christ, a being satisfied with all that God is for us in Christ. When these things are missing, there is no worship, no matter what forms or expressions are present.[18]

Implications

Now consider four implications of this for the experience of worship and its expression in worship services.

1. *The pursuit of joy in God is not optional. It is our highest duty.* Millions of Christians have absorbed a popular ethic that comes more from Immanuel Kant than from the Bible. Their assumption is that it is morally defective to seek happiness—to pursue joy, to crave satisfaction, and to devote ourselves to seeking it. This is absolutely deadly for authentic worship. The degree to which this Kantian ethic flourishes is the degree to which worship dies, for the essence of worship is satisfaction in God. To be indifferent to or even fearful of the pursuit[19] of what is essential to

18. Don't take me to mean that the true Christian never struggles with low and almost dead and barren seasons of spiritual affections. We do. See especially the crucial discussion of three levels or stages of worship in Piper, *Desiring God*, 85–87. There can be faint echoes of the worth of God that shine through even when we are hanging on to hope in him by our fingernails. He is honored by the pitiful, dying woman who drowns in her own vomit (I speak from pastoral experience) and does not curse God but submits, if with screams, and hopes against hope that this horror is not wrath but the last ghoulish terror before everlasting dawn.

19. I am keenly aware of the criticism that the direct pursuit of joy by taking one's eyes off The Enjoyed is deadly. I am not commending that you go to the Grand Canyon of God's greatness and sit on the rim with your finger on your pulse and your mind on your inner condition. That would cancel out the Canyon. Give yourself up to the Canyon. See it. Revel in it. Absorb it. Ponder it. That is the kind of pursuit I have in mind. God's all-satisfying glory is not experienced by focusing on the experience but on the glory.

worship is to oppose worship—and the authenticity of worship services (in any culture or any form).

Not a few pastors foster this very thing by saying things such as, "The problem is that our people don't come on Sunday morning to give; they only come to get. If they came to give, we would have life." That is probably not a good diagnosis. People ought to come to get. They ought to come starved for *God*. They ought to come saying, "As a deer pants for flowing streams, so pants my soul for you, O God" (Ps. 42:1). God is mightily honored when a people know that they will die of hunger and thirst unless they have God. It is the job of pastors to spread a banquet for them. Recovering the rightness and indispensability of pursuing our satisfaction *in God* will go a long way toward restoring the authenticity and power of worship—whether in solitude, in a group of six elders in Uzbekistan, in a rented garage in Liberia, in a megachurch in America, or on the scaffold in the last moment just before "gain."

2. *Another implication of saying that the essence of worship is satisfaction in God is that worship becomes radically God-centered.* Nothing makes God more supreme and more central than when people are utterly persuaded that nothing—not money or prestige or leisure or family or job or health or sports or toys or friends or ministry—is going to bring satisfaction to their aching hearts besides God. This conviction breeds a people who go hard after God on Sunday morning (or any other time). They are not confused about why they are there. They do not see songs and prayers and sermons as mere traditions or mere duties. They see them as means of getting to God or God getting to them for more of his fullness.

If the focus shifts to our giving to God, subtly it becomes not God at the center but the quality of our giving. Are we singing worthily of the Lord? Are our instrumentalists playing with quality fitting a gift to the Lord? Is the preaching a suitable offering to the Lord? And little by little the focus shifts from the utter indispensability of the Lord himself to the quality of our performances. We even start to define excellence and power in worship in terms of the technical distinction of our artistic acts.

Nothing keeps God at the center of worship like the biblical conviction that the essence of worship is deep, heartfelt satisfaction in him and the conviction that the expression and pursuit of that satisfaction are why we are together. No outward act can replace this. The act can only express it (which we call a service of worship) or substitute for it (which we call hypocrisy).

3. *A third implication of saying that the essence of worship is satisfaction in God is that this essence protects the primacy of worship by forcing us to come to terms with the fact that worship is an end in itself.* If the

essence of worship is satisfaction in God, then worship can't be a means to anything else. We simply can't say to God, "I want to be satisfied in you so that I can have something else." Such an expression would mean that we are not really satisfied in God but in that something else, and that would dishonor God.

For thousands of people and pastors, however, the event of worship on Sunday morning (that is, the worship service) is conceived of as a means to accomplish something other than worship. We "worship" to raise money; we "worship" to attract crowds; we "worship" to heal human hurts; we "worship" to recruit workers; we "worship" to improve church morale. We "worship" to give talented musicians an opportunity to fulfill their calling; we "worship" to teach our children the way of righteousness; we "worship" to help marriages stay together; we "worship" to evangelize the lost among us; we "worship" to motivate people for service projects; we "worship" to give our churches a family feeling, and so on.

If we are not careful, when we speak of aiming at these things "through worship," we bear witness that we do not know what true worship is. Genuine affections for God (the essence of worship) are an end in themselves. I cannot say to my wife, "I feel a strong delight in you so that you will make me a nice meal." That is not the way delight works. Delight ends with her. It does not have a nice meal in view. I cannot say to my son, "I love playing ball with you . . . so that you will cut the grass." If your heart really delights in playing ball with him, that delight cannot be performed as a means of getting him to do something else.

I am not denying that worship (the essence and the service) may have a hundred good effects in the life of the church. It will, just as true affection in marriage makes everything better. My point is: The degree to which we "do worship" for these reasons is the degree to which worship ceases to be authentic. Keeping satisfaction in God at the center guards us from that tragedy.

4. *Finally, the last implication of saying that the essence of worship is being satisfied with God is that this definition accounts for the fact that Paul considers all of life an expression of worship.* All Christian behavior (in every culture at every level) is to be done out of satisfaction in God and with a view to preserving and increasing satisfaction in God. I devoted a chapter in *Desiring God* ("Love: The Labor of Christian Hedonism") to justifying that sentence, but let me commend it to you with one word from the Lord Jesus.

In Luke 12:33, Jesus says, "Sell your possessions, and give to the needy. [And thus] provide yourselves with moneybags that do not grow old, with a treasure in the heavens that does not fail." I understand "treasure in the heavens" to refer to increased measures of joy at God's right hand and pleasures in his fellowship in the age to come. Jesus says that we are to provide ourselves with that—in other words, make efforts to increase our joys with God in heaven. He says that the way to do so is by selling our possessions and giving alms. That is illustrative of all the ways we sacrifice and love in the Christian life. We are to live this way so as to provide ourselves with treasures in heaven.

In other words, we should aim in all we do to maximize our satisfaction in God—now and in the age to come. If someone asks, "Is it loving to give alms to others with a view to maximizing our own joy in God?" the answer is a resounding yes, because in giving up worldly things so that we can meet the needs of others, our aim is to persuade them that the treasure of God, which frees us to give in this way, is so valuable that they too should embrace it and live for it and so join us in the joys of heaven. Everyone who falls in love with God because they have seen in us that God is more precious than things will make our satisfaction in God all the sweeter. Which is one reason why missions is one of the most deeply satisfying callings in the world. "It is more blessed to give than to receive" (Acts 20:35).

So I believe it can be shown biblically that all our behavior should be motivated by a deeply freeing taste of God's goodness and a thirst for more and more satisfaction in God. Therefore, the root of Christian living and the root of congregational praise are the same, which is why for Paul worship simply cannot be merely or even mainly thought of in terms of Sunday services but of all of life. His is an absolutely God-saturated vision of Christian existence. When our whole life is consumed with pursuing satisfaction in God, everything we do highlights the value and worth of God, which simply means that everything becomes worship. May God make himself—manifest fully in Jesus Christ—that precious to us.

That is what I am referring to when I say, "Missions is not the ultimate goal of the church. Worship is." Our goal is to see that experience happen among all the peoples of the world. May the power of the gospel waken the dead, bring them from darkness to light and from the power of Satan to God, so that they see him and savor him with all their hearts. And may they be so radically satisfied in him that they are freed from the fears and pleasures of this world and follow Jesus on the Calvary road of love. Then others will see their good works and give glory to their Father in heaven—and the Word will go on from glory to glory.

Conclusion

The ultimate goal of God in all of history is to uphold and display his glory for the enjoyment of the redeemed from every tribe and tongue and people and nation. His goal is the gladness of his people, because God is most glorified in us when we are most satisfied in him. Delight is a higher tribute than duty. The chief end of God is to glorify God and enjoy his glory forever. Since his glory is magnified most in the God-centered passions of his joyful people, God's self-exaltation and our jubilation are one. The greatest news in all the world is that God's ultimate aim to be glorified and our aim to be satisfied are not at odds.

Worship

The goal of missions, therefore, is the gladness of the peoples in the greatness of God. "The LORD reigns, let the earth rejoice; let the many coastlands *be glad*!" (Ps. 97:1). "Let the nations *be glad and sing for joy*!" (Ps. 67:4). The missionary command to be happy in God is simply a command for the consummation of praise. Professed praise of God without pleasure in God is hypocrisy.

Therefore, worship is the fuel and the goal of missions. Worship is the goal of missions because in missions we aim to bring the nations into the white-hot enjoyment of God's glory. It is the fuel of missions because we can't commend what we don't cherish. We can't call out, "Let the nations *be glad*!" until we say, "*I rejoice* in the Lord." Missions begins and ends in worship.

Prayer

This means that God is absolutely supreme in missions. He is the beginning and the end. He is also the one who sustains and empowers the entire process. "From him and through him and to him are all things. To him be glory forever" (Rom. 11:36). God's moment-by-moment sustaining of the Christian movement preserves his supremacy, because the one who gives the power gets the glory. Let him who serves serve "by the strength that God supplies—in order that in everything God may be glorified through Jesus Christ" (1 Peter 4:11).

This is why God has ordained prayer to have such a crucial place in the mission of the church. The purpose of prayer is to make clear to all the participants in missions that the victory belongs to the Lord. "The horse is made ready for the day of battle, but the victory belongs to the LORD" (Prov. 21:31). Prayer is God's appointed means of bringing grace to the world and glory to himself. "Call upon me in the day of trouble; I will deliver you, and *you shall glorify me*" (Ps. 50:15). "Whatever you ask in my name, this I will do, *that the Father may be glorified in the Son*" (John 14:13).

Prayer puts God in the place of the all-sufficient Benefactor and puts us in the place of needy beneficiaries. Therefore, when the mission of the church moves forward by prayer, the supremacy of God is manifest and the needs of Christian missionaries are met. In prayer, he is glorified and we are satisfied. "Until now you have asked nothing in my name. Ask, and you will receive, *that your joy may be full*" (John 16:24). The purpose of prayer is the Father's fame and the saints' fullness.

Suffering

God himself is the fullness we live on and the fountain of life that we commend in missions. He is our treasure. His "steadfast love is better than life" (Ps. 63:3). Therefore, the greatness of his worth is seen most clearly when we are willing to give up our lives for the sake of his love. We measure the worth of a treasure by what we will gladly give up in order to have it.

Suffering alone proves nothing, but suffering accepted because of the "surpassing worth of knowing Christ" and losses embraced in order to "gain Christ" (Phil. 3:8) prove that Christ is supremely valuable. "Blessed are you when others revile you and persecute you. . . . Rejoice and be glad, for your reward is great in heaven" (Matt. 5:11–12). The extent of our *sac-*

rifice coupled with the depth of our *joy* displays the worth we put on the reward of God. Loss and suffering, joyfully accepted for the kingdom of God, show the supremacy of God's glory more clearly in the world than all worship and prayer.

Therefore, God ordains that the mission of his church move forward not only by the fuel of worship and in the power of prayer but also at the price of suffering. "If anyone would come after me, let him deny himself and take up his cross and follow me" (Mark 8:34). "A servant is not greater than his master. If they persecuted me, they will also persecute you" (John 15:20). "If they have called the master of the house Beelzebul, how much more will they malign those of his household" (Matt. 10:25). "The Son of Man must suffer many things" (Mark 8:31). "As the Father has sent me, even so I am sending you" (John 20:21). "Behold, I am sending you out as sheep in the midst of wolves" (Matt. 10:16). "I will show him how much he must suffer for the sake of my name" (Acts 9:16).

Is Knowing Christ Crucial?

Because the price is so high, one may well ask, Is it really necessary? If the goal of God in history is to uphold and display his glory for the enjoyment of the redeemed, may it not be that he will redeem people without missions? Could people come to praise the true God from hearts of saving faith while still ignorant of Jesus and his saving work? Could nature or other religions lead people into eternal life and joy with God?

The biblical answer we have seen is no. It is a stunning New Testament truth that since the incarnation of the Son of God, all saving faith must henceforth fix on him. This was not always true. Before Christ, the people of Israel focused faith on the promises of God (Rom. 4:20) summed up in a coming Redeemer. And the nations were allowed to walk in their own ways (Acts 14:16). But those times were called the times of ignorance. With the coming of the Son of God into the world, Christ was made the conscious center of the mission of the church. The aim of missions is to "bring about the obedience of faith *for the sake of his[1] name* among all the nations" (Rom. 1:5). God's will is to be glorified in his Son by making him the center of all missionary proclamation. The supremacy of God in

1. The context makes it crystal clear that "his" refers to Jesus Christ: "[He] was declared to be the Son of God in power according to the Spirit of holiness by his resurrection from the dead, Jesus Christ our Lord, through whom we have received grace and apostleship to bring about the obedience of faith for the sake of *his* name among all the nations" (Rom. 1:4–5).

missions is affirmed biblically by affirming the supremacy of his Son as
the focus of all saving faith.

People or Peoples?

Since the eternal destiny of every individual hangs on knowing Christ and
embracing him gladly as the highest value of life, is then the task of missions
to maximize the number of people redeemed or the number of peoples
reached? The biblical answer is that God's call for missions in Scripture
cannot be defined merely in terms of crossing cultures to maximize the
total number of individuals saved.[2] Rather, God's will for missions is that
every people group be reached with the testimony of Christ and that a
people be called out for his name from among all the nations. It may be
that this definition of missions will, in fact, result in the greatest possible
number of white-hot worshipers for God's Son. But that remains for God
to decide. Our responsibility is to define missions his way and then obey.

The ultimate goal of God in all of history is to uphold and display his glory
for the enjoyment of the redeemed from every tribe and tongue and people
and nation. The beauty of praise that will come to the Lord from the diversity of the nations is greater than the beauty that would come to him if the
chorus of the redeemed were culturally uniform or limited. Moreover, there is
something about God that is so universally praiseworthy and so profoundly
beautiful and so comprehensively worthy and so deeply satisfying that God
will find passionate admirers in every diverse people group in the world. His
true greatness will be manifest in the breadth of the diversity of those who
perceive and cherish his beauty. The more diverse the people groups who
forsake their gods to follow the true God, the more visible God's superiority
over all his competitors.

By focusing on all the people groups of the world, God undercuts ethnocentric pride and throws all peoples back upon his free grace rather than
on any distinctive of their own. This humility is the flip side of giving God
all the glory. Humility means reveling in his grace, not in our goodness. In
pressing us on toward all the peoples, God is pressing us further into the

2. David Doran, in his book, *For the Sake of His Name: Challenging a New Generation
for World Missions* (Allen Park, Mich.: Student Global Impact, 2002), 131–54, has written a
chapter called "The Territory of the Great Commission." In it he gives a corrective to a lop-
sided emphasis on the people-group focus in missions at the expense of the geographic focus.
In spite of our interaction, I do not think it necessary to change anything I have written. But I
do alert the reader that Doran interacts with me in his book and so may provide a perspective
that I am neglecting.

humblest and deepest experience of his grace and weaning us more and more from our ingrained pride. In doing this, he is preparing for himself a people—from all the peoples—who will be able to worship him with free and white-hot admiration.

Therefore, the church is bound to engage with the Lord of glory in his cause. It is our unspeakable privilege to be caught up with him in the greatest movement in history—the ingathering of the elect from every tribe and language and people and nation until the full number of the Gentiles comes in and all Israel is saved and the Son of Man descends with power and great glory as King of kings and Lord of lords and the earth is full of the knowledge of his glory as the waters cover the sea forever and ever. Then the supremacy of Christ will be manifest to all, and he will deliver the kingdom to God the Father, and God will be all in all.

Afterword

The Supremacy of God in Going and Sending

TOM STELLER

There is a wonderful passage in the often neglected epistle of 3 John that sums up the burden of this book beautifully. We want to leave you with its truth ringing in your mind and heart. There are only two ways for us to respond to the truth we have been considering about the supremacy of God in missions. We must either go out for the sake of his name, or we must send and support such people who do, and do so in a manner worthy of God. Listen to the words of the apostle John, who heard the heartbeat of Jesus as he leaned on his breast and who listened with his own ears to the giving of the Great Commission.

> The elder to the beloved Gaius, whom I love in truth. Beloved, I pray that in all respects you may prosper and be in good health, just as your soul prospers. For I was very glad when brethren came and bore witness to your truth, that is, how you are walking in truth. I have no greater joy than this, to hear of my children walking in the truth. Beloved, you are acting faithfully in whatever you accomplish for the brethren, and especially when they are strangers; and they bear witness to your love before the church; and *you will do well to send them on their way in a manner worthy of God. For they went out for the sake of the Name, accepting nothing from the Gentiles.*

Therefore we ought to support such men, that we may be fellow-workers with the truth.

3 John 1–8 NASB

It is worth noting what makes a godly old man happy. The apostle John, who refers to himself simply as "the elder," is overjoyed. He has just received word that Gaius, one of his spiritual children, is walking in the truth. There is no greater joy than this!

What evidence compels this old apostle to be convinced that Gaius's soul is prospering? What is the truth in which Gaius is walking? Apparently some itinerant evangelists/missionaries, whom John knew, had visited Gaius and were loved by him in a special way. They returned to the church of which John was a part and testified that Gaius treated them well, even though they were strangers to him. This so moved John that he wrote Gaius a letter to encourage him for walking in the truth and for acting faithfully. He wanted to urge Gaius to continue all the more. "You will do well to send them on their way in a manner worthy of God."

Gaius was admonished by the apostle to be a sender. This phrase, "to send on one's way," occurs nine times in the New Testament, and each one occurs in a missionary context.[1]

The most descriptive verse is found in Titus 3:13. In this verse, Paul writes to Titus, "Diligently help Zenas the lawyer and Apollos on their way so that nothing is lacking for them" (NASB). From this verse we can learn that sending is something to be done diligently and is all inclusive— "so that *nothing* is lacking for them."

In 3 John, this diligence and thoroughness is captured in the phrase "in a manner worthy of God" (v. 6). This elevates the importance of sending as high as can be imagined. It is a commandment of God (notice the "ought" of verse 8). The reason we must send them in a manner worthy of God is that they go out for the sake of the name. The name of God is at stake in how we treat our missionaries. God is glorified when we support them substantially with our prayers, our money, our time, and myriad other practical ways (notice the "whatever" in verse 5). God is not glorified when our missionaries are simply a name on the back of the church bulletin or a line item in the budget.

It is not of secondary importance to be engaged in this ministry of sending. It is a very high calling. It is walking in the truth. It is the mani-

1. See especially the uses of *propempō* in Acts 15:3; Rom. 15:24; 1 Cor. 16:6, 11; 2 Cor. 1:16; and Titus 3:15.

festation of a healthy and prospering soul. Senders are fellow workers with the truth. To send in a manner worthy of God is a call to excellence in the support of missionaries. It is a direct participation in God's purpose. The cruciality of sending cannot be overemphasized. Therefore, it must not be done in a shoddy manner but in "a manner worthy of God."[2] There is a world of difference between a church "having" a missionary and a church "sending" a missionary. When we send missionaries in a manner worthy of God, God is glorified, our souls prosper, and we are fellow workers with the truth. We are in sync with God's heartbeat and his purpose to be glorified among all the peoples.

But just as there is a God-centeredness to sending, there is also a God-centeredness to going. In fact, the two are intimately related. Listen to the apostle John's flow of thought. "You will do well to send them on their way *in a manner worthy of God. For* they went out *for the sake of the Name,* accepting nothing from the Gentiles. *Therefore* we ought to support *such* men." According to this text, only a certain kind of person is to be supported and sent to the mission field (notice the word "such"). Only those who go *out for the sake of the name* ought to be supported.

Here is perhaps the best definition of a missionary in the New Testament. A missionary is someone who goes out for the sake of the name, accepting nothing from the Gentiles. Private material gain must not be the motive. Even genuine humanitarian concern, though crucial, must not be the driving motive. Rather, a missionary is propelled by a deep love for the name and glory of God. Like the apostle Paul, a missionary's aim is to "bring about the obedience of faith among all the Gentiles, *for His name's sake*" (Rom. 1:5 NASB).

The purpose of this book has not been merely to inform you of the supremacy of God in missions. Rather, from start to finish we have sought to invite you to become more personally engaged in the cause of missions with a heartfelt, God-centered passion. Our aim has not been to exalt the missionary but to exalt God and to exalt his mission. The precise nature of your engagement in the cause of missions will be different from that of any other person. Whether you go as a missionary or stay as a sender is a secondary issue. The primary issue is that whatever you do, you do it for

2. John Stott, commenting on verse 6, says, "They are not just to be received when they arrive, but to be so refreshed and provided for (no doubt with supplies of food and money) as to be sent forward in a manner worthy of God. . . . Such thoughtful sending forth of missionaries on their journey is not only a 'loyal thing' (v. 5 RSV), but a 'beautiful' thing (v. 6, *kalōs poiēseis, you will do well*)." *The Letters of John: An Introduction and Commentary*, Tyndale New Testament Commentary, rev. ed. (Grand Rapids: Eerdmans, 1989), 225.

the glory of God (1 Cor. 10:31) and for the advance of his kingdom (Matt. 6:33) and with a view to its consummation, which will embrace every tribe and tongue and people and nation (Matt. 24:14; Rev. 7:9).

David Bryant calls one who has this mind-set a "world Christian."[3] Not every Christian is called to be a missionary, but every follower of Christ is called to be a world Christian. A world Christian is someone who is so gripped by the glory of God and the glory of his global purpose that he chooses to align himself with God's mission to fill the earth with the knowledge of his glory as the waters cover the sea (Hab. 2:14). Everything a world Christian does is with a view to the hallowing of God's name and the coming of God's kingdom among all the peoples of the earth. The burning prayer of the world Christian is, "Let the peoples praise you, O God; let all the peoples praise you!" (Ps. 67:3). So whether we are those who send or those who go, let us glory in the supremacy of God in missions, and let us link arms together as we join in the refrain of old, "Let the nations be glad!"

Tom Steller is Pastor for Leadership Development,
Bethlehem Baptist Church, and Dean of Bethlehem College
and Seminary, Minneapolis, Minnesota.

3. David Bryant has helped define and popularize the notion of "world Christian" in his book *In the Gap: What It Means to Be a World Christian* (Downers Grove, Ill.: InterVarsity, 1979).

Subject Index

African Christians, 16–18
amillennialism, 75n9
annihilationism, 134, 135n3, 138,
    142–43nn15–16, 234
  texts against, 138–45
apathy, 117–18
atonement
  necessity for salvation, 99–100, 145–47, 205
  universality of, 134, 145
austerity, 67–68

blessed to be a blessing, 197
bogus theology, 30

calling people to maximum joy, 31
cap your expenditures, give the rest away, 23
China, 17, 62, 87
Christ
  came to glorify God, 43
  his name the only name, 52–53
  and missions for his name, 57–58, 149–50
  and necessity of his work, 135, 145–47
  as only hope for salvation, 138
  summary statement of his necessity, 257
  supremacy in missions, 131–76
  as treasure, 31
  as true temple, 241
come-see religion in the Old Testament, 27–30
compassion
  not at odds with passion for God, 52–54,
    233–38
  seeks to show people glory of Christ, 236
  and zeal for God, 61–62
Cornelius, not saved before hearing gospel, 78,
    156–62
covenant, new, 77–78

diversity
  how magnifies God, 221–24
  intended and eternal, 220–21
dying as gain, 31

election
  focused now on Christ, 149–50
  for God's glory, 40
  see also predestination
eternal security, 66
ethnos, 183–86
Europe and America, no longer Christian cen-
    ter of gravity, 16
evangelism
  E-1, E-2, E-3, 218
  see also missionary, missions

faith
  fight of, 66
  nature of, 235–36
  as necessary for salvation, 135–37, 147–74
  strengthened by suffering, 108–10
families of the earth, 190–92
  size of, 214–15
first edition (1993), 15
fundamental task of missions, 32

general revelation, as way of salvation, 136nn6–
    7, 137
Global South, 16–20
glory of God
  as chief end of God, 39–46, 84, 228–29, 247
  as goal of prayer, 79–80
  relation to worship, 229–31
glory of God's help, 24

265

Person Index

Alexander, John, 75
Anderson, James N. D., 148n23

Baldo, Suleyman Ali, 103
Barrett, David B., 97, 97nn3–4, 180n3, 181, 181n8, 213, 213nn29–30
Barth, Karl, 217n38
Baxter, Richard, 74
Beale, G. K., 208n24
Bergin, G. Fred, 90n19
Beyerhaus, Peter, 60, 60n19
Bitterman, Anna, 114
Bitterman, Brenda, 114
Bitterman, Chet, 113, 114
Bitterman, Esther, 114
Blomberg, Craig, 112n12
Bonhoeffer, Dietrich, 96, 96n2
Boyd, Greg, 143n16
Brainerd, David, 59, 60, 60n17, 74, 74n7, 94, 112
Brant, Albert, 161
Bridge, William, 75n9
Bromiley, Geoffrey, 190n16, 240n2
Brown, Delwin, 134n3, 144n17
Bruce, F. F., 163n31, 188n13, 223, 223n48
Bryant, David, 264, 264n3
Bunyan, John, 74n7
Burroughs, Jeremiah, 75n9

Cain, Glen, 161
Calvin, John, 152n25, 246, 246n10
Campos, Martinho, 120, 121
Card, Michael, 115, 116n19
Carey, William, 38, 73, 74, 94, 154

Carlisle, Thomas, 198
Carmichael, Amy, 131
Carson, D. A., 134n1, 148n23
Collison, Patrick, 246
Conzelmann, Hans, 163n31
Cowper, William, 74n7
Cranfield, C. E. B., 166n33
Crockett, William, 134n3
Crockett, William V., 136nn5–6, 137, 137n8

Dawson, John, 61, 61n20, 62
Deng, Xiaoping, 87n16
Dibelius, Martin, 188n13
Dixon, Larry, 134n1
Dolan, Bonnie, 19n13
Doran, David, 258n2
Dowsett, Dick, 148n23
DuBose, Francis, 217n38
Duewel, Wesley, 62, 62n21
Duff, Alexander, 74

Eddy, Sherwood, 131
Edwards, David, 134n3, 136n5, 139n10, 140n13, 142n14, 144n18
Edwards, Jonathan, 46, 46n7, 48, 48n10, 60n17, 74n7, 111, 112n12, 144, 144n19, 176n46, 227–28, 228nn1–3, 229n4, 233, 233n7, 234, 234nn9–12, 235, 235n13, 236, 237, 237n16
Einstein, Albert, 36
Eliot, John, 73, 74
Ellenberger, John, 175, 175nn42–44, 176, 176n45
Elliot, Elisabeth, 113n14, 113n16
Elliot, Jim, 89, 113, 113n14

Erickson, Millard, 136, 136n7, 137, 156, 156n28, 168
Estes, Steve, 114n17

Fackre, Gabriel, 148n23
Fernando, Ajith, 134n1, 136n6, 148n24
Fleming, Pete, 113
Fudge, Edward William, 134, 134n1, 135n3
Fuller, W. Harold, 161n30

Geivert, R. Douglas, 148n23
George, Timothy, 38n4
Gerstner, John, 144n19, 234n9, 235n13
Gonzalez, Justo, 20n19
Gonzalez, Ondina, 20n19
Goodwin, Thomas, 75n9
Graham, Billy, 115
Greeven, Heinrich, 240n2, 242n4
Grenfell, Lydia, 95
Grudem, Wayne, 21n22

Haenchen, Ernst, 163n31
Hawthorne, Steven C., 59n16, 180n4
Hebblethwaite, Brian, 135n4
Hein, Rolland, 134n2
Hick, John, 135, 135n4, 137
Hitt, Russell T., 113n14
Hodge, Charles, 136n7, 156n27, 166, 167, 167n36, 168, 169n40, 176, 176n47
Horton, Michael, 19, 19n12
House, Paul R., 148n23
Howard, David, 89, 90n18
Howard, Philip E., Jr., 60n17
Hulse, Erroll, 72n4

Jenkins, Philip, 16, 16nn3–4, 17n5, 19
Johnson, Todd M., 97n4, 213nn29–30
Johnstone, Patrick, 11, 11n4, 87n16, 212, 213, 213n28, 216
Judson, Adoniram, 74

Kant, Immanuel, 251
Kelly, Stanford, 126
Kittel, Gerhard, 190n16, 215n33
Kraft, Charles, 148n23
Kraft, Heinrich, 208n24
Kulichev, Hristo, 121
Kurian, George T., 97n4, 213nn29–30

Lenski, R. C. H., 188n13
Lewis, C. S., 68, 68n2, 248, 249n17
Lewis, Norman, 126n24

Lewis, Peter, 72n4
Livingstone, David, 74, 130
Longenecker, Dwight, 163n31
Lull, Raymond, 128–29, 129n28
Luther, Martin, 246, 246n11

MacDonald, George, 134, 134n2, 137
Mahmud, Ushari Ahmad, 103
Mandryk, Jason, 11, 87n16, 213n28
Marshall, Frank (pseudonym), 119–20
Martyn, Henry, 93–96, 112–13
Mather, Cotton, 74, 74n6
Mathis, David, 13
Maxwell, Joe, 19nn14–15, 20nn16–17, 20n18, 21n21
McCully, Ed, 113
McKnight, Scot, 139n11
McVeigh, Malcolm J., 148n23
Misner, Charles, 36
Mohler, Albert, 156n27
Moo, Douglas, 166n33
Moon, Lottie, 131
Morgan, Chris, 134n1, 144n19
Morris, Leon, 139, 140n12, 208n24
Moule, Handley, C. G., 127, 127n27
Mounce, Robert, 208n24
Mueller, George, 90, 90n19
Murray, Andrew, 60, 60n18
Murray, Iain, 38n4, 75n9
Murray, John, 166, 166nn33–34, 167, 167n35, 168, 169n40

Nash, Ronald H., 148n23, 156n27
Netland, Harold, 135n4
Newton, John, 127n27, 156n27
Noll, Mark, 17, 17nn7–8, 18, 18nn9–10

Okholm, Dennis L., 148n23
Olshausen, Hermann, 169n41
Otis, George, 97

Packer, J. I., 72n4
Parry, John, 135n4
Paton, James, 109n11
Paton, John G., 74, 74n8, 109, 109n10, 110n11, 129–130, 130n29
Peterson, Robert, 134n1
Pettit, Norman, 60n17, 74n7
Phillips, Timothy R., 136n5, 148n23
Phillips, W. Gary, 148n23
Phiri, Isaac, 19n13, 19n15, 20nn16–18, 21n21
Pierson, A. T., 88, 89n17

Scripture Index

Genesis

1:27 49
3:5 49
10:5 220n44
10:20 220n44
10:31 220n44
11 220n44
12:1–3 190
12:2–3 153
12:3 73, 188, 190–91, 191n17,
   192, 198, 218, 218n39
14 174
17:4 185
17:4–5 199
18:18 190–91, 191n17, 192
18:18 LXX 189n15, 209n25
22:18 190, 191n17
22:18 LXX 189n15, 209n25
25:23 214
26:4 190, 191n17
26:4 LXX 189n15, 209n25
28:14 190, 191n17
49:10 73

Exodus

6:14f 212n27
6:14–15 214
6:17 192n18
14:4 42
14:17 42
14:18 42
19:5 LXX 189n15
20:13 107n9
23:22 LXX 189n15

23:24 244
23:27 LXX 189n15
33:16 LXX 189n15

Leviticus

20:24 LXX 189n15
20:26 LXX 189n15
26:12 208

Numbers

1:44 192n18
3:24 192n18
14:21 84
18:1 192n18
25:14–15 192n18

Deuteronomy

2:25 LXX 189n15
4:6 LXX 189n15
4:19 LXX 189n15
4:27 LXX 189n15
7:1 185
7:6 LXX 189n15
7:7 LXX 189n15
7:14 LXX 189n15
10:15 LXX 189n15
11:23 LXX 189n15
14:2 LXX 189n15
26:19 LXX 189n15
28:1 LXX 189n15
28:10 LXX 189n15
28:37 LXX 189n15
28:64 187

28:64 LXX 189n15
29:23 LXX 189n15
30:1 LXX 189n15
30:3 LXX 189n15
30:6 86
32:8 221n47
32:43 201

Joshua

4:24 LXX 189n15
7 214
7:14 190, 214
22:14 192n18
23:3 LXX 189n15
23:4 LXX 189n15
23:17 LXX 189n15
23:18 LXX 189n15

1 Samuel

8:20 LXX 189n15
10:20–21 214
12:20 42
12:22 42

2 Samuel

7:23 42

1 Kings

6:20–22 28
6:38–7:1 28
7 28
7:48–50 28

A Note on Resources

❄ desiringGod

If you would like to further explore the vision of God and life presented in this book, we at Desiring God would love to serve you. We have hundreds of resources to help you grow in your passion for Jesus Christ and help you spread that passion to others. At our website, www.DesiringGod.org, you will find almost everything John Piper has written and preached, including more than thirty books. We have made over twenty-five years of sermons available free online for you to read, listen to, download, and in some cases watch. In addition, you can access hundreds of articles, listen to our daily internet radio program, find out where John Piper is speaking, learn about our conferences, discover our God-centered children's curricula, and browse our online store. John Piper receives no royalties from the books he writes and no compensation from Desiring God. The funds are all reinvested into our efforts to spread the gospel. Desiring God also has a whatever-you-can-afford policy, designed for individuals with limited discretionary funds. If you would like more information about this policy, please contact us at the address or phone number below. We exist to help you treasure Jesus Christ and his gospel above all things because he is most glorified in you when you are most satisfied in him. Let us know how we can serve you!

Desiring God
P.O. Box 2901
Minneapolis, Minnesota 55402
888-346-4700
mail@DesiringGod.org
www.DesiringGod.org